The WORKING WOMAN'S *Guide to* MANAGING STRESS

J. Robin Powell, Ph.D., CSW
with Holly George-Warren

PRENTICE HALL
Englewood Cliffs, New Jersey 07632

Prentice Hall International (UK) Limited, *London*
Prentice Hall of Australia Pty. Limited, *Sydney*
Prentice Hall Canada, Inc., *Toronto*
Prentice Hall Hispanoamericana, *S.A., Mexico*
Prentice Hall of India Private Limited, *New Delhi*
Prentice Hall of Japan, Inc., *Tokyo*
Simon & Schuster Asia Pte. Ltd., *Singapore*
Editora Prentice Hall do Brasil, Ltda., *Rio de Janeiro*

ISBN 0-13-969205-3 (case)

Prentice Hall
Career & Personal Development
Englewood Cliffs, NJ 07632
Simon & Schuster, A Paramount Communications Company

PRINTED IN THE UNITED STATES OF AMERICA

BIOGRAPHIES

Dr. Robin Powell is a clinical social worker who specializes in stress and chronic pain management. She maintains a private psychotherapy practice that draws on her expertise in relaxation, visualization, and mind/body integration. She is also associated with The St. Mark's Place Institute for Mental Health in New York City. Dr. Powell teaches stress reduction and relaxation training classes and workshops at The Chronic Fatigue Syndrome Clinic and other institutions. She is a faculty member at New York University with specialties in body therapy, dance, and fitness. Certified in the body therapy Kinetic Awareness, she is a founding board member of the Kinetic Awareness Center, Inc. Dr. Powell is the co-author of *Coping For Kids*, a comprehensive stress management guide used in schools throughout the country.

Holly George-Warren has contributed to a variety of magazines and books. Currently she is Editor of Rolling Stone Press.

for
Mac & Jackie Powell
for their continued love and support
Ian
whose presence makes life joyful
and Robi
whose furry warmth comforted me while I wrote

CONTENTS

Chapter Eleven

MASTERING THE WORK-HOME BALANCE   237

Appendix

Index   273

QUICK GUIDE:

Common Work-Related Problems and How to Solve Them

The following are common problems working women experience. Each specific problem is discussed in the chapters listed under "Solutions". Chapters that contain information that help support your efforts are listed under "Support." Chapters 1, 2, and 11 directly discuss, for example, how to deal with a demanding workload. Assertiveness, a technique helpful for coping with your workload, is found in Chapter 7. Naturally, a healthy lifestyle—exercise, eating properly, practicing relaxation, and good support systems—will help you cope with all these stressors.

Problem	Solution	Support
Overwhelming workload	Chapter 1	Chapter 9
	Chapter 2	Chapter 7
	Chapter 3	Chapter 8
	Chapter 11	
Speaking up in meetings	Chapter 7	
	Chapter 4	
Demanding supervisors	Chapter 9	Chapter 7
Too little responsibility	Chapter 9	
	Chapter 11	
Sexual harassment	Chapter 9	Chapter 7
Experiencing stress symptoms	Chapter 1	
	Chapter 2	
	Chapter 10	
Feeling you'll never get ahead	Chapter 4	
	Chapter 8	
Difficulty balancing work and home	Chapter 11	
Forgetfulness on the job	Chapter 8	
Being late for work	Chapter 8	
Failure to meet deadlines	Chapter 8	

ACKNOWLEDGMENTS

Pursuing a healthy lifestyle is an ongoing process and this book represents my journey to date. There are many individuals who greatly contributed to this book. Charles Lawrence has been a guide and mentor for many years. Elaine Summers initiated my journey, introducing me to Kinetic Awareness and a wealth of avenues for pursuing physical and mental health. Dr. C. Norman Shealy, and the staff at the Shealy Stress and Pain Reduction Clinic in Springfield, Mo., introduced me to many of the principles and methods in this book. Dr. Henry Rucker's spirit and teachings were with me throughout. And of course, Ted Hoffman, who shared his knowledge and patience in teaching me to write.

The following individuals read various chapters and offered their expertise in their respective fields: Charles Lawrence, Lena Furgeri, EdD, CSW Mike Murrell, MSC, and Sara Powell, PT. Harvey Perlow, DDS, and Charles Vogel, DDS, offered valuable information as did Anna H. Griffin, RD, MSN, and April Palmieri. Clients, friends, and family have served as invaluable models and examples throughout the book. I wish to thank them all.

Both authors wish to thank Deborah Kurtz, our original editor at Prentice Hall, for her initial conception of this book. We greatly appreciate the editorial expertise offered by our Prentice Hall editor Ellen S. Coleman. Also, thanks goes to our agent Sarah Lazin for her counsel and support. Holly wishes Robert Warren to know she could not have completed the project without him.

Introduction

WHY YOU NEED A STRESS MANAGEMENT PROGRAM

Life would be quite boring without stress. Having that deadline, balancing career and family, motivates and challenges us. We wouldn't want to completely rid our lives of stress. But for many of us, our stressors limit us, wear us out, leave us feeling overwhelmed, instead of the healthy, vibrant people we'd like to be. Working women are especially at risk for high-stress lives because we often struggle with dual roles, trying to be everything to everybody—with no time left over to just *be*.

If you're trying to juggle career and family, I'm sure you understand the feeling of not knowing whether you're coming or going. Wanting both—career and family—you work hard on the job and strive to be the perfect mate and/or mother as well. If you're single, you have your own overbooked schedule with which to contend. Driven to get ahead professionally, putting in long hours at work, pushing hard to stay fit, and maintaining friendships and an intimate relationship, it's no wonder that you feel exhausted, without enough time to get everything done. What's more, in addition to being exposed to the same pressures as working men, you have additional, different types of stressors and resources for coping, which relate to your gender, roles, biology, and perception of what is stressful.

Most likely, the highly competitive arena of the workplace cannot satisfy all your needs. You may worry that pursuing a fast-paced career may limit your ability to settle down, get married and have kids. Sometimes it may seem next to impossible to give all to a job and be involved in an intimate relationship at the same time. Attempting to balance the two often causes a seemingly never-ending struggle to weave relationships, career, personal identity, and intellectual growth.

Women can find themselves overwhelmed when they try to be all things to all people. Men have tended to accept the price they pay for getting ahead professionally, sacrificing their family involvement, without much consideration of their loved ones' wishes. Women, on the other hand, usually place more emphasis on relationships and a sense of community. Seeking fulfillment through family and relationships and competing in the workplace, where there may be conflicting standards for women, leaves them often feeling pressure on all fronts.

In addition, women usually must work harder than their male colleagues to build a career. While preparing for yours, you may have found yourself limited by outdated customs, sexism, and poor training. From the first day you entered the workplace you probably got mixed messages about your behavior on the job. Rewarded for being passive, caring, helpful, obedient, and helpless, most women find that conformity and being popular are emphasized over assertiveness and competitiveness—traits needed in the workplace. When aggressive and confrontational at work, a woman is often accused of being unfeminine and uncaring. Where she's labeled a "bitch," her male counterpart is seen as shrewd or simply doing his job. Building self-esteem and self-image is a complex and confusing process for today's woman. Pleasing others often leaves you with an identity loss and poor sense of self—unable to speak up at meetings, say no to overloads of work or personal demands, or initiate discussions about raises.

Women and their work roles consistently have been viewed by society as less important than men's. At your office, for example, are you often talked down to, talked over, and/or interrupted by men? You may face work discrimination in many forms, from blatant to subtle. Have you been regularly passed over for promotion or denied certain positions? Pregnant women in particular are frequently seen as a liability. Though only recently publicized, sexual harassment, a form of discrimination, has been regularly experienced by women for decades.

Occupations in which there is little control or power, such as secretaries, nurses, waitresses, teachers, and social workers, tend to fall to women, while their male counterparts are managers, doctors, restauranteurs, principals, and supervisors. Though very demanding, traditional "female" jobs are low in benefits, power, and control, making them more stressful than many "male" jobs.

When coping with stress in the workplace, you may find that you tend to be more negative in your self-evaluation than your male colleagues. Do you often take responsibility for failure, blaming it on something personal rather than attributing it to outside forces? In solving problems, you may be more emotionally focused—seeing the stressor as something that must be tolerated—rather than problem-oriented and aimed at changing the stressor. This can lead to feeling overwhelmed.

Because the workplace was designed for men without taking into account women's life cycles and/or their needs, women are penalized for responding to their biological clock and having children. Work schedules are designed for men who have no home responsibilities. Mothers who return to work after raising children often must compete with eager, aggressive young men. When women seek connectedness and fulfillment through a family relationship, their careers usually suffer.

Biologically, women have stressors such as pregnancy, menstruation, and menopause, which physically affect the body, the emotions, and one's ability to cope with stress. In addition, many women pick up the bad habits traditionally considered those of working men—cigarette smoking, excess alcohol consumption, and lack of exercise. More women suffer from heart attacks than in decades past.

Chances are you entered your own stressful work environment unprepared for encountering discrimination and harassment, without enough assertiveness necessary to compete, and perhaps with a poorly defined self-image in relation to your role at the workplace. Do you cope with these stressors by going home at the end of the day, putting your feet up and relaxing for the rest of the evening? If you're like most women, you probably find even more responsibilities at home, especially if you are a parent.

THE SECOND SHIFT:
THE WORKING WOMAN'S "OTHER" JOB

How did everything get so screwed up? After all, what's the big deal about working? In general, societal expectations have not changed as quickly as have lifestyles. Historically, men have been providers and women cared for the children and household. The man was seen as the strong "breadwinner," whereas the woman was viewed as the submissive "little homemaker." This male/female role stereotype has been passed down to the 1990's—even though reality today is very different than in decades past. Over the past twenty years, patterns of family life have been changing rapidly, resulting in more two-career relationships, delayed marriages, and later childbearing than ever before. Frequently, women opt to retain their jobs after they give birth or re-enter the job market when their children are still young. In addition, with the increase in divorce, more women must support themselves and their children. In fact, it is estimated that more than half of all American children born in 1980 will probably spend some time living in a single-parent household before reaching the age of eighteen. The majority of these households will be headed by women.

It has been said that women get off work and go home—to work. While women may work as many hours as men, they usually carry the responsibilities of the household too. Even when there are no children, it is usually the woman who assumes the majority of "homemaking" chores. Men who have been raised to see themselves as the breadwinner often refuse to take on household chores and nurturing duties. For them it is "women's work," not in keeping with their self-image. As long as men do not accept equal responsibility in the home, working women will experience excess stress, especially if they have young children.

The dilemma of working both outside and inside the home—this dual-role conflict—is one that faces many women today.

Although in general working outside the home improves psychological health by providing a sense of accomplishment and satisfaction and increasing self-esteem, the positive effect holds true only when the roles of family and work are well-integrated and when a marriage is satisfying. It is important to note that for women, *family stress*, combined with work, is often an important factor in determining mental health. If you are having difficulties with your mate and/or family members, undergoing financial problems, or raising a child with special needs, you take with you extra stressors. Women with young children who don't get much help and support from their mate (or the father of their children), and who have a less supportive work environment, find their dual role ultra-stressful and may suffer more for it.

Therefore, a stress-management guide for working women must take into account all areas of the working woman's life. In this book we will be looking at causes and solutions for stressful situations both on the job and off.

WHAT THIS BOOK WILL DO FOR YOU

Working women often underestimate how stressed they are. You may never seem to have time to stop and take a break, but still be unaware of the adverse effects your hectic schedule is having on you, accepting exhaustion as part of your daily life. Have you ever thought, "If I'm going to play in a man's world and still fulfill my role as mate and/or mother, do I have to accept being exhausted?" Has being stressed out simply become a part of your life? Though you may feel you're accomplishing something by over-extending yourself, it is not a healthy way to consistently live your life. Taking simple steps to understand how you can better support your busy lifestyle will guarantee that you will be affected less adversely by the negative effects of stress.

Although every woman will respond differently to stress, depending on her genetic makeup, background, and coping methods and resources, there are certain general aspects of a working woman's life that are particularly stressful. They are:

◆ too many roles—being many things to many people

◆ too many responsibilities—balancing family and career

◆ too many choices

◆ not enough preparation for making choices

◆ not enough support once choices are made

Techniques and skills needed by working women for successfully managing stress are:

◆ awareness

◆ healthy diet

◆ exercise

◆ relaxation methods

◆ assertiveness

◆ time management

◆ problem-solving capabilities

◆ good support systems

◆ positive self-image

The stress-management program in *The Working Woman's Guide to Managing Stress,* in which each of the aforementioned techniques will be discussed in detail, is designed to increase your awareness of stress and its effects. Identifying the stressors in your life is the first step toward managing them. The chapter that follows will show you how to determine your stress level by checking off items on the Common Stress Symptoms Checklist, taking the Daily Stress Test, and going over the Major Life Event Stress Scale. Once you have discerned your needs, you can begin using the *Guide* to plan your own personal stress-reduction program.

Managing your stress doesn't mean simply eliminating all your stressors. In this book you will learn when to avoid, eliminate, alter, or accept stressful situations. Changing a situation is an effective means of coping with stress. You can *change* your habits, environment, and relationships (your behavior—not others'). As described in Chapter 6, you may find that you want to *alter* your diet by reducing sweets and caffeine and increasing your whole grains and vegetables. You (hopefully) may wish to *quit* smoking. At work you might find that by *developing* assertiveness skills and improving your communication techniques (detailed in Chapter 7), you can better cope with a difficult co-worker or too many demands. *Restructuring* your work area may take pressure off your body and improve your stamina (see Chapter 9). One means of changing, discussed in Chapter 4, involves *altering your perception* of a situation—thinking about it in another way. A deadline that seems overwhelming, for example, may be *reconsidered* and put into perspective.

Learning relaxation techniques will help you respond less intensely to stressful situations. For instance, when stuck in traffic on the way to work, you have two options: You can rant and rave and worry—pumping adrenaline into your system and speeding up bodily functions—or you can take a deep breath and practice the techniques presented in this book. The former wears out your body and sets you up for health problems, and the latter engages the relaxation response and helps improve your mental and physical well-being.

Here, you will learn that you *do* have a choice when dealing with the many stressors in your life. Through the acquisition of some new skills, plus rethinking your lifestyle, you can cope effectively with stress. First, a few suggestions before you start.

A Note From The Author

I've learned from friends and family—and, in the past, from myself—that although everyone seems to acknowledge that stress exists, and many realize how it adversely affects them, they still deny that it impacts their health. When they get a cold or stomachache during an emotionally or physically stressful period, they will deny any connection. One friend, for example, worried constantly about returning to work after having a baby, and her first week back became stricken with the flu. She insisted that everyone was sick at work, refusing to admit that she had stressed her immune system by fretting over her child's well-being.

We mistakenly feel that if we get sick from being stressed, we are somehow weak, that we should have been able to overcome our stressor(s). This is, in part, because we have grown up with the traditional medical model that sees disease and illness as something that comes from outside and can therefore be treated by "outside" elements such as pills or surgery, prescribed by a doctor. Today, more and more physicians recognize that all ailments have a stress component and that we play an important part in our own health. In fact, medical literature suggests that anywhere from 65 percent to 85 percent of all visits to a doctor have a stress factor.

You do have the power to change *many* of the things in your life that contribute to your health. But keep in mind that this involves a gradual and continual process of growth and learning. Also remember, not all things can change. Many so-called "new age" thinkers have put a great deal of responsibility for illness on the individual, tying specific physical ailments to certain emotional conditions. I've known cancer patients who were so convinced by this line of thinking that they blamed themselves for the inability to cure themselves. This is a dangerous view. Yes, you are responsible for your own health, and it is possible to change many old habits and beliefs. Don't expect it to happen overnight, though, and if it doesn't work at the speed you wish, do not blame yourself. Remember, it's taken you a lifetime to develop the habits you now have: Give yourself time to slowly but surely make positive changes. By using this process, the stress-reduction steps you take will become part of your life, not just another fad to try.

HOW TO USE THIS BOOK

The Working Woman's Guide to Managing Stress is designed to help you move from feeling helpless and out of control to taking an active role in responding to and dealing with stress. You can't always control your world, but you can influence your perception of and response to it. Within these pages, you will find proven-effective stress-management methods, presented in a way to help you integrate them into your busy life. I hope you will approach this book's material with a joyful perspective and make stress reduction a pleasurable activity.

To get the most from this book, I suggest that you first read through the book once, then go back and focus on aspects that are particularly relevant to your life. Since time is a commodity in short supply for most working women, you may be unable to read the book from cover to cover immediately. If that's the case, I strongly advise that you start by reading "Identifying the Stress in Your Life" (Chapter 1) and the first half of "Using Relaxation to Decrease Your Stress" (Chapter 2). This information is the foundation upon which the rest of the book is built. Then choose what interests you; you may want to focus on exercise and improving your diet, which go hand in hand, before learning the relaxation techniques. Many women do not know how to be assertive. If setting limits or asking for what you need is difficult, read "How Assertiveness Can Lead to Stress Reduction" (Chapter 7). If you suspect that emotions such as anger, depression, or boredom are affecting you, turn to "Using Your Mind to Decrease Stress" (Chapter 4). You can refer to the Quick Guide: Common Work-Related Problems and How to Solve Them on page ix as a handy chart for locating specific problems.

The book is designed so that you can flip back and forth; each chapter has self-contained information. Often, I'll suggest that you go to another chapter for more detail on a particular aspect of a topic. For example, if you determine that headaches are a symptom of your work stress, you may want to skip to Chapter 10 to read "Rx and Exercises for Stress-Related Problems." Near the end of the book, Chapter 11 Mastering the Work-Home Balance" gives helpful ideas about incorporating into your life the techniques you've been learning. Different suggestions should apply to your own personal situation, whether you are single, part of a two-career household, married with children, or a single mother.

As you read through the chapters, keep in mind that making major lifestyle changes to accommodate stress-reduction techniques can at first be stressful. It's important to make changes *gradually*—don't try to do everything at once. Focus on a few aspects at a time. You may want to start with goal planning to set priorities, then find you need time-management skills; both are addressed in Chapter 8. Developing clear goals, getting organized, and learning to ask for what you want may be just the ticket for decreasing work stress. Relaxation training is *guaranteed* to reduce stress. It does take practice, though, to learn the techniques and discipline to incorporate them into your schedule. The rewards are well worth the trouble it takes, however.

Along the way to de-stressing your life, acknowledge your efforts. Don't criticize yourself for not exercising or eating healthfully every single day if you are at the moment concentrating on learning relaxation methods. Instead, applaud yourself for your accomplishments. Too often we see only where we have to go—not how far we have come. The fact that you've picked up this book and started reading it is in itself a step in the right direction.

Congratulations on your decision to make your life less stressful—and good luck in your endeavors!

Before Starting This Program

If you are experiencing physical symptoms—heart palpitations, migraines, high blood pressure—be sure to consult a physician. Even though you suspect there is a stress component to your complaint and that relaxation training will be beneficial, get a check up before beginning this program.

Chapter One

IDENTIFYING THE STRESS IN YOUR LIFE

Kristine, 38, is the production manager of a small graphic arts/typesetting firm. Because of the recession, the company has been doing badly and employees are very nervous about losing their jobs. Finally, hope arrives in the form of an extremely large account, which unfortunately requires more workers than the company has to complete the job on time. So, to meet the deadline, Kristine and her staff must work overtime every day and on weekends. As the liaison between top management and the employees, Kristine feels an inordinate amount of pressure. If she and her staff do not complete the job punctually, they could lose the account, which would result in staff cuts.

To make matters worse, she feels extra pressure to perform because she is a woman. Previously Kristine's job was held by a man, and the top management personnel are male. Lately co-workers have praised her predecessor, emphasizing that he handled things differently. As a woman, Kristine feels she has to constantly prove herself, which adds to the already stressful situation.

Soon Kristine's entire life begins to revolve around her job. Because she has a one-hour commute, she wakes up every morning at 5 A.M. to get to work. She usually stays at the office until 7 or 8

P.M., so by the time she drives home, she has little time for anything before retiring. Emotionally exhausted, Kristine barely communicates with her husband. In the evening, she chugs down a few beers and stares at the TV until going to bed. This bothers her since her relationship with her husband is very important to her. Another priority is keeping a clean and organized home, though lately it has become a mess.

Kristine has begun putting on weight, which really disturbs her since she struggled to lose twenty-five pounds the year before. Junk food and sweets are so easy to grab as she rushes through the day. Her self-esteem, affected by criticisms at work, is lowered more by feeling unattractive and sluggish. What concerns her most, though, is her lower back. It has begun to hurt unbearably. This tires her further, making her even more irritable. Even though she knows her problems derive from overwork, it doesn't make the pain any more tolerable, and she is concerned about long-term damage to her back.

Anyone in Kristine's position—male or female—would experience some side effects from such a work load. As a woman, however, Kristine also experiences excess stress as she struggles not only to compete with the male managers but to maintain her marital relationship and home. Unfortunately, like many women, it is her physical and mental health that suffers.

Kristine's experience perfectly exemplifies stress and its negative effects. Because of her ongoing, unrelieved stress, her body, which had been giving her such warning signs as fatigue, edginess, and food and alcohol cravings, is finally letting her know that it is in distress, causing her back muscles to tense to the point of excruciating pain. Modeling herself after the men around her, she continues to overwork, underestimating the toll it is taking.

All of us experience and respond to daily stressors, though not always as extreme as in Kristine's case. When excess tension builds up and there is no release, as with Kristine, you may find yourself experiencing such symptoms as fatigue, inability to concentrate, irritability, upset stomach, insomnia, high blood pressure, backaches, headaches, and frequent colds and flu's.

In this chapter, you will be looking at what stress is and how it affects your body. You will identify stressors in your life and your particular stress symptoms. Identifying areas where you can make changes will allow you to develop your own personalized plan to better manage your stress. Awareness and understanding are the first step. We will also look at the steps Kristine can take to de-stress her life both at home and on the job.

WHAT IS STRESS?

Stressed-out. Stress queen. Stressed to the max. The word "stress" has become almost a cliché in today's fast-paced, busy society. Most of us use the word freely, usually to describe what we think is causing the way we feel. But what is stress, really?

Stress is the nonspecific response of the body to any demand made on it. What does that mean? The term, defined by stress researcher Hans Selye, simply refers to your response to any change or demand made upon you—mental, physical, chemical, or emotional. It's a chemical reaction that allows us to adjust, resist, or adapt to stressors in our lives in order to maintain our natural balance, or "homeostasis." You can't avoid it and wouldn't want to. But the cumulative demands of everyday life can build up and the body may not be able to maintain its balance, leaving you unable to function to your maximum potential.

Let's clear up an important misconception: The idea that stress is all in your mind simply isn't true. Stress is always associated with a release of adrenaline into the bloodstream, which speeds up bodily functions, prompting the name the "wear-and-tear disease." Intense or prolonged stress causes the body's balance to become upset and malfunction. This leads to the breakdown of bodily functions and lowers resistance to illness.

Anything that causes stress is a "stressor." A myriad of things can produce stress: your environment, physical strains, emotions. Environmental stressors include cold and hot temperatures, noise, air pollution, overcrowding, and poor working conditions. Illness, injury, infections, overexertion, sedentariness, poor nutrition, and lack of sleep are all physical stressors. For most of us, however, our primary source of stress does not lie in the external realm, but *inter-*

nally—within our emotions, thoughts, and perceptions. The way we perceive a situation will determine whether we respond with a stress response or instead maintain a balanced state.

Not everyone reacts to individual stressors in the same way. What is a recognizable stress to one person may cause little response in another. For example, too little responsibility on the job may suit one woman but disturb another. Many women thrive on deadlines, whereas others feel overwhelmed by them and constantly worry if they will finish.

The same stressor that has a marked effect on you one day may not affect you at all the next week. Presenting a report at a meeting may bolster your self-esteem one week; the following month the same responsibility can leave you feeling completely overloaded. Its impact is relative to the number of stressors you have encountered simultaneously and their cumulative effect. Your age, health, personality, ethnic background, and your own parents' responses to stressful situations also influence your stress response.

Many people tend to think that only negative experiences cause stress. This isn't true. Any demand made on the body will be a stress; how you respond to and recover from the event is what counts. Exercise, for instance, is a healthy stress, although too much of it, of course, can be damaging. If you decide to start exercising after work—a healthy idea—you must adjust to the changes it places on your schedule and body. Getting a promotion, though positive, can cause stress since it creates changes in your routine, as well as new demands. So does starting a promising new job or being given a challenging project. In fact, you'll see in the Major Life Event Stress Scale on pages 21–23 that getting married rates higher on the stress scale than being fired from your job! What's important is being aware that even something good in your life can wear you out, so you can learn to tune in to your body's needs.

Stress should not be viewed entirely as a bad thing, however. Yes, "negative" stress, or "distress," can indeed cause problems, depending on how one reacts to it. But it can also be positive and stimulating. In fact, a completely stress-free life would be a great big yawn! We all need challenges to help us focus, perform, and feel alive. Therefore, we don't want to rid our life of stress completely, but we do want to learn how to manage it. To summarize:

1. Many things can cause stress—illness, poor nutrition, lack of exercise, too much exercise, noise, cold, air pollution, vacations, holidays, worry, fear.

2. Not everyone responds to stress in the same way: what stresses one woman doesn't necessarily stress another.

3. What stresses you one day may not stress you next week.

4. A positive event can be stressful.

5. Stress can be "distressing," or conversely, it can be challenging.

How Stress Affects You

Today it is readily accepted that stress plays an important role in most illnesses. Emotional responses translate into physical symptoms, and stress may actually cause such conditions as peptic ulcers, bronchial asthma, high blood pressure, headaches, and backaches. In other situations emotional turmoil causes susceptibility to organic disease and infection. The fatigue, poor concentration, and irritability you feel, your overreaction to situations, and a negative attitude are your first signs of stress.

Now's a good time to use the Common Stress Symptoms Checklist (below) to pinpoint your own symptoms of stress.

COMMON STRESS SYMPTOMS CHECKLIST

Check all the reactions to stress that you have experienced recently

Muscular

❑ sore/tense muscles   ❑ aches and pains   ❑ headaches
❑ backaches   ❑ TMJ (jaw pain)   ❑ teeth grinding

Sleep Disturbance

❑ insomnia   ❑ wake up early
❑ wake up in the middle of the night and unable to return to sleep

Infection

❑ frequent colds/flu   ❑ herpes

(continued)

Appetite/Weight Change

❑ increase/decrease   ❑ increase alcohol,
   in food intake   tobacco, drug use

Stomach Disturbances

❑ digestive upset   ❑ queasiness   ❑ diarrhea
❑ constipation   ❑ ulcers   ❑ colitis

Skin

❑ cold hands and feet   ❑ hives   ❑ rash
❑ itchy skin

Physical

❑ fatigue/low energy   ❑ high blood pressure   ❑ restlessness
❑ trembling/twitching   ❑ tightness/pain in chest ❑ lump in throat
❑ pounding heart   ❑ weakness/dizziness   ❑ abnormal sweating
❑ stuttering   ❑ dry mouth/throat   ❑ easily startled by
                                                    small sounds

Behaviors

❑ nail/lip biting   ❑ clumsiness   ❑ accident proneness
❑ foot-tapping/finger drumming

Addictions

❑ work   ❑ sex   ❑ alcohol/drugs/
                                                    caffeine/sugar

Mental

❑ poor concentration   ❑ preoccupation   ❑ negative attitude
❑ negative self talk   ❑ procrastination   ❑ forgetfulness

Emotional

❑ anger   ❑ anxiety   ❑ worry
❑ depression   ❑ mood swings   ❑ frustration
❑ sadness   ❑ feelings of emptiness ❑ overreacting to
                                                    situations

Understanding The Stress Response

The body's physical reaction to stress is known as the "fight or flight response," because the body immediately reacts to threat or danger—regardless of whether the hazard is real or perceived. In emergency situations this response results in quick bursts of energy to flee or else stand and meet the challenge. Primitive humans, who were constantly escaping from or fighting predators, needed this instinctive response to survive.

Few situations faced today require such a strong response, however. But it still occurs; our bodies respond as if we need to elude a saber-toothed tiger, rather than finish a presentation for an important board meeting. We therefore lack the physical outlets of primitive man or animals. Think about it: When your boss yells at you, or your child-care provider calls in sick, you usually won't have the opportunity to run around the block to work off the effects of that extra adrenaline that's just kicked in.

During the fight or flight response the following series of changes occur:

♦ Adrenaline and other hormones are released into your bloodstream

♦ Your heart rate increases

♦ Your blood pressure goes up

♦ Your breathing becomes shallow and accelerated

♦ Your muscles tense for activity, especially the neck, jaw, shoulders, and back, often leaving stiff shoulders and an achy back as a painful souvenir

♦ Blood flow is restricted to the digestive organs, which eventually can result in such problems as stomach ulcers

♦ Blood flow is constricted in the hands and feet, which explains why they may feel cold

♦ The liver releases sugar, which elevates energy levels

♦ Blood flow increases to the brain and major muscles

♦ The body perspires to cool itself.

This response can be triggered wholly or in part. If you've ever been in a car that just barely missed having an accident, you probably recall the full-blown response in which your heart raced, stomach knotted, palms sweated, muscles tensed, and breathing became shallow. In such a case, the response was appropriate for the situation. After the danger passed, you then began to calm down and return to normal; the danger signals were no longer being sent to the nervous system.

Most of us don't often experience life-threatening events. But we do encounter daily ongoing real or perceived threats that keep the body in a constant state of arousal, preventing the stress response from being turned off and returning to a balanced state. Constant worry about the quality of your work, deadlines, unpaid bills, and confronting a tyrannical boss—all of which may be perceived as threatening—inappropriately trigger the stress response.

There is always some physical response associated with stress. No matter the degree of the response, the body releases hormones, such as adrenaline and (under chronic stress) cortisone, which eventually wear down specific areas of the body. The immune system becomes unable to fight off infections and disease. Medical studies have linked stress and contracting a cold. Many of us catch a flu; some get herpes infections. Some people tend to engage the muscle-tension aspect of the stress response and suffer backaches or headaches. Stomach ulcers are another manifestation, particularly for those who have difficulty expressing anger and who engage in poor eating habits, such as eating when tense. When stress goes unchecked, more serious problems can occur. Stroke and heart disease—our society's biggest killers—have been linked to stress.

Identifying Your Daily Stressors

Your performance on the job is affected not only by pressures at work but by all the other factors in your life. Every day we're assaulted by stressors that are so insidious that we don't even realize their effect on us. What happens, though, is that each one builds on top of another, so that soon the accumulation begins to affect our health. Poor dietary habits, such as eating junk food and drinking caffeinated beverages and alcohol, combined with environmental stressors, like air pollution and noisy traffic, added to emotional stressors, can eventually result in an avalanche of stress. Receiving criticism on a report you wrote may send you over the edge if you've had little sleep, skipped breakfast, and have been drinking coffee all morning. Be aware of each of these variables, so that you can eliminate those you *can* control—to better deal with those that you cannot. Just because you are not consciously aware of any physical or emotional reactions to stressors does not mean that your body isn't reacting. The Daily Stress Test below will help you determine the day-to-day stressors in your life. It will help you to identify the areas of your life where you can reduce stress.

DAILY STRESS TEST

Read each item and circle whether it is: (0) False/Never (1) Sometimes True (2) Often True (3) Almost Always True (4) Always True

Stress From Your Diet

1. I usually start the day with sweet rolls, pancakes,
   or sugared cereal   0 1 2 3 4

2. I regularly eat desserts and/or sweet snacks during
   the day, especially when I'm tired   0 1 2 3 4

3. I drink coke or other soft drinks often   0 1 2 3 4

4. I heavily salt my food   0 1 2 3 4

5. I eat salty, fried foods such as potato chips, salted nuts   0 1 2 3 4

6. I drink more than two cups of coffee or tea (or other
   caffeine drinks) a day   0 1 2 3 4

   I eat a well balanced diet of fresh fruits and vegetables
   and whole grains

   (Subtract half of a point from your total score.)

Stress from Drugs and Alcohol

1. I smoke 20 or more cigarettes a day   0 1 2 3 4

2. I take tranquilizers or sleeping pills regularly   0 1 2 3 4

3. I often have a drink at night to relax   0 1 2 3 4

4. I drink more than 1 ounce of alcohol (or 4-5 oz. of wine
   or beer) a day   0 1 2 3 4

   I do not smoke

   (Subtract half of a point from your total score.)

(continued)

Stress From the Environment

1. I live in a city of 300,000 or more   0 1 2 3 4
2. I live in a climate that is uncomfortable for me   0 1 2 3 4
3. I have little privacy   0 1 2 3 4
4. I am exposed to other people's cigarette smoke   0 1 2 3 4

Stress From Lack of Exercise

1. I do no regular exercise   0 1 2 3 4
2. I get some exercise (1 or 2 days a week)   4 3 2 1 0
3. My way of relaxing is to watch TV each night   0 1 2 3 4
4. I am overweight (or underweight) by more than 10 lbs.   0 1 2 3 4
   I do regular aerobic exercise
   (Subtract half of a point from your total score.)

Stress From Lack of Sleep

1. I get less than 7 hours of sleep   0 1 2 3 4
2. I never relax except when I'm sleeping   0 1 2 3 4

Personal Relations and Social Activities

1. I am in a stressful relationship   0 1 2 3 4
2. I never have time to see my friends   0 1 2 3 4
3. I rarely do something just for fun   0 1 2 3 4
4. I feel unsatisfied with my personal relationships   0 1 2 3 4
   I make time for enjoyable activities with friends and family
   (Subtract half of a point from your total score.)

Job Stress

1. I feel frustrated at my job   0 1 2 3 4
2. I work more than 40 hours per week   0 1 2 3 4
3. I sit most of the day   0 1 2 3 4
4. I have little control over my job and responsibilities   0 1 2 3 4
5. I feel overworked   0 1 2 3 4
6. I feel bored at my job   0 1 2 3 4
7. I have little opportunity for advancement   0 1 2 3 4
8. I am underpaid for my job   0 1 2 3 4
9. I have conflicts with my boss or co-workers   0 1 2 3 4

(continued)

10. I work more than one job   0 1 2 3 4
    I derive satisfaction from my job
    (Subtract half of a point from your total score.)

If your score was 25 and below you have a low level of stress in your life;
35 you have mild stress in your life; 55 and over you have many sources of
stress with which to contend.

Change As A Stressor

For most of us, it is daily ongoing stress that tends to wear us out.
We cope with it, accepting allergies or mild aches and pains. But
what may tip the balance between staying healthy and getting sick
are events or changes we encounter. There are certain circumstances—both joyful and sorrowful—that can add extra stress. The
more changes in your life, the more susceptible you will be to experiencing stress symptoms. The following standardized scale, derived
through research, demonstrates the degree of stress brought on by
certain major life events. The number following the event shows the
stress impact, on a scale of 1-100. Notice how many changes you
have recently undergone; if you have encountered major changes in
your personal life, it will impact your performance at work.

MAJOR LIFE EVENT STRESS SCALE
(THE MODIFIED HOLMES/RAHE STRESS SCALE)

Circle all of the following that have occurred in the past year. Then add up
your score.

Life Event	*Scale*
Death of your spouse	100
Divorce	73
Separation from your mate	65
Death of close family member	63

(continued)

Major personal illness/injury	53
Getting married	50
Being fired at work	47
Marital reconciliation with mate	45
Major change in the health/behavior of family member	44
Pregnancy	40
Sexual difficulties	39
Gaining a new family member (birth, adoption)	39
Starting a new company	39
Your company is merging with a larger company	39
A new worker seems to be vying for your position	39
Your boss is fired	38
Major change in financial state (better or worse)	38
Death of close friend	37
Changing to different line of work	36
Major change in number of arguments with spouse	35
Buying a home	31
Foreclosure on a mortgage/loan	30
Receiving a promotion	30
Major change in work responsibilities	29
Son or daughter leaving home (college, marriage, etc.)	29
In-law troubles	29
Getting an award for work achievement	29
Major change in living conditions (renovations, etc.)	25
Revision of personal habits (dress, habits, etc.)	24
Troubles with boss	23
Major changes in working hours or conditions	20
Change in residence	20
Major change in type or amount of recreation	19
Major change in church/spiritual activities	18
Major change in social activities	17
Major change in sleeping habits	16
Major change in number of family get-togethers	15
Major change in eating habits	15
Christmas	13

Vacation	12
Minor violations of the law (traffic ticket)	11

Total Score _____

The more change you have in your life, the higher your score, and the more likely you are to get sick.

Adapted from and reprinted with permission from Journal of Psychosomatic Research, Vol 11, Thomas A. Holmes, Richard H. Rahe, Elsevier Science Ltd., Pergamon Imprint, Oxford, England, 1967.

ARE YOU PRONE TO STRESS?

Have you ever noticed how some people seem to take life's little upsets in stride while others stay constantly wound up? Some women can handle several stressful situations before the stress response affects them; others react immediately. Are you afraid you won't look good for your important meeting? Do you worry that you won't get any recognition for your work? Do you complain to others around you at the supermarket when the person in the "Express" checkout line has more than the allotted number of items? Are you a horn-honker when the car in front of you hasn't pulled away quickly enough at a traffic light? Do you get upset if your meeting has been rescheduled, even though the switch is more convenient? If you can relate to any of these behaviors, you may be experiencing stress from inner sources.

Certain personality types, or temperaments, are more stress-prone than others. To find out if your personality is particularly susceptible in responding to stress, answer the following questions:

1. Are you over-scheduled? Do you take on more than you can do? Are you unable to say no, and therefore have no time of your own? Do you over-commit?

2. Are you a perfectionist? Do you try to be the perfect employee, lover, wife, mother? Are you always hard on yourself and feel you could have done better?

3. Do you worry about what people think? Do you go over how you looked, acted, sounded? Do you rerun conversations in your head?

4. Do you hate to wait? Do you have difficulty waiting—for a colleague to finish a report, at the copying machine, in line at the bank, supermarkets, department stores, in traffic jams, waiting for friends to show up?

5. Are you a constant worrier?

6. Are you unable to take time for yourself? Do you need constant stimulation?

If you answered "yes" to two or more of these questions, chances are that stress has become a way of life for you.

One stressful trait particularly common among women is perfectionism. Our culture sends messages that women are to look and act perfect. Most women are taught beginning in childhood to be patient and nonassertive. This is an impossible (and undesirable) goal in any era, but it is even more so today as most women juggle careers and homemaking. Author and popular speaker Dr. Joan Borysenko began a lecture I attended by asking the audience to think of their worst fear. Without hesitation I thought, "Making a mistake." I was instantly horrified at my response, but as I learned, this is not an uncommon feeling. A fear of making mistakes is tied to feelings of inadequacy and the need for approval. We are afraid that people will find out that we're not as good, smart, or competent as we are trying to make them think we are (because deep down we believe we are inadequate). The fear that we won't meet a deadline, turn in a good proposal, or be a good enough mother, for example, leaves us feeling defensive and unable to tolerate criticism. These fears in turn trigger the fight or flight response. And so the stress-response cycle continues.

How we feel about ourselves, low self-esteem, and lack of confidence can lead to feelings of helplessness and loss of control, influencing how the body recovers from stress. Helplessness suppresses the immune system and decreases our resistance to disease. In fact, some researchers believe the inability to feel in control is more damaging than the stressful event itself. People who experience a sense of being in control have greater coping capacities and experience fewer harmful effects of stress. The implications for women are obvious.

Stress And Your Emotions

The following emotions have been linked to stress:

Fear is one of the most powerful negative emotions. It impedes your life if you constantly think about things that might happen: "If I don't do good work on this project, I may lose my job, and then I won't have the money we need. Jane won't be able to take music lessons, and John won't be able to go on the school trip, and I will be a failure both in my job and as a mother." Lecturer and developer of "Attitudes For Attunement," Dr. Henry Rucker calls fear "a fantasy of what might be." It's not based on real facts because, ironically, what we fear rarely comes true. Yet, if you are constantly frightened and think the worst, you will set up the conditions for bad things to happen (you'll be too stressed to do a good job on the report) as well as constantly trigger the stress response.

Chronic worry is tied to fear and its recurring thought, "what if." Reflecting a lack of self-confidence, chronic worry is extremely fatiguing. It takes your mind off what you should be doing, whatever task is at hand.

Anger can be a self-destructive emotion when out of proportion to the situation and/or when it is inappropriately expressed. Frustration, irritation, and impatience at others or at situations set you up to constantly push and over-schedule yourself. Since the Sixties there has been controversy over the pros and cons of expressing anger. In the 1960s and early 1970s, a popular school of thought encouraged people to let out their anger, or "ventilate." More recently, however, it is thought that the expression of anger isn't as important as whether or not the person constantly feels angry. Chronic hostility is a problem, and continually expressing it can lead to an habitual response to any annoying situation. Conversely, and equally problematic, there are individuals who never experience anger, or they feel it but cannot express it. I believe that being in touch with your feelings, and recognizing and acting upon them is vital to good health. In the real world, everyone gets angry—and everyone should express this anger. The key is to determine whether or not the anger is appropriate to the situation and how you plan to express it. You may not even be aware of why you are angry. Consider: Are you angry about waiting in line at the video store because you have been passed over by the clerk, had a fight with a co-worker, or because you always feel frustrated and angry at having to wait? Look for patterns.

Keep a log of your anger: what makes you angry, who makes you angry and to whom you express it, your anger's duration, and any thoughts that accompany it. Deal with your anger directly. If possible, confront the person with whom you are angry, rather than taking it out on someone else or complaining about it to another person. If a co-worker constantly makes the same mistake, confront her with it. If you can't confront the person or situation, take several deep breaths and relax your muscles; exercise after work. Don't brood about what makes you angry. It only keeps you in a stress response and can lead to health problems. Ask yourself: Is it worth getting upset about? If it is, deal with it. If you are unable to work it out, reframe your attitude, and calm yourself with relaxation. Take steps to avoid the anger-producing situation.

STRESSBUSTER: HANDLING ANGER

Studies have shown that women who use exercise to cope with angry feelings are emotionally healthier than those who turn to other outlets such as food, alcohol, or cigarettes. If your boss is driving you crazy, play racquetball, jog, or take an aerobics class after work.

Impatience, which is often related to hostility, causes people to be intolerant of others. You expect others to conform to your standards of perfectionism and are impatient when they don't. It is nearly impossible to relax if you are impatient with yourself and others.

Rigidity/Inflexibility gives a false sense of control and strength. It limits your choices and sets you up for failure. We can control our universe only by our ability to respond to it. In martial arts, for example, you learn to move and flow with your opponent; you learn when to yield, avoid, or punch.

Perfectionism is a sure way to stay continuously disappointed. You (or others) will never be able to live up to your expectations—and this is extremely fatiguing.

Fear, chronic worry, anger, impatience, inflexibility, and perfectionism, all lead to an inability to relax, which causes wear and tear on the mind and body and leaves you susceptible to stress-related symptoms.

Are You Stress-Hardy?

Psychologists Suzanne Kobasa and Salvatore Maddi, in a seven-year study of illness patterns and stress among business managers, found that certain qualities or attitudes affected whether or not an individual was likely to become sick after a stressful event. They found that people who have a sense of personal commitment to what they are doing, and (again) who feel in control of their lives, and who believe life to be challenging, tend to be resistant to many kinds of illness. Labeling these individuals as "stress-hardy," Kobasa and Maddi believe that certain stress-resistant skills—hardiness, commitment, sense of control, and enjoyment of challenge—actually can be taught to people. In determining your own stress level, think about how you approach your job. Do you need to adjust your attitude, changing from stress-prone to stress-hardy?

STRESSBUSTER: SUPPORT AND STRESS

Women are especially sensitive to and benefit from social supports. When social contacts are strengthened, so is the immune system. Research has shown that support systems, such as friends, family, and support groups, actually can increase the number of T-cells (which control and coordinate the immune system).

DESIGNING YOUR STRESS REDUCTION PLAN

Using the example of Kristine from our chapter opening, let's look at how a stress-reduction strategy devised for her can be applied to your own situation. After taking the Daily Stress Test, Kristine determined many stressful areas in her life—not only at work, though her job pressures had triggered many of her symptoms, but in her personal life as well. She identified these stress contributors: overwork on the job; a poor diet including excess alcohol consumption; lack of exercise; and no time for personal relationships. Here's how Kristine plans to decrease her stress level and susceptibility to fatigue, backache, weight gain, and edginess.

Job Stress

Although Kristine can't change her situation—excess overtime to complete her project—she can change her *perception of the stress* and her emotional response to the situation. Kristine, as the liaison between top management and the employees, has begun to feel over-responsible for the workers and their plight if the job doesn't get done. Certainly, this reflects a caring attitude, but her worry doesn't contribute to productivity; it only detracts from it. Kristine must accept that she is doing the best job she can and that others must accept responsibility too. If she's not working at her top potential, that's the place to focus. She may need to develop better time management or assertiveness skills. Likewise, worrying about the deadline only causes more stress. Kristine can *reframe her attitude* to see it as a challenging opportunity rather than a constant source of stress. She can use affirmations to help support this attitude and keep her calm (see Chapter 4).

Kristine also feels pressure from the male managers because she is a woman. Sexist remarks from her colleagues bother her, making her feel she must do an even better job than her male predecessor. Although she knows that everyone is under pressure and the remarks may be their reaction to stress, she does not have to ignore them. Instead of simply snapping a retort, Kristine can go to the top manager(s) and say she has heard their remarks concerning her (in relation to the last person who had the job). She can then ask if management is happy with the way she is handling her position. If there is dissatisfaction with her performance, she should ask how to improve her work, and discuss the situation clearly and in a professional manner. In this way she is dealing with the situation in an assertive rather than aggressive manner. Kristine also needs to evaluate her role in the situation. Does she question herself because as a woman she has been conditioned to do so? Self-esteem issues come into play here. Kristine will need to reaffirm her self-image and her confidence that she does a good job. She needs to remember that she was hired for her ability.

In addition, Kristine must take better care of her body. She should take breaks and stretch during the day. She can walk around the building to stretch her legs. Instead of eating a sandwich while she works, she needs to make sure she takes a lunch hour. During her lunch hour or on a ten-minute break, she can practice some relaxation exercises. On her commute she should make her ride as comfortable as possible, use an orthopedic pillow to support her back, practice breathing exercises, and keep her muscles relaxed.

On-the-job stress reducers for Kristine include:

• Changing her perception of the stress
• Reframing her attitudes
• Asserting herself
• Enhancing her self-esteem
• Taking breaks and evaluating her physical environment
• Practicing relaxation techniques

Diet

Eating junk food and drinking too much alcohol, Kristine's responses to stress, are actually causing her even more stress. In this case she can *avoid* and *limit* her stressors. Using the guidelines in Chapter 6, Kristine can improve how she feels, increasing her stamina and concentration by changing her diet.

Exercise

Because of Kristine's schedule she will have little time for exercise until the account is completed. She may want to do some physical activity on Sunday, such as taking a walk with her husband or practicing stretching exercises. Because of her back condition, however, she will need to do some basic back-care exercises. She can choose some of the exercises beginning on page 226 (Chapter 10) and do them when she gets up in the morning (about ten minutes) or when she comes home at night.

Relaxation

Kristine's response to her stressful situation—long hours plus a long commute—is excess muscle tension in her back, which creates a painful condition. Progressive muscle relaxation (Chapter 3) will help her feel and release the excess tension. Once she learns the technique, she can practice relaxing her muscles on the way to work as well as during the day. Kristine should combine breathing and progressive muscle relaxation with her back-care exercises.

Relationship With Her Husband

Kristine is concerned that she rarely sees her husband and that they spend little time together just having fun. Exhausted by Sunday, Kristine ends up doing laundry and taking care of household chores with no time or energy left for entertainment.

Having always taken care of the house, Kristine still tries to do so, even though she is now working more than her husband, Dave. They need to sit down and divide responsibilities. Although Kristine needs more help now, this division should be permanent. Because both are working, they may want to use a drop-off laundry service and hire household help every two weeks to do heavy cleaning. This would leave more time for leisure.

The two of them need to do something together as a couple rather than just attending to chores. On Sundays they should plan to see a movie or engage in a hobby they enjoy. Recreation will be very important for Kristine, whose life is totally involved with work at this point. Also, no matter how tired they are they can spend time together at night, reading in bed or sitting together watching TV.

Kristine has several areas of her life in which she can reduce stress. First she will need to set priorities. She should write down the things she wishes to change and what steps she can take and then state them as goals. She might state them by saying, as an affirmation, "I choose to have a healthy, balanced diet," or "I make time to be with Dave." If she thinks her husband will be resistant to helping around the house, she may want to start by changing her diet so she will feel better and be less irritable. Learning to be assertive on the job may take some practice, but changing her perception of the stress and taking deep breaths throughout the day can have immediate effects. For Kristine a priority is her back, and she needs to address that issue right away.

Your Stress-Reduction Program

Now that you have identified some of the stressful areas in your own life using the Daily Stress Test, Major Life Event Stress Scale, and Common Stress Symptoms Checklist, and have answered the questions regarding how stress-prone you are (page 23), you—like Kristine—can begin to make a plan of action. List the areas where you need to make changes using the Personal Stress Reduction Program Form (below). You may have found from the Daily Stress Test that although you eat a healthful diet, and get some exercise, you are only getting six hours of sleep a night. On the Common Stress Symptoms Checklist you may find you checked off fatigue, irritability, accident proneness, forgetfulness, and inability to concentrate. If caffeine is not the culprit in your insomnia, getting more sleep may require that you manage your time better (Chapter 8), or say "no" to extra work on the job and/or projects outside of work (Chapter 7). Or you may be unable to fall asleep because you are thinking about work projects or your relationship with your boyfriend. In that case, practicing relaxation would be your first step (Chapter 2). If worry and perfectionism seem to be keeping you constantly in a stress response, relaxation techniques, reframing your attitude, and using affirmations and visualization can help you break the pattern.

PERSONAL STRESS REDUCTION PROGRAM

Using the space provided, write down your stressors. Writing them down helps clarify them, increases your awareness, and will make it easier to begin to make changes.

Work:

_____

_____

_____

(continued)

Personal:

_____

_____

_____

Relationships/Family:

_____

_____

_____

Habits (eating, sleeping, exercise):

_____

_____

_____

STEPS TO TAKE FOR EACH

Work:

1. _____

2. _____

3. _____

4. _____

5. _____

Personal:

1. _____

2. _____

3. _____

(continued)

4. _____

5. _____

Relationships/Family:

1. _____

2. _____

3. _____

4. _____

5. _____

Habits:

1. _____

2. _____

3. _____

4. _____

5. _____

We all have the resources to combat stress, especially by eating right, exercising, maintaining a positive attitude, and getting plenty of rest and relaxation. Yet many of us persistently maintain continuous, ongoing stress, which keeps us worn out. When numerous stressors occur simultaneously, something has to give. In upcoming chapters, you will learn how to recognize and eliminate potential stressors and replace them with healthy behaviors.

Chapter Two

USING RELAXATION TO DECREASE YOUR STRESS

Sometimes we get so caught up in what we're doing—busily running from one task to the next—that it's hard to tell just how our body really feels. Suddenly, one telltale sign—or several—lets us know that we are overdoing it. If you responded "yes" on the "Stress Symptoms Checklist" to such conditions as fatigue, irritability, lack of concentration, headaches, high blood pressure, or insomnia, relaxation training should be part of your stress-reduction strategy.

Perhaps you have been taking some kind of medication—aspirin, tranquilizers, coffee, or alcohol—to help alleviate your symptoms. This is the quick fix many of us turn to when we have problems. But, as you may have discovered, medications provide only short-term "relief" and often cause unwanted side effects and/or problems of their own.

Regularly practicing relaxation techniques, on the other hand, can engage your own innate mechanisms to help you balance and heal the body and the mind. Relaxation is the foundation of any stress-management program. Everyone can benefit from some type of relaxation; the beauty of it is that mastering relaxation enables you to voluntarily produce an alternative to the stress response and reverse its negative effects.

Relaxation is good for you. It's a much-needed activity for over-stimulated minds and bodies. Under stress, your muscles tense, breathing becomes shallow, heart rate increases, blood pressure elevates, fat is released into the system; during relaxation the opposite happens. In a relaxed state your body doesn't have to work as hard; you need less oxygen, your pulse rate slows, and your blood pressure goes down. Levels of blood lactate—the chemical in your system that causes anxiety—also decrease. As the physical systems slow down, so do the brain waves. During relaxation, brain-wave frequency often changes to alpha, which creates a feeling of emotional well-being. The important benefits of relaxation are:

• A decrease in your heart rate

• A decrease in your blood pressure

• A decrease in your respiration rate

• A decrease in oxygen intake and carbon dioxide expulsion

• A decrease in blood cholesterol and lactate

• A decrease in potential muscle action

• An increase in alpha brain waves

• An increase of the galvanic skin response (the measure used on lie-detector tests)

The Medical Benefits Of Relaxation

Medical researchers have documented the health benefits of relaxation, particularly for people suffering from migraine, tension headache, essential hypertension, and insomnia. Chronic pain patients are regularly taught relaxation to help reduce pain and their body's response to it (usually manifested as muscular tension).

Besides relieving mental and physical tension, a relaxation regimen can strengthen the immune system and produce a range of other medically beneficial changes. A number of studies have documented how the regular practice of relaxation techniques can increase levels of helper T-cells that fight against infectious disease. Since the cardiovascular system is greatly affected by stress, it's no surprise that relaxation training can lower blood pressure and cholesterol levels and lessen the severity of angina attacks. People with adult-onset diabetes, which is related to obesity and diet, benefit from relaxation since the technique improves the body's ability to regulate glucose. Many hospitals, in fact, provide patients with videotapes of relaxation exercises during their stay.

Unfortunately, even though the benefits of relaxation have been proven, many doctors, untrained in relaxation or the effects of stress on the body, overlook or fail to recommend it to their patients as a means of improving their health. Many believe their patients aren't motivated enough to spend time practicing relaxation, and that people prefer just taking a pill. Many of us have been conditioned to agree with this attitude. For most working women, however, pills cannot begin to help with their ongoing response to excess stress, nor can they truly relieve their symptoms. Practicing relaxation has been found to be the best means of preventing and controlling stress-related complaints.

What Is Relaxation?

Relaxation means various things to people. Taking a walk in the country can be very relaxing; so can soaking in a hot bath after a long day. When I use the word "relaxation," though, I am referring to a state of being, initiated by you, in which there are actual physiological and psychological changes. Just feeling relaxed may not mean you are. If you operate at a high arousal level, you will benefit from a relaxing day or evening, but you will not have achieved an actual physiological change activated by the nervous system. In other words, your body is still in the stress-response cycle rather than in the relaxation-response condition.

Taking A Nap Just Isn't Enough

Some people feel if they just take a nap or get a good night's sleep they are counteracting the wear and tear of the stress response. But for many it isn't enough to break the stress cycle. When you regularly practice relaxation, on the other hand, you remain in a more relaxed state after each session as compared to where you began. In addition, if you are tired, twenty minutes of deep relaxation has been found to be as beneficial as two hours' sleep.

Five Major Benefits Of Relaxation Exercises

1. RELAXATION DECREASES YOUR BODY'S AROUSAL LEVEL. Because stress is cumulative, your body may be constantly functioning at what is called a high level of arousal. That is, you never turn off the stress response and allow the body to go back to normal. When the body is in this state, it takes little to further aggravate it. Many people are unaware of being "stressed," but may be bothered by and overreact to little upsets and hassles. For instance, someone misspelling a word on a report may send you into a rage, or you may find yourself steaming while waiting in line at the bank during your lunch hour or in traffic after work. A simple mistake like dropping or forgetting something may trigger more anger and frustration than is warranted.

2. RELAXATION ALLOWS YOU TO RESPOND CALMLY TO STRESS. When your body is less aroused, your "normal" response to a stressful situation also will be lowered. The more you practice relaxation, the easier it will be to remain calm during stressful situations (because you are generally more relaxed and now know how to stay that way). Daily, unavoidable upsets will appear less stressful (because there is less of a cumulative effect), and major ones will be more easily coped with. When your boss tells you she needs the *other* report finished (she was sure she had told you), when you are kept waiting and you are there to help *them* out, when there are only express buses and no locals and you wonder if you'll make it to work on time, you can respond to the situation at hand without fuming, "awfulizing" (thinking the worst), or grinding your teeth.

3. RELAXATION HELPS DURING A CRISIS. The more you practice relaxation, the easier you will find it to relax during stressful situations. For example, you may find yourself taking a deep breath when you're feeling overwhelmed by a deadline at work, or you may laugh off your impatience at being stuck in a traffic jam, turn up your favorite song on the radio, and take a moment to relax your muscles. If your meeting is rescheduled and you find it frustrating, you will remember to notice your reactions, take a deep breath, and reframe the situation—you can use the time to finish another project, do your breathing, or organize your desk.

4. RELAXATION AIDS IN YOUR RECOVERY FROM STRESS. There are times when you will respond fully to a stressful situation. We can't and

don't want to rid our lives of all stressors. Using a relaxation exercise after an incident, however, will help you recover more quickly. All of us have had work deadlines and have pushed ourselves to the max. After such a period, be sure and get back on track by doing your relaxation exercises to return the body to neutral.

5. RELAXATION INCREASES YOUR AWARENESS. As you begin to experience what relaxation feels like, you will become more sensitive to your physical responses to stress and thus notice them sooner. Practicing progressive muscle relaxation helps you learn to feel the difference between tension and release; breathing techniques allow you to become aware of shallow breathing and when you hold your breath. You may become more observant, for example, that you are tensing your neck and jaw muscles and restricting your breathing while reviewing a report; instead, by releasing the jaw and deepening your breathing, you can ward off a full-blown headache.

STRESSBUSTER: BACKSLIDING TIP

Sometimes stress will "win out," and you'll feel like giving in to your past responses, falling back into old bad habits: you eat sweets and drink too much coffee and then relax with a drink, rather than doing exercises and practicing relaxation. Fortunately, your regimen of regular relaxation, a balanced diet, and adequate exercise will enable your body to withstand the havoc and recover with fewer harmful effects. (Be careful not to let bad habits take over, though!)

"I Need To Be Charged Up To Work"

Some people feel they must be charged up to function well. Actually, the reverse is true. When you are relaxed, you have a greater capacity to react appropriately; you can process more information and have a higher degree of concentration. In addition, you will feel more alert and have more available energy.

In one of my lunch-time relaxation seminars, a participant reported that she needed a cup of coffee following the session, because she felt she was too relaxed afterwards to go back to work.

She was not accustomed to experiencing relaxation, much less functioning in a relaxed state. Therefore, she felt she needed to become charged up, to get that adrenaline pumping.

This is not uncommon. Many of us use caffeine to simulate real alertness. In the beginning, the sensation of relaxation may feel like fatigue or collapse. This may be in part because you are tired and are allowing yourself to feel it. You may need to slow down and pay attention to what your body needs. Also it is a new state of being and you may just need to get used to it.

The Art Of Relaxing

Being able to relax is a skill and, like any skill, it takes patience and practice. The more you practice, the easier and faster it will be to perform the steps to relaxation, such as relaxing your shoulders, feeling heaviness in your hands, or staying focused on a word. Of course, the ability to completely relax will not happen overnight, but you should have a general sense of relaxation each time you finish an exercise. The more you practice, the longer this feeling of relaxation will stay with you. It may take several weeks to begin seeing any noticeable changes (give it three months to make real changes in your physical condition or symptom). Each relaxation session should last at least ten minutes, though fifteen to twenty minutes is optimum. Practicing every day should be your goal, but in the beginning, start working it into your schedule three times a week.

The goal of doing a relaxation exercise is to lower your general stress level and allow you, under stress, to respond appropriately. Part of the process involves paying close attention to your physical responses. During the day, stop and notice your breathing. Take mini-relaxation breaks. Push your chair back from your desk, close your eyes, and consciously go through and relax each of your major muscle groups. Combining this with practicing full-length relaxation exercises will set you on the road to a more relaxed state of being.

Guidelines For Practicing Relaxation

1. FIND A QUIET ENVIRONMENT. Look for a place that is free from distraction. At work, shut your door, find an empty conference room or office and ask not to be disturbed. At home, put the answering

machine on, or take the phone off the hook, close the door, tell your family or roommate that you should not be disturbed and will be unavailable for ten to twenty minutes.

2. GET COMFORTABLE. You may do relaxation either sitting or lying down (see "Positions for Practicing Relaxation" on page 42). Some people like lying down in the beginning because they are not distracted by upper back and neck aches. Also, it is easier to feel the sensation of your breathing when lying down. If you find yourself falling asleep, sit up. Sleeping is relaxing, but it does not help regulate your body's response to stress in the same way. If you have sleep-related problems, however, try doing relaxation before bedtime to help you fall asleep. Regular practice (when you are awake) will help to eliminate insomnia. If you do practice relaxation lying down, make sure that you sit up part of the time. Since we spend most of our days sitting, we need to associate sitting—as well as lying down—with being relaxed.

3. DON'T WORRY ABOUT YOUR PERFORMANCE. In the beginning you will find it difficult to concentrate during the relaxation period. Thoughts will come into your head. This is normal. Notice them, and then let them go. The more you practice, the easier it will become to clear your mind. Instead of thinking about what you're going to have for dinner, where you're going to go food shopping after work, how you'll get home in time to fix it (with all the work you have to do), and how relaxed you'll be after dinner, you will learn to have a momentary thought about dinner and then let it go.

4. ACCEPT YOURSELF. When you quiet your mind and focus on your body, you will feel any tension, stiffness, or pain that you have. This can be very uncomfortable. Recognize that you always have this discomfort but have not been aware of it. We have the ability to block out physical and emotional feelings. Relaxation coupled with movement-awareness exercises will help alleviate your discomfort. Similarly, feelings and emotions may come up when you begin to relax. You may even feel sad or depressed. These are real feelings that need to come to the surface, so don't try to repress them. Instead, acknowledge them. The exercises will help you deal with them.

5. STAY FOCUSED. As I've mentioned before, you may start to daydream. To remain focused, say a word to yourself or aloud. When my mind starts wandering during relaxation exercises, I find it helpful to do a count breathing (as described later in this chapter). In the

---

STRESSBUSTER: TIPS FOR EASEFUL RELAXATION

♦ Make a special time to practice relaxation that fits into your schedule.

♦ Find a quiet, comfortable place free from distraction.

♦ If possible, practice in the same spot each time.

♦ Use music or a taped sequence to enhance relaxation.

♦ Stay focused, using a mental device to help concentration.

♦ Don't worry about how you are doing.

♦ Spend at least ten minutes on your relaxation exercises.

---

beginning, sticking to one device may be difficult, so if you have trouble, switch to another means of focusing. Begin by watching your breath, then go to count breathing. If your mind begins to wander, you may want to feel heaviness in your hands and feet. I recommend more active techniques in the beginning, such as progressive muscle relaxation or autogenics (described in Chapter 3). Then gradually work into the more passive techniques, such as meditation (page 69). You may feel that you are just fighting thoughts and not getting anywhere, but you are. Focusing on sensations, calming thoughts, or a word changes your consciousness and trains your concentration. Stick with it.

6. SET ASIDE A REGULAR TIME JUST FOR RELAXATION. If you wait until you have a free moment to do your relaxation, you will never do it. Experiment with the best time for you, and then try to stick to it. In the beginning plan ahead day to day, or week to week. Once you fit it into your schedule, it will become part of your regular activities. Many single women or women without children like to do their relaxation before going to work in the morning. If your mate is busy getting ready for work also or you have children, you may want to find another time. If you have a quiet place to go at work, try practicing it there. Take a twenty-minute break in the afternoon when you need a pick-me-up. Be consistent; if you do it regularly, your co-workers will get used to it and know it is part of your routine. If you value it, they will also; if you don't, they won't. You may want to split it up, practicing two times a week at home and two at work.

7. USE THE POWER OF SUGGESTION. As you establish a regular routine, you will begin to associate relaxation with a place, a piece of music, or a combination of conditions. These things will "suggest" relaxation and help the process, which is another reason why it is good to have a regular time and place. Work with a few tapes and only use them for relaxation.

Positions For Practicing Relaxation

While practicing relaxation, your body should be straight. Do this by sitting in an armchair, a straight-back chair, a stool, or lying down.

When sitting:

+ Use a comfortable chair where your back can be supported and your feet are on the ground, with your knees bent. Your back needs to be straight, either by sitting at the edge of the chair or by being supported by pillows or the chair itself. Since it is often difficult for people to sit up straight without strain, I recommend using a pillow to support the small of the back.

+ Let your hands rest on your legs or the arms of the chair.

+ Feel your head as free on top of your body, perhaps imagining it as a helium balloon.

+ Lengthen your spine.

When lying down:

+ Lie flat on the floor with your arms extended at your side.

+ Keep your legs apart about hip width.

+ You may want to place a small pillow under your neck (if you have an exaggerated curve, or feel strain) and/or your knees, especially if you have low back pain.

+ Make sure you are warm enough, and use a cover if necessary.

This is a good position if you have many aches and pains. Some people find themselves falling in and out of sleep in this position, however, and if that's the case, use the sitting position.

Relaxation Tapes Make Beginning Easier

In the beginning it's easier if you work with an audiotape—of your own voice, soft music that you've recorded, or a commercial relaxation tape. Tape-record the exercises I will describe, so you don't have to think about what comes next. Use your own voice or have a friend record the exercises for you. (If you do it yourself, you may have to become accustomed to hearing your recorded voice.) When taping, be sure to go slowly and give yourself plenty of time after each instruction or suggestion to experience the sensations. At the end of the tape, give the suggestion that you will be relaxed but alert when you finish. It's nice to use music in the background of your tape.

There are commercial relaxation tapes that you can order; a list is offered in the Appendix. Holistic bookstores and centers often sell tapes, too. Though you don't want to become dependent on the tapes—since the goal of relaxation is to be able to relax anywhere—they are a good learning tool. Also there are times when you will find it more difficult to concentrate, and tapes come in handy then.

To enhance and deepen relaxation, I recommend using specially designed musical accompaniment when practicing relaxation. The music blocks out background noise and helps increase concentration. It designates the time as relaxation time, and as you practice, you will begin to associate relaxation with the particular piece of music. Use music that has a calming effect. Many recordings are designed for relaxation. Holistic bookstores and some health food stores carry musical tapes. Most large record stores now have a New Age section that offers a variety of selections. The music should not be emotional or dramatic and needs to avoid rhythmic changes or changes in pitch. Recordings of sounds, such as the ocean, are also calming. See the Appendix for suggestions.

Classes Or Seminars

Enrolling in a class or seminar is a good way to learn more about relaxation techniques. Questions can be answered, plus you have a chance to hear how others respond to stressful situations. Classes are often offered through YWCA's and YMCA'S, YMHA's, adult learning centers, and holistic learning centers.

STRESSBUSTER: TAKING CONTROL

Gaining control over your body will help you learn to let
go! This sounds like a paradox, doesn't it? Yet, relaxation
is initiated by you, and your ability to relax is improved by
practice—the more control over your relaxation response,
the more release you will achieve.

Don't Give Up

These techniques will help you learn to relax under pressure and to
halt and prevent further distress to your system. The hardest part is
taking the time—not doing the techniques themselves. Most of us
can find ten minutes to relax during our day or evening but actually doing it is the challenge. Pick a time that works best for you.
Though some relaxation consultants advise clients not to practice
relaxation on a full stomach, I feel that *whenever* you can and do
work it into your schedule is the best time—because you are *doing*
it. If, after dinner, you have the time, then that's when to do it.
Maybe later, another time will come up that is better. Some people
like to get up a little early in the morning and relax before breakfast.
Nancy, a mother of two, gets up before her kids do so she can meditate for twenty minutes; this prepares her for her busy day as the
secretary to a demanding business executive. Bedtime is not as good
a time because you could begin to associate relaxation with sleep.
Also, remember to combine relaxation sessions with short relaxation
mini-breaks throughout the day.

Working directly on the body calms both the body and the
mind. By achieving one aspect of the relaxation response, you can
elicit a whole response. In this and following chapters I will describe
a variety of proven relaxation techniques. You can start with deep
breathing, or by simply focusing on a word, as in Transcendental
Meditation (Chapter 3). Everyone is different, and some techniques
will work better for you than others. I have found that most everyone responds to breathing exercises, but some people prefer progressive relaxation over autogenics (Chapter 3); others like visualization better (Chapter 4). You may want to vary what you do, or do
one for a while and then try another, until you find the one with
which you are most comfortable. Most important, though, is to start

today. In developing your stress reduction program also keep in mind techniques that best address your particular symptoms. If you respond to your boss by tensing your back muscles, then progressive relaxation will be good for you, as will doing the small, slow movements found in the body therapy, Kinetic Awareness (Chapters 5 and 10). If your reaction to stress is a migraine, try hand temperature warming (Chapter 3). If too many responsibilities keep you worrying and you simply feel worn out, breathing and some of the meditation techniques might be right for you.

STRESSBUSTER: RELAXATION VS. AGGRAVATION

Relaxation training is a useful way of coping with things that you can't change. Instead of complaining and fuming about the committee work you despise but are required to do, practice relaxation, breathing deeply throughout the meetings. Reframe your attitude toward your deadlines, but support it by practicing relaxation during your day.

USING BREATHING EXERCISES TO RELAX

Proper breathing is essential for good physical and mental health. It supplies the body with the necessary energy to sustain life; without the exchange of oxygen and carbon dioxide in your lungs, your tissues' cells would stop functioning. Yet few of us breathe freely and deeply. You may not realize it, but you can consciously affect your breathing patterns. Learning to breathe freely and deeply is the first step in learning to relax. In fact, "breathing work," or learning to breathe more efficiently, serves as an integral part of most stress-reduction programs because it is the quickest and easiest method of slowing down the nervous system and inducing relaxation. You may, without noticing it, typically experience shallow breathing, known as chest breathing, which is a symptom of the stress response. If you slow down your breathing, however, you can kick in a whole relaxation response.

Although your breathing is automatic in that you can't voluntarily shut it down, you can control the quality of breath—the amount of air that reaches your lungs. Emotions, tension levels, physical activity, posture, and habit affect how much air you bring into the lungs. If you have an insufficient amount, your body will not function as well as it should; your heart and lungs must work much harder, waste products won't be removed from your system as efficiently (causing toxins to stay in your system), digestion will be impeded, and your complexion will be affected. And experts agree that if you are not breathing deeply, you are not relaxed.

The most efficient breathing is from the diaphragm, which allows you to breathe deeply enough to bring air into the lower lobes of your lungs. The diaphragm is a large dome-shaped muscular sheet that attaches to the base of the rib cage and the muscle mainly responsible for respiration. When you breathe diaphragmatically, your abdominal muscles expand and release to allow the diaphragm to move up and down. As you inhale, the lower ribs expand, and the diaphragm pulls down; when you exhale, the ribs release and the diaphragm moves back up. Diaphragmatic breathing is the deepest, most efficient, and natural way to breathe. If you are chest breathing, or breathing shallowly from your chest, the air stays in the upper part of your lungs.

How are you breathing right now? Take a moment and try this. Put one hand on your chest and one hand on your stomach (midsection). Take a deep breath. Which moved first and which moved the most—your stomach, or your chest? If it was your chest, you will need to make some adjustments in your breathing. When you constantly breathe from the chest, you may be preventing yourself from relaxing.

Leaving your hands on your chest and stomach, try and make your hand rise by expanding your stomach on the inhalation, keeping your chest still. Your goal should be to learn to expand your stomach and your low abdomen when you breathe. Keep your shoulders relaxed and dropped. If your shoulders rise when you inhale you are chest breathing and using excess shoulder tension.

Learn To Breathe Like A Baby

Proper breathing can best be seen in babies. If you watch an infant, you will see her/his abdomen rise and fall; actually the whole body seems alive with healthful energy. When a baby is unhappy and crying, breathing becomes shallow and moves into the chest, but when the baby is comfortable again, changed, fed, and held, the breathing returns to the lower abdomen. Ideally, that is how we should all breathe: respond to a situation with the kind of breath we need and then return to normal abdominal breathing. But for most of us, our breath has become conditioned to respond in only one way—shallow.

How does this happen? As children, when we were scolded, or were fearful or nervous, we held our breath. Many factors—being slow in school, having parents who fight, looking different—can kick in the stress response and affect the way a child breathes. So by high school, a youngster may have already developed poor breathing habits. Ideas about our appearance also affect our breathing. As women, we constantly get the message that we must have a flat stomach and a big chest. We've learned to hold in our stomach and lift our chest. Holding in your stomach won't make it flat, though; only exercise and diet will do that. And, worst of all, holding in the stomach will make deep breathing next to impossible.

Try this for a moment. Pull in your stomach, and hold it. Now take a deep breath. What happened? You probably found it difficult to breathe and that all of your breath was in your chest.

Your posture contributes to the quality of your breathing too. If your body isn't aligned, the muscles needed for breathing can't work properly. Forcing the neck forward, for example, blocks off the amount of air coming into your lungs. Sitting slumped in your chair interferes with the diaphragm's ability to draw in air. (See Chapter 5 for more on posture.) In my stress-reduction seminars, many people are unable to sit up straight even when they try. With their body collapsed, they can't achieve the necessary expansion of the abdomen. For this reason, it's helpful to begin your practice of breathing while lying down, so you can experience the expansion of the abdomen.

From one day to the next, there are varying conditions that will affect your breathing. Illness, lack of exercise, weather, and air pollution will influence how deep or regular your breathing will be. Aerobic exercise, for instance, will improve the efficiency of your lungs and support you through these various conditions.

The same mechanism that interferes with our breathing, however, also enables us to change it. By becoming aware of your breathing patterns, practicing exercises, and remembering to take deep breaths throughout the day, you can elevate the quality of your breath and, in turn, increase energy and mental clarity, improve your mood, and help your body function more efficiently.

Guidelines For Breathing Practice

Before you begin practicing the following breathing exercises, here are a few guidelines:

- Always use your nose to breathe in when you inhale. You can breathe out through your nose or mouth when you exhale.
- Be sure to breathe normally between deep breaths, since repeated deep breaths can make you feel dizzy or lightheaded.
- It's easier to practice breathing while lying on your back. Once you have learned the exercise, practice when sitting and standing.
- If you are accustomed to shallow breathing, you may find yourself yawning as you start to breathe deeply. This is just your body's way of helping establish an equilibrium between the oxygen and carbon dioxide in your body. Don't stifle the yawn. It's usually a sign you are beginning to let go.
- When doing any breathing exercise (or relaxation exercise), begin by noticing what your breathing is like before you start, its speed and depth. When you finish, take note of any changes in your breathing, your feelings, and tension levels.

Breathing Awareness Exercise

This first exercise is designed to help you become attuned to your breathing and aware of subtle changes. Try it before attempting the other exercises. Observation, rather than changing your breathing, is the goal:

1. Begin by lying down (see positions for relaxation on page 42) and closing your eyes.
2. Observe your breathing:
   - What is the speed? Is it fast or slow?
   - What is the depth? Is it shallow or deep?
   - Where do you feel movement?
   - Notice where you feel the most breath and where you feel the least.
   - Is your breathing regular or irregular?

3. Focus on inhaling. Observe what it feels like. How much effort does it take? Do you have to force it to inhale? Does it flow on its own?

4. Now focus on exhaling. Notice what the exhalation feels like. Do you take enough time to fully exhale? Are you doing anything to interfere with the flow? Are inhalation and exhalation the same? Do you like one better than the other?

5. Explore your breathing:
   ◆ Place your hand on your chest and take several breaths, noticing how it feels to breathe in and out of your chest.
   ◆ Place your hand on your midsection, and repeat the same process.
   ◆ Place your hand on your abdomen, and breathe into it.
   ◆ Think about how each felt. Ideally you should breathe in the midsection and/or low abdomen (see Abdominal Breathing below).

6. Leave your hand on your abdomen and continue breathing this way for several breaths.

7. Go back to your regular breathing. Has it changed in any way since you started? Are you more aware of it?

Abdominal Breathing

The goal of deep, or diaphragmatic, breathing is to bring air into the lower parts of your lungs rather than just the top part. This is perhaps the most important breathing exercise you will do. It is designed not only to increase your breathing capacity and initiate a relaxation response but to train you to breathe this way normally. As an exercise, practice ten to fifteen minutes a day. You can combine this breathing with the other exercises. Concentrate on taking easy, smooth breaths. This exercise may be difficult at first. It is the opposite of what we all have been taught—to pull in our stomach and lift and breathe from the chest and use the shoulders.

1. Start by noticing your breath without changing it. Notice the speed and depth.

2. Place your right hand on your upper abdomen, spread your fingers with the little finger touching the navel, and let the left hand rest comfortably on your chest.

3. As you inhale, breathe into your right hand, extending your abdomen but not forcing it. Your chest should move only slightly on the inhale. Exhale fully, letting your abdomen relax.

4. Repeat, slowly inhaling and exhaling several times. Breathe normally after several deep breaths.

5. Repeat the process, but take away your left hand and continue breathing into the right.

6. You can continue with this breathing, passively watching your slow even breaths, or add one of the other exercises.

NOTE: Your hands are to help you initiate abdominal breathing; once you've learned the technique, do it without the hands or return to using your hands to check your progress. Practice this exercise sitting up.

VARIATION: When you become skillful at breathing into the upper abdomen, lower your hand, with your thumb on your belly button and fingers on the low abdomen, and breathe in and out. Once you are comfortable with slow, even, diaphragmatic breathing, you can add an increase in the exhalation. Breathe out for longer than you breathe in. For example, breathe in four counts and out six to eight.

TIP: It's easier to tell if your shoulders are moving when sitting. Watch yourself in the mirror to see what it looks like when you breathe.

Three-Part Breathing

This exercise is designed to encourage filling the lungs fully. To do this, visualize your lungs in three parts: lower, middle, and top.

1. Take a deep diaphragmatic breath, and visualize your lower lungs filling with air. Feel your ribs expanding front and back.

2. As you continue to inhale, see the middle lung filling with air. Focus on both the front and back of your body.

3. Finally, visualize the top of your lungs filling completely.

4. As you exhale, see the air leaving the top of your lungs, moving down to the middle and finally to the bottom.

Count Breathing: 2 to 1

I like to use this breathing when my mind starts wandering. Focus on saying the counts (to yourself or aloud), as well as paying attention to your breathing. The breathing can be done alone or in combination with other exercises. The goal is to breathe out twice as long as you breathe in.

Breathe in slowly three or four counts, pause, and then let the breath out slowly for six to eight counts. Notice how your breathing responds to the deep breath by just watching your next breath or two. Then repeat.

As your breathing deepens, increase the counts and increase how long you pause between inhalation and exhalation. If you can't take three or four slow breaths, start with two and work on increasing them.

Count Down

This is a good exercise if you're having difficulty falling asleep. Start with the number 10 and count down to 1. As you breathe in, visualize the number on both the inhalation and the exhalation. Take long, slow abdominal breaths. Suggest to yourself that as you go down in numbers you will become more and more relaxed.

Fat Breathing

When you have become comfortable with diaphragmatic breathing, try this one; it brings the breath even lower in the abdomen:

1. Place your right hand on your abdomen, with your thumb on your navel.

2. On the inhalation, slowly blow up your belly like a balloon (gently, don't force).

3. Exhale fully.

4. Repeat this several times. Then breathe normally.

5. Expand the abdomen, and then hold the inhalation for as long as is comfortable.

6. Breathe normally for several breaths, and then repeat.

Container Breathing

Using the above breathing technique, start with the breath low in the abdomen, and move it slowly up through your body. Imagine your torso as a container that you gradually fill up with air. Focus on the whole torso, front and back.

Color Breathing

In this exercise, you will imagine breathing in a color, which fills your torso. Experiment with what color best suits you, your mood, your needs. This can be soothing or energizing, depending on the color you choose. Yellows and oranges are warming colors, and can stimulate you or increase your sense of well-being. Blue and green are cooler and may calm you down. Each person is different, so you'll need to try out the colors for yourself.

Passive Watching

For me, this is the most difficult exercise of all. The goal is to just passively watch your breath. Using the awareness-breathing guidelines, see how long you can stay focused on your breathing without letting your mind wander too much:

1. Begin by noticing the speed and depth of your breath.

2. Notice where you feel any blocks, where it feels free.

3. Notice how the air feels coming in the nostrils.

4. Continue to stay with just watching your breath, observing how it feels and how it changes or stays the same.

5. Notice any thoughts or feelings that arise, and then go back to focusing on your breath. Do not criticize yourself for losing your concentration.

6. Be aware of any changes in your feelings and mental state.

Combination Exercises

When I began learning relaxation, I found it difficult to stay focused (and at times still do), and I think others do too. For this reason I like to combine several exercises. This helps you stay focused, while training you to concentrate. When practicing any exercise, don't force yourself or constantly judge how you are doing:

1. Start by noticing your breathing without changing it. Passively watch it, knowing that your concentration will create the conditions for it to begin to slow down.

2. Focus on diaphragmatic or low abdomen breathing. Take several deep breaths. Breathe normally and repeat again.

3. Extend the exhalation. Use a ratio of 2:1. Exhale twice as long as the inhale. You can do this by using the count breath: in 3 or 4, and out 6 to 8.

4. Inhale and hold your breath for as long as you can. Let out the air.

5. Inhale and pause, and then let the air out with a hiss. Force the air out of your mouth with a sound like a snake. This will deepen the exhalation.

6. You can stop here or add one of the other exercises.

7. Return to your normal breathing. Notice any changes.

BREATHING: ON THE JOB Breathing is the first place to start implementing relaxation on the job. It is perhaps the easiest and most natural way to elicit a relaxation response. In addition, you needn't stop and do anything special, and you can concentrate on your breathing while doing other tasks, such as listening in a meeting, reading a report, talking on the phone. Try these on-the-job tips:

+ Attach a note to your desk or computer reminding you to breathe throughout your day.

+ Every time you check your watch or worry that there's no time to finish (or you're so bored you can't wait for a break), take several deep breaths or do the "stop watch" breathing technique (below).

- Use the "stop watch" breathing technique during the day. Count the number of times you breathe in a minute. Then slow it down. If you are breathing diaphragmatically, it's normal to breathe about six to eight times a minute. Once you know how many slow breaths you can breathe per minute, take minute-long breathing breaks throughout the day.

- Notice your breathing during meetings, while listening to others speak, when working on projects, when typing, and while on the phone. Take slow, easy breaths whenever you can.

- Take a two-minute break when you are feeling overloaded or have been at the computer for more than an hour. Go through several of the breathing exercises listed earlier.

- If you feel tired during the day and need a pick-me-up, do nasal breathing. With your finger, close off one nostril and breathe in and out of the other. Take several breaths. Change sides and repeat. Now breathe in one nostril and out the other, using your finger to close off one and then the other. This should make you more alert. Be sure and take normal breaths in between to avoid feeling light-headedness.

Once you begin using breathing exercises throughout your day and evening, you're on your way to developing the relaxation response. Practice will increase your awareness, improve your concentration and control, and make the relaxation exercises described in the next chapter all the more natural.

Chapter Three

TEACHING YOURSELF TO RELAX

How many times has someone at your office told you, "Just relax"? Usually that advice, although well-meaning, is easier said than done. Most people have forgotten how to truly relax, and many are not even aware of how unrelaxed they are. When you are tense and unable to wind down, you undoubtedly wish there was something you could do to calm yourself. In this chapter, we will present some methods that have proven successful for doing just that—progressive muscle relaxation, autogenic training, biofeedback, and meditation. These techniques can help you control the physical symptoms associated with the stress response.

In progressive muscle relaxation, you learn to release muscular tension in all parts of your body. With autogenic training, you gain the ability to warm your hands and feet (which increases blood flow), deepen your breathing, and slow your heartbeat. Biofeedback relays information about physical processes to aid you in controlling your body's response. Meditation uses focused awareness to achieve a state of inner calm. The thread linking all of these techniques is your ability to increase your awareness of the body and its functions.

How To "Feel" Your Body

Being aware of physical tension is the first step toward reducing it. Most of us, however, don't notice the physical sensations in our body, because we've been conditioned early on to block out most of them unless they hurt. To live in our modern world—sitting all day in front of a computer or standing for hours at a cash register or teller window—we have learned to shut out our body's physical messages. Focusing on finishing an overdue report, without taking a break, you may not notice your body's distress signals because you are not paying attention to your physical cues. Therefore, you fail to move, stretch, or get up and walk around when necessary. Your body doesn't know that your break isn't for another hour; it wants to move or stretch now! Unfortunately, muscle tension dulls your ability to perceive your body's sensations, thereby creating a vicious cycle. Increasing your awareness skills can help break this cycle.

When practicing relaxation and body awareness techniques, you will focus on how your body feels in very subtle ways, including sensations that range from pleasant to neutral to uncomfortable. In the following exercises I'll use certain words to describe the process of concentrating on the body; for example, I'll ask you to "sense" or "feel" your body. Naturally we all feel our body and its positions to some degree, but we are talking about the ability to perceive accurately bodily information. Concentrating on a body part can help you discern a range of bodily feelings and sensations, as well as emotional discomfort.

Being aware of your body is a skill that takes a little time to develop. The more you practice, the easier it will become. As your perception of your body increases, you may become aware of tensions you didn't know existed. As a result, you may even feel worse for a while. But this awareness will also help you to release the tension, so stick with it! Awareness can—and should—be practiced all the time, at work and at home. The more you increase your awareness, the more you'll begin to see how you create unnecessary tension and discomfort.

RELIEVE TENSION WITH PROGRESSIVE RELAXATION

Muscle tension is a major component of the stress response and one of the more easily recognizable physical symptoms of stress. Muscles that tense in response to the fight or flight response often do not fully release after a stressful situation; under chronic stress the muscles may remain constantly contracted. This prolonged contraction can actually perpetuate the stress response by keeping the body charged up. If, over a period of time, you walk around with tense muscles, you may not even notice the tightness unless you have a particularly arduous day at work, lift a heavy file, or take an evening exercise class and feel the tension.

But consider, for example, what it's like when you're trying to finish a project quickly so that you can leave work on time. Notice how your body responds to the demands. What happens when you're on the phone with a client or customer? Take note of where your shoulders are; how much tension is there in your neck or your back? Do you grind your teeth while typing or put excess effort into your arms and hands when hitting the keyboard? With progressive muscle relaxation, you'll learn to recognize the tension and release it.

How do you release tight, contracted muscles? The first step is learning to notice and feel the degree of your tension. One of the best ways to do this is to put excess energy or tension into a part of your body, feel it, and then release it. By tensing a muscle and then releasing it, you can feel the difference between the two states, which will help you learn to initiate relaxation in your body.

Indian yogis have used this technique for centuries, but it was Edmund Jacobson, a Chicago physician, who first utilized the method specifically for stress reduction related to anxiety-provoking thoughts and events. He found that the emotions can be changed by working directly on the muscles, and he had apparent success with many stress-related disorders, including anxiety, hypertension, and insomnia, which are symptoms experienced by many overextended women. Backaches, headaches, and tight muscles from overwork or poor body positions respond well to this technique.

Today, the method of tensing and releasing ten to twenty muscle groups, a technique referred to as "progressive relaxation," is one of the most effective and widely used relaxation methods. Regularly practicing progressive muscle relaxation will allow you to become more aware of your tension and release it before it becomes a full-fledged backache or neck spasm.

Progressive relaxation is a good technique with which to begin because it is very specific and active. If you have difficulty feeling parts of your body separately, or if you have trouble concentrating and find your mind wandering when doing breathing or focusing techniques, progressive relaxation is particularly helpful.

There are two forms of progressive relaxation, active and passive. The active process involves physically tensing and releasing the muscles. In the passive method, you focus on the muscle and its sensations and use your concentration to release it. Here, awareness combined with a conscious decision to relax the muscles achieve the desired results.

I prefer the passive technique for several reasons. Often when practicing active muscle relaxation, people tend to emphasize the tensing rather than the releasing. Tension is more familiar and easier to feel. On the other hand, during the passive technique, concentration is focused on the sensation of relaxing, which is more powerful. Another advantage is that the passive method can be practiced anywhere: at your desk, on the way to work, while talking on the phone. Learning the active technique first, however, is a stepping stone to the passive method. The more you practice, the easier it will become, and you will train your body to relax by simply concentrating on it.

Don't be discouraged if you don't immediately feel relaxed. The benefits of this technique are cumulative. Ideally, in the beginning you should practice once a day, for fifteen to twenty minutes, or do mini-sessions at work of five minutes' duration. It should take about two weeks of regular practice before you really master the technique. If you can't do it every day, then do it as often as you can. Even two or three times a week is a good start.

Active Progressive Relaxation

In this technique, you will focus on a body part, sense it, and then slowly put tension into it. You control the tension, progressively putting tension into the body part, rather than just tightening up. You will hold the tension for a few moments, then slowly release, focusing on feeling the sensation of release. For example, you will tense for six to eight seconds (becoming tense and holding the sensation), and then slowly release and relax for fifteen to twenty seconds before tightening again.

Whether at home or at work, begin by making yourself comfortable; if possible, loosen your clothing, take off your shoes. Make sure you are warm enough—practicing relaxation often lowers your body temperature. Practice in a quiet place free from distraction; at work, find an empty office or conference room. Choose a comfortable position either sitting or lying down.

Close your eyes. Always begin any exercise by noticing how you are feeling at the moment. What is your breathing like? Before changing it, notice the speed and depth. Watch it for a moment. Then take a slow, easy abdominal breath. (I recommend tape-recording the following instructions, so you can play them back rather than having to read them.)

RELEASING THE HANDS: Notice and feel your right hand. Make a fist, or with your hand extended, put tension into it. Feel the tension in your hand, hold, then release it and relax your hand. Notice how the relaxation feels, take a deep breath, let go of the tension even more, and feel the release. Now tense again, really putting a lot of tension into your hand, and hold it. Notice how your whole body responds to the tension. What happens to your breathing, your shoulders? Release, and feel the relaxation in your hand and your arm. Take time to feel the sensation. Repeat the process. Now just take a moment without tensing, to focus on the release. Feel your hand as very relaxed. Let it rest heavily on your legs and feel relaxation in your arm as well.

Turn your attention to your left hand and compare it to your right. Then focus on your left hand, putting tension into it, feeling the tension and then releasing (hold six or seven seconds; release and sense for fifteen seconds). Continue the same process that you used on your right hand. Finish by noticing both hands and arms and feeling them as relaxed.

Bend your elbow, and tense your biceps. Tighten them (keep the neck relaxed), and then straighten and let the process of relaxation move through your arm. Repeat this three times and then do the other arm. To further the relaxation in your hand and arm, extend your arm and spread your fingers, then release the fingers and release the arm. Think of the arm and hand as feeling heavy, and rest them on your thigh. Repeat on the left side. Breathe, and feel the relaxation in both arms and hands. They may feel longer, heavier, and tingling from increased blood flow.

RELEASING THE FEET AND LEGS: Now turn your attention to your feet. Focus on your right foot. Put a little tension into your foot by gently curling the toes. Don't use too much tension, though, as that could cause cramping. Feel the tension, and then let it go. Feel the whole foot: toes, ball, and instep. As you focus on the release, consciously send the direction of relaxation to your foot. Don't force it; by simply noticing it, you can induce relaxation. Repeat this three times. End by just focusing on your foot. Compare your right to your left foot. Then shift your attention to your left foot and repeat the process.

Go back to your right foot. Flex the foot by lifting the toes up toward your ankles, slowly flex until you feel the tightness in your calf. Hold. Then release from the top of your calf, letting the muscles relax. Think of the muscles as lengthening. Feel the relaxation. Take a deep breath, and as you exhale, let go of the tension even more. Feel the relaxation, and then repeat two more times.

Now, with the same foot, point your toe, feeling the tension running up the front of your leg. Do the same as before, releasing from the top, lengthening and feeling the release. Point and release two more times. Repeat the process on the left leg, both flexing and pointing.

Move your attention to your thighs. Tighten your upper leg. If you have trouble isolating this area, extend your leg out and feel the tension. Then release. Let go of the tightness, and feel the difference. Do this twice, and repeat on the other leg. Finish by feeling the relaxation in both legs and feet. Feel them lengthened and relaxed.

You may want to stop here, especially when you are first learning the active progressive relaxation technique. If you've been taking your time and really sensing each part and focusing on relaxation, it may take ten minutes to get up to this point. This can be a complete exercise in itself when you spend time watching your breathing at the beginning and end, as well as noticing the changes in your body's sensations. Another variation—perfect for a work break—is to do the hands and feet only, then move to the upper body, shoulders, and neck. For the full sequence continue with relaxing the torso.

RELAXING THE TORSO: Tighten your buttocks, hold and then release. Breathe and, if you are seated, feel your "sitz" bones (the bones you sit on). Let the small of your back widen. Repeat two times. Slowly pull in your stomach muscles, hold, and release. Now do a few abdominal breaths. Pull in your stomach again, then try to take a deep breath. If you tighten your stomach, you will not be able to breathe properly. Take a few more deep breaths. Feel the breath without the tension. Feel your abdomen and back as relaxed.

Focus your attention on the area between your shoulder blades. Breathe into the area. Slowly pull your shoulder blades together, and hold. Then release and feel the widening. Breathe into the open area. Repeat three times. See your shoulders as wide, your collarbone as extending outward.

Now notice your shoulders. Gently lift your shoulders up toward your ears, hold them there, then let them go. Notice how good it feels to let them go. Let them go even further by deeply feeling the release. Breathe. Repeat three times.

Turn your attention to your neck. Tense your neck muscles and notice how it feels. Release. Since most of us have so much tension in the neck already, tensing it even more isn't as valuable as gently moving it in all directions. Slowly move your neck and feel any tension, but concentrate on letting it go. Move it in all the directions in which it can go. Bring your head back to center and feel it as long and released. Focus your attention on your jaw. Slowly open your mouth, and feel the tension in the open position. Then slowly close it back to a relaxed position, with your lips slightly parted, finally closing it completely. Repeat this process, slowly opening and then closing to find the relaxed position. Now move your jaw around in all directions.

Move your attention to your forehead, wrinkle the forehead, then release as you visualize your forehead being smooth and open. If you tend to wrinkle your forehead, do this a few times to learn the pattern. If not, just focus on smoothing the wrinkles. Tighten around the eyes, and release. Open your eyes wide, and feel the tension, then release. Do the same thing with your eyebrows: lift and then release. Purse the lips and release. We put a great deal of tension into our face, and this can become a habit, which in turn can cause unnecessary lines and wrinkles. Doing this exercise helps you to change these patterns. Now conclude this part by going through the face again but without tensing. Starting at the top of your head, feel the sense of relaxation moving from the top to bottom; keep the eyes, cheeks, and jaw relaxed. It will improve your appearance.

Now take a moment to notice how you feel. Scan your body. Do you feel different from when you started? What is your breathing like? Notice areas that still feel tense; they may be places that will need extra work. Pay attention to them during your daily routine. Feel the tense part(s) now and breathe into it (them). Take a deep breath in, and slowly let it out. Open your eyes and stretch.

Passive Relaxation

Find a comfortable position, either sitting or lying down. Take your time going through this exercise. Close your eyes. Observe your breathing. Without changing it, watch it for a moment. Focus inward, letting go of thoughts and concerns. Take a few gentle abdominal breaths. (Again, it's helpful to tape-record the following steps.)

Starting with your forehead, feel it as wide. Let the wrinkles smooth; see any wrinkles between your eyebrows disappear. Feel space in your forehead. See your forehead as open, wide.

Now notice the area around your eyes, feeling the sockets. Let the skin around the eyes expand as wide as the sockets (don't actually move this area, just permit yourself to feel this happen). Allow the area around your eyes to become relaxed and open, letting any wrinkles smooth out.

Spread the sensation of relaxation down to your cheeks, feeling the skin soften. Focus on your jaw, letting go of any tension. Let your lips part, feel the jaw (joint), teeth, tongue. Relax your lips and let them soften. Feel your whole face as relaxed, soft, wrinkle-free, and expanded.

Move down to your neck. Feel the back of the neck as lengthening. Let the head be free on top of your shoulders; as the muscles in front of the neck soften, the throat opens and relaxes. Keep your face relaxed, lips parted, neck lengthened.

Now sense the shoulders, and release them by allowing them to drop. Your attention to how they feel and where they are in space will be enough to let them relax and sink back into the chair or the floor. Stay with this feeling of relaxation in your shoulders.

Let the sense of relaxation flow from your shoulders into your arms. Feel the arms lengthen, as the sensation of relaxation moves down to your elbow. As the elbow releases, feel the relaxation move into your lower arm. Feel the wrist, the bones, and skin. Sense the hands, the thumb, and each finger, as the relaxation moves toward the finger tips. Take a deep breath, and feel the relaxation in your shoulders, arms, and hands. Feel the shoulders dropped and the arms longer than when you started.

Take another breath, and notice the front of your body. Let go as you exhale. Do this again. Take a slow abdominal breath and gently release any holding in the chest, diaphragm, and abdomen. Let the shoulders widen.

Now focus your attention on your upper back. Feel the muscles on either side of your spine. Relax by releasing them downward toward your tailbone. Lengthen the muscles all the way down your back.

Feel the small of the back, and see it widen. Sense the buttocks muscles, and let them go. Feel your hip joint (where your pants crease at the top of your leg when you bend your knee). Let that area soften. See the joint as widening, letting the muscles expand.

Next allow a feeling of relaxation to travel down both legs. Starting at the top of the thighs, see the muscles lengthening outward. The loosening feeling moves into the knees, and they relax, softening the back of the knees as well. When the relaxation moves down the lower leg, the calf releases, the shin muscles let go. Feel your ankles, as the sensation of relaxation moves into the feet, the heels, the instep, the ball of your feet, and the toes. Now, the whole leg and foot feels relaxed.

Scan your body, and notice how you feel. You should be relaxed from head to toe. Some areas may be harder to relax than others, however, and will take practice. What is your breathing like? Take a slow breath in and out.

Give yourself the suggestion that you are very relaxed and that you will be relaxed and alert throughout your day. Say to yourself, "When I open my eyes I will be relaxed and alert." Take another deep breath, then open your eyes and stretch your body, feeling calm and refreshed, ready to stay relaxed throughout your day.

STRESSBUSTER

You may find yourself having difficulty concentrating. This is natural. Simply return your thoughts to the exercise when you find your mind wandering. Sometimes it helps to take a few deep breaths. The better you know the exercise, the easier it will become. If you are doing your relaxation at work, it helps to have practiced at home first to get used to doing it.

ACHIEVE BALANCE WITH AUTOGENIC TRAINING

With autogenic training you induce physical sensations associated with relaxation by using concentration, visualization, and suggestion. The goal of autogenics is to balance your physical, mental, and emotional processes, which—because of the effects of stress—may be out of equilibrium. Autogenic training along with progressive relaxation is used extensively in stress-reduction programs and in conjunction with biofeedback training. Autogenics has been effective in relieving a variety of respiratory, gastrointestinal, and cardiac problems, including bronchial asthma, peptic ulcer, migraines (more common in women than men), constipation, colitis, spastic colon, racing heart, high blood pressure, as well as pain, insomnia, Raynaud's syndrome (a condition characterized by cold hands and feet), and anxiety. Autogenics will help as well with milder work-related symptoms such as impatience, overreacting, poor concentration, and restlessness. As a working woman you may be experiencing one or more of these physical problems.

Autogenic training was developed in the 1930s by J.H. Schultz, a German psychiatrist. Schultz (later joined by Wolfgang Luthe) identified a group of physical sensations that are the opposites of those caused by stress. Schultz labeled this the "autogenic state." With Luthe, he then developed a technique to teach people to reproduce these sensations, by repeating a set of six "phases," or directives:

- ◆ My arms and legs are heavy
- ◆ My arms and legs are warm
- ◆ My heartbeat is calm and regular
- ◆ My breathing is free and easy
- ◆ My solar plexus is warm
- ◆ My forehead is cool

This technique takes longer to master than breathing exercises or progressive relaxation (some practitioners estimate three to ten months). But you should be able to experience heaviness in your limbs right away, and, from the beginning, your concentration on the sensations will help induce relaxation and give you more control over your mind and body. So give yourself a month of regular practice to get going. (Again, I advise tape-recording the following instructions.)

The Autogenics Technique

Before beginning, assume a comfortable position, sitting or lying down. Loosen your clothes. Close your eyes. Notice how your body feels and what your breathing is like. Take a gentle deep breath in and out. Focus on a particular body part, and use the images to induce the desired result. Say the phrases before, after, or with your images. Repeat phrases at least three times. Pause after saying them. Use the following concepts:

CONCEPT: TO FEEL HEAVINESS IN THE LIMBS

Focus: Concentrate on your right hand with the idea of feeling heaviness.

Image: Use an image that suggests heaviness and giving into gravity.

You may see your hand as too heavy to lift. Sense the heaviness as relaxing.

Phrase: "My hand is heavy."

+ Repeat this with your left hand.

+ Repeat the above images with your feet using the phrase, "My feet are heavy."

+ Finish with the phrase, "My arms and legs are heavy."

CONCEPT: TO FEEL WARMTH IN THE LIMBS

Focus: Concentrate on the right hand (unless you are left-handed).

Image: Use the image of sunlight or warm water to induce warmth.

Phrase: "My hand is warm."

+ Sense your hand, and imagine the sun beaming down on it, warming it. Imagine a pleasant environment. If you have difficulty, find another image, such as relaxing in front of a warm fire or by a warm stove. Fill in as many details as possible, but stay focused on your hand. Really feel it warming.

+ Repeat on other hand.

+ Repeat with feet.

+ Repeat with arms and legs.

+ Finish with "My arms and legs are warm."

CONCEPT: TO SLOW AND REGULATE HEART RATE

Focus: Feel your heartbeat.

Image: See your heartbeat as slow and steady. Imagine it slower. See a pendulum, a slow clock or a slow steady drum beat.

Phrase: "My heartbeat is calm and regular."

> NOTE: If you are uncomfortable concentrating on your heartbeat go on to the breathing concept.

CONCEPT: TO SLOW AND DEEPEN BREATHING

Focus: Concentrate on your breath. Feel the rise and fall of your abdomen.

Image: Imagine your breath as being automatic and without effort. Imagine the waves of the ocean filling you up and then washing out of you.

Phrase: "My breathing is free and easy."

CONCEPT: TO WARM THE CENTER OF THE BODY

Focus: Feel deep within your belly (around or slightly above your bellybutton).

Image: Use a golden light deep within the center of your body warming you.

Phrase: "My solar plexus is warm."

> NOTE: Do not use this exercise if you have any abdominal problems, ulcers, diabetes, or during the last trimester of pregnancy. Instead say to yourself the phrase, "I am calm and relaxed."

CONCEPT: TO COOL THE FOREHEAD

Focus: Feel your forehead.

Image: Imagine a cool breeze blowing across your forehead, or a cool, damp cloth placed on your brow.

Phrase: "My forehead is cool."

After going through these six phases, scan your body and notice how you feel. Do you feel different from when you started? Notice your breathing. Take a few deep breaths in and out. Finish by saying the following phrases to yourself a few times:

♦ "I feel calm and relaxed."

♦ "When I open my eyes I will be relaxed but alert."

Open your eyes, and stretch, moving your arms, shoulders, neck, and legs.

STRESSBUSTER:
HOW TO FOLLOW THE PATH TO RELAXATION

Don't be discouraged if you find some autogenic techniques difficult. I found it hard to warm my feet, for example. For some, learning to feel heaviness and warming their hands comes rather quickly, but feeling warmth in the solar plexus or slowing the heartbeat is much harder. Attempting to cool the forehead is important. You don't want a warm forehead, since that can increase blood flow and may trigger a headache if you are a migraine sufferer.

It does take time to get the hang of autogenics, but—as in many things in life—the process of learning the technique can be helpful too. You'll probably find yourself relaxing and becoming much more aware of your body's signals as you learn each phase. As you continue to practice you will find that at work you can simply take a moment and feel heaviness in your arms and legs and instantly feel more relaxed. At your desk you can slow your breathing and heartbeat while experiencing relaxation in your limbs. This will give you more energy and presence of mind throughout your day.

RID YOUR BODY OF STRESS-RELATED PHYSICAL SYMPTOMS WITH BIOFEEDBACK

Biofeedback can be used to control physical symptoms associated with stress, including such problems as headaches, backaches, bruxism (teeth grinding), TMJ (pain in the jaw muscles), Raynaud's syndrome, anxiety, and chronic pain.

With biofeedback, instruments are connected to the body, which then record, amplify, and transmit on a screen or use sound to indicate levels of your heartbeat, skin temperature, brain waves, or muscle tension. When you concentrate on changing the sound or patterns on the screen, by tuning in to your body, focusing on breathing, relaxing a muscle group, or increasing your hand temperature, you can create changes that are then picked up by the machine. For example, electrical signals from your muscles can be transformed into flashing lights or a beep that goes off when your muscles tense. The machine acts as a guide and coach, letting you know how much tension you have and when you increase or decrease it. It is a good technique for women who have difficulty tuning into physical sensations or who have problems concentrating.

We all use feedback as a learning tool. When you learn a new computer program, for example, you are receiving information about your ability, physical and mental, and take action accordingly. In biofeedback, information about how your body is functioning is fed back to you. When you receive this data, you can zero in on the response and gain control over it.

One of the major contributions of biofeedback has been to document the control of bodily functions previously thought to be under the autonomic, or automatic, nervous system. For centuries yogis in the Himalayas have been able to slow their heart rate and change their brain waves, blood pressure, and metabolic rate, but the scientific community remained skeptical. With instrumentation they were able to document these changes. Although most of us don't have the amount of time yogis do to practice and perfect physical and mental control, you can learn to regulate your heart rate, blood pressure, and brain waves.

Basically, biofeedback just teaches you to relax by showing you bad habits such as tensing your jaw, lifting up your shoulders, or using more effort than necessary when moving. It indicates a change in your stress response when you do relax your jaw, droop your shoulders, or stay calm even though your mind is on the argument you had with your supervisor. It can also demonstrate an increase in your blood pressure when your thoughts turn to an emotional event.

Psychologists, psychiatrists, and other health-care professionals often use biofeedback training along with progressive muscle relaxation and autogenic training. If you have difficulty sticking with a technique, need more concrete feedback, or your problem does not respond with progressive relaxation or autogenics, you may find relief with biofeedback. For information on finding a biofeedback practitioner, see the Appendix.

Keep in mind that biofeedback is simply a tool to help teach you things you can do on your own. As you practice the techniques in this chapter, you will see that it is not necessary to use a device or machine to learn the relaxation response. By following the other suggestions in this book, you eventually will be able to achieve the same results.

FIND PEACE THROUGH MEDITATION

Like other relaxation techniques, meditation works by focusing the mind away from external events and emptying it of conscious thoughts, thereby achieving an inner awareness. In meditation, as in relaxation, when one focuses inward, certain physiological changes occur that contrast with the stress response. Meditation leaves you with a feeling of calm and peacefulness. Many meditators report a feeling of "oneness" with nature and the world. During meditation (as in deep relaxation) your brain-wave frequency changes from waking beta to alpha, or theta, which has been referred to as an altered state of consciousness. An altered state simply means you are deeply relaxed and aware of inner sensations and feelings.

It is difficult to distinguish between relaxation and meditation. Some people use the terms interchangeably, others see them as distinctly different—the former as physiological and the latter as a state of deep personal awareness. What's indisputable is that you should find it very rewarding. Twenty minutes a day of meditation has proven successful with a wide range of ailments including high blood pressure, hypertension, insomnia, chronic pain, depression, and anxiety. Meditation helps improve your ability to concentrate and enhances your alertness, a plus for today's overscheduled working woman. It allows you to tune in to more subtle feelings and thoughts as you quiet your conscious, intellectual mind.

As a method of achieving internal awareness, meditation can aid in gaining a better understanding of yourself and your potential. For the purpose of this book, we will be looking at meditation's use as a stress-reduction method rather than as a spiritual tool.

All forms of meditation require some type of focus to achieve inner attention or awareness. In the practice of Transcendental Meditation (T.M.), mantras, or words with spiritual meaning, such as the sanskrit word, *Om,* are repeated. Other schools of meditation focus on an object, such as a candle flame, or an image or pattern. In Sufi meditation, movement induces a meditative state.

As a focus, you can use any word or phrase with which you have pleasant associations or that have some meaning to you. Cardiologist Herbert Benson, the first physician to incorporate meditation into a stress-reduction program, developed his relaxation response technique by adapting the principles of T.M. In his book *The Relaxation Response,* he instructs people to breathe in and out and repeat the count of one.

Stress-reduction expert Jon Kabat-Zinn, Ph.D. a professor of behavioral medicine at the University of Massachusetts Medical School, teaches a type of meditation called mindfulness. Dr. Kabat-Zinn uses this technique with people suffering from chronic pain and stress-related disorders. In mindfulness, you pay attention to your breathing and physical sensations, which increases your concentration and your ability to relax. Dr. Kabat-Zinn believes focusing on your breathing is more useful than focusing on a mantra, because you can practice this method in all stressful situations. In focusing on sensations and bodily processes, you become aware of your "wholeness," an important aim of this method.

Learning To Meditate

To practice meditation, you need a quiet environment, a passive attitude, a comfortable position, and a focus for your concentration, such as breathing, physical sensations, or a word or image.

For successful meditation, you must be motivated and willing to spend time practicing. Meditation is perhaps the most difficult relaxation technique to master because it is so passive, and, as a result, you may find your mind wandering.

The trickiest aspect of meditation—or any relaxation, for that matter—is eliminating distracting thoughts. Let the thoughts come and go. Don't hold on to them. Even though you may get an idea for how to solve a specific problem, for example, just acknowledge it, but don't stay with it; say to yourself that you will remember it. Notice what you're thinking about or feeling, but don't judge these thoughts or emotions.

You may sometimes become anxious when you meditate. Because you are all alone with your thoughts and feelings, you may worry about what you have to do or should have done. Dr. Joan Borysenko calls this the "anxiety parade." Just let the thoughts and feelings come in and go out without grabbing on to them.

In addition, you may start experiencing aches, itchiness, or restlessness. Many people never stop to simply focus on their own body, nor do they try not to think. In the beginning, you may find this process of inner concentration uncomfortable, and you may become distracted. If so, try practicing some of the more active relaxation techniques, such as progressive relaxation, to grow accustomed to the process. When you are more comfortable, try meditation.

Positions For Meditation

When you are meditating you want to be as comfortable as possible so you can turn your focus inward. First, find a position in which you can relax most easily without falling asleep, feeling stiff, or causing discomfort. There is no one correct position.

SITTING IN A CHAIR. Sitting in a straightback chair with your feet on the floor gives support for your body.

LEANING AGAINST WALL. Using the wall for support is a good position since you don't have to use excess effort to sit up. You can extend your legs or sit with them crossed.

LYING DOWN. This position is fine as long as you don't fall asleep. Lying down takes pressure off your back, hips, neck, and shoulders and is a good position for people with back or shoulder pain.

SITTING CROSSLEGGED ON CUSHION. This position is more common among meditators who are in good physical condition and exercise regularly.

LOTUS. In this position you sit with your feet crossed and on the opposite thighs. Don't attempt it unless you have been doing yoga regularly or have very loose joints.

Practicing Meditation

1. QUIET ENVIRONMENT. Find a quiet place, with dim lighting, free from distractions. If you live with other people, let them know you are meditating and not to be disturbed. The room should be a comfortable temperature. You may want to use environmental sounds such as waves or rain falling or some meditation music. Give yourself fifteen to twenty minutes. Set a timer.

2. FIND A COMFORTABLE POSITION. Choose among the positions listed above. Find the best one for you.

3. CLOSE YOUR EYES. Closing your eyes helps you focus inward.

4. RELAX YOUR BODY. Go through and relax each part of your body. I recommend practicing progressive relaxation and mastering that technique before you begin meditation.

5. BE AWARE OF YOUR BREATHING. Begin noticing your breathing. Use the techniques for watching your breath in Chapter 2, on pages 48 and 49.

6. FIND A FOCUS. Choose a focus. You may want to stay with breathing and simply notice changes in your body as in the mindfulness technique; you may prefer to stare at a candle flame, or choose a word or phrase to repeat. When using a phrase, coordinate your breathing with your word or phrase. You can use a phrase such as "I am calm" or "I am at peace," breathing in on the "I am," and out on the "at peace."

STRESSBUSTER

You may find meditation helps you become more focused at work. Research suggests that meditation improves brain functioning because it encourages a balance between the two hemispheres of the brain, the left-hand side, responsible for logical, rational thought, and the right-hand side, which is creative and imaginative.

The previous exercises are guaranteed to elicit the relaxation response. Now that you know the 1-2-3's of relaxation, it's time to determine how to incorporate them into your hectic workday. The next section should help.

FITTING RELAXATION INTO YOUR BUSY SCHEDULE

You only need fifteen to twenty minutes to practice relaxation. For most women it's not difficult to find this amount of time, but rather to fit it into their schedule—to plan it and follow through.

Working overtime for a special account, Kristine, as you may remember from Chapter 1, had an hour commute, requiring her to arise at 5 A.M. to reach work on time. When she first considered her schedule, it seemed as if it would be impossible to squeeze in any relaxation in the morning. Upon a closer look—and after making stress-reducing changes—she discovered she could make some adjustments.

Kristine was taking at least twenty minutes in the morning just trying to wake up, then showering and getting dressed. When she cut down on her nightly sweets and alcohol consumption, she found that, although she was tired when she woke up, she wasn't as wiped out. Instead of spending so much time over coffee, she cut back to ten minutes; now she takes a shower and begins doing some loosening-up exercises under the hot water. After her shower, ten minutes of back care exercises followed by ten minutes of practicing relaxation prepare her for her busy day. She then has twenty-five to thirty minutes to get dressed and leave.

During her hour commute, Kristine listens to relaxing music on tape and continues practicing breathing and progressive muscle relaxation. She then thinks about what she needs to accomplish during the day and mentally prepares herself. For the last twenty minutes, she puts on upbeat popular music to perk her up as she enjoys the drive through lush farmlands.

In the past, Kristine would arrive at work early, to get ready for the day, munching a sweet roll and sipping two or three more cups of coffee, mulling over what work had to be done. Now, in place of a sweet roll or sugared muffin, Kristine takes whole grain cereal and fruit with her, limits herself to one or two cups of coffee, which she has while beginning her work. Instead of arriving ten minutes early, she prepares during her regular hours and simply asks not to be disturbed during that time. Although she usually feels she needs a second cup of coffee, she plans to cut back to one when the extra work is finished. During the rest of the day she drinks decaf. When she begins to drag in the afternoon, she goes outside to walk around the block or sits in a nearby park for a breather.

Several working women I know dovetail by meditating in the bath or shower. Lee, one of my clients, has found that meditating in the shower leaves her free from distraction and prepares her for her hectic day as the owner of a graphic design firm. She sits and lets the water run over her as she breathes and focuses inward. It allows her husband to go about his morning routine while Lee spends time taking care of herself.

Cindy, a speech therapist, likes to soak in the tub. After practicing relaxation at different times and in different settings, she has found that her most profound and deep meditation comes when she is in the tub, so she now includes it in her morning routine. Cindy has a timer and sets it for fifteen minutes to ensure that she spends the time she needs in a relaxed state. After her meditation, she washes her hair and takes a quick shower. Soaking warms up her body and facilitates the stretching and strengthening exercises that follow.

To practice relaxation in the bath, you need to have a tub in which you are comfortable. Purchase foam squares for your head and hips or a commercial bath pillow. Make sure the water is not so hot that it drains you but warm enough that you don't get chilled. After soaking for a while, watch that you don't stand up too quickly, as you might get dizzy. Try the following tips:

♦ Prop your legs up on the wall or keep them comfortably bent. Make sure your neck is in a position that does not cause strain. You will have to experiment. Keeping the water level low sometimes helps.

Use passive progressive relaxation, starting with your feet. Then focus on your breathing. Use an active relaxation technique such as countdown breathing.

♦ Visualize yourself in a peaceful environment: at the beach, in a meadow, by a stream, on top of a mountain. See all the details, colors, sounds, textures, of what you are doing.

Or:

♦ Visualize any wrinkles in your face smoothing out.
♦ Finish by saying affirmations.

NOTE: Once you are comfortable with relaxation in the tub, you can go to more meditative techniques.

If you practice relaxation in the morning, take a quick shower afterwards to get you started for the day and make you more alert. If you do the bathtub relaxation in the evening, dim the lights, and use candles and music for an extra treat. Ensure that your bathroom is a place in which you enjoy spending time. Paint it a pleasant color, put pictures on the wall. Keep it clean and neat.

Remember: A hot bath is relaxing and a nice thing to do, but unless you use a mental relaxation technique you will not be reversing the physiological effects of the stress response. Also, this shouldn't be the only place you practice relaxation; remember to practice breathing and releasing muscles throughout your work day.

Many women I know like to meditate in the morning before they go to work: it prepares them for the day and they usually have fewer distractions. The most beneficial schedule is combining home practice with relaxation at work. If you work long hours or find yourself getting tired and stressed out by afternoon, practicing on the job is a good idea. Finding a quiet, comfortable area free from interruptions and the distractions of your work can be a challenge. Marilyn, a secretary in a legal firm, uses the conference room when it is empty; when it's not, she borrows an empty office belonging to a lawyer who's usually in court.

You don't have to do a "full blown" relaxation sequence, however, for it to be beneficial. In fact, at least once a day you should consider each part of your body, notice your breathing, practice progressive relaxation and/or visualize yourself in a pleasant place. I know a computer programmer who input calming phrases that periodically appear on the screen telling her to relax.

Fitting relaxation into your schedule requires that you look closely at how you use your time. Use tips from Chapter 8 on time management to help you. Then devise a plan and stick to it. Start by working it in at least three days a week. When you succeed, you can add more time, or you may want to practice relaxation three times a week and do aerobic exercise three days as part of your stress-reduction plan. One thing is certain: It will be worth your efforts.

STRESSBUSTER:
INCORPORATING RELAXATION INTO YOUR WORKDAY

Regularly practicing relaxation will lower your general stress level—that high arousal rate that causes you to overreact to stressful situations. And incorporating relaxation into your work day will help you better cope with the daily hassles that all working women face, enabling you to have the energy and peace of mind you deserve. Give these ideas a try.

+ Practicing relaxation teaches you about your tension levels and breathing. Use this information to help increase your awareness of physical sensations and responses to stress during your work day.

+ Put a note on your desk or computer—wherever you will see it—to remember to take deep breaths throughout the day—then do it! Use the stop watch breathing technique from page 53—taking slow breaths in and out for a minute.

+ When you feel anxious or rushed, pay attention to that feeling and respond either by stopping and doing a count breath (going from ten to one) or by doing a progressive muscle relaxation—or both. The two minutes you spend doing this will be time well spent. A good way of doing progressive relaxation is to associate a number with a body part. Say the number (1 for your head, 2 for neck, etc.) as you feel that part. It will reinforce the release and you will begin to associate your relaxation with the numbers.

+ If you work alone and do a lot of typing or entering data into a computer, listen to relaxation music on your Walkman (see Appendix for music selections).

+ If you're under pressure to meet a deadline and feel increasingly drained, don't reach for a cup of coffee; instead, take a short break by walking and listening to a relaxation tape on a Walkman. The movement combined with hearing the relaxing voice will revive and relax you.

- If you feel too distracted at work to practice a full relaxation sequence, do a "physical meditation." Following the guidelines for neck and shoulder exercises beginning on page 202, close your eyes, breathe deeply, and slowly go through the exercises, focusing on how your body feels. This will rejuvenate you and get the kinks out of those tight muscles.

- Practice slowing your breathing during meetings, when listening to others, and while talking on the phone. The more you do this while engaged in an activity, the more it will become a natural response.

- If you find yourself constantly looking at the clock (either because you are bored and want to go home or because you have so much work and feel rushed), train yourself to take two very long breaths every time you check the time. Let it become a trigger to breathe deeply. You may need to make a note at first. Doing this will remind you to begin breathing and working in a calm manner. If you habitually watch the clock, this will help you break the habit, replacing it with a healthier one.

Make relaxation a work habit—you'll be more productive and creative in the long run. The more you incorporate relaxation into your day, the more skillful you'll be at it and the easier it will become.

Chapter Four

USING YOUR MIND
TO DECREASE STRESS

Leslie, 35, a secretary for an insurance company, once again is out
sick from her job. A succession of colds and flus continually cause
her to miss work, further complicating an already stressful situation.
Leslie often argues with her co-workers, and complains her boss
overloads her and treats her with little respect. This is her fifth job in
as many years; work always seems to end in the same way. Each job
starts out well, but soon problems arise with her boss and co-workers. She tries to do a good job, but unable to say no and set limits,
she gets overloaded, resentful, and then blames others. With a very
negative view of life, Leslie expects the worst in people.
Emphasizing the dark side of everything, she sees outside forces as
the cause of all her troubles; she expects people to treat her poorly
and they often do. This attitude keeps her constantly stressed, wearing down her immune system and leaving her susceptible to illness
and injury. A vicious cycle of anger and anxiety, poor health, and
conflicting relationships has become the norm.

YOU ARE WHAT YOU THINK

What you think affects how you feel. Why? As I've pointed out, stress
is a physiological response to one's various mental activities. Your

thoughts will affect your emotions and influence your actions. If we think primarily positive thoughts, we generate positive feelings, and in turn tend to draw positive experiences. Conversely, anxious, negative thoughts will produce undesirable feelings and behavior. Does this sound like a Pollyanna idea? Research has actually shown that a happy person may really be a healthier one.

The belief that your frame of mind can affect your behavior is shared by many contemporary thinkers from Norman Vincent Peale and Dale Carnegie to cancer specialist Bernie Siegel, from religious to psychological thinkers, to a wide range of alternative healing practitioners. All these individuals emphasize that we have the ability to change our attitudes and thought processes and therefore influence our lives.

If worrying can trigger a stress response, then you could expect that ending fearful, irrational thoughts would lower your stress rate and improve how you feel. In this section we will be looking at ways to overcome a negative mindset that keeps you in a chronic cycle of stress.

FOOD FOR THOUGHT
It's not—what you think you are
But rather—what you think *you are*.
Brian Tracy

If you want to improve your behavior and make changes in your thinking, you need to cultivate healthy thoughts, as well as replace old negative ones. This can be done by *listening* to what you say to yourself (gaining awareness), *understanding* where your beliefs come from, *cleaning* up your language, *replacing* thoughts with more healthy and realistic statements, and *repeating* affirmations to break the cycle of negative thinking and encourage positive images. *Visualization* is used to support your actions and put in the picture of how you want to respond.

How To Recognize Negative Self-Talk

The first step is paying attention to your self-talk. Self-talk consists of all the things we constantly tell ourselves about our experiences and feelings. Almost every minute you are engaging in self-talk. Yet many of us think negative, limiting thoughts that keep us from reaching our full potential. In fact, some experts have found that up to 75 percent of what we say to ourselves may be working against us. Phrases such as "I can't," "I doubt," "I'm sorry," or "I tried" all indicate failure. How often do you think, "I probably won't be able to finish this in time and then I'll have to...," "it's not as good as it could be and they probably won't think I'm good enough," "I wish I had more energy so I could do...," "if I'm late I'm not going to get what I need from...and then I won't...." The tendency to take a situation to its worst possible conclusion has been labeled "awfulizing."

What's wrong with "what if" and "if only"? Often we don't react to a situation as it is now, but instead respond with old negative attitudes and beliefs. These conditioned reactions bring up emotions that in turn trigger the stress response and can set off or continue a vicious cycle of anxiety and chronic stress. It's important to remember that such feelings appear to be real. But awfulizing isn't based upon what is real—it's a habit or an old belief—and we need to learn to break the cycle.

Being aware is essential. You may find you have a pattern; either you "awfulize," "personalize," and/or "absolutize." When you personalize, you are both awfulizing *and* taking it personally. For example, say your real estate client is in a bad mood and unhappy with everything you show her, so you assume it's your fault that she doesn't like any houses, and therefore fear she will drop you for another agent. When you absolutize, you think everything must go a certain way. This ties in with perfectionism. You think things like "I should" do this, "I must," "I ought." If you or someone else fails to live up to your standards, you consider you both to be bad. You think, "I should not have shown that house, I ought to have known better," or "that client really makes me mad, she is so picky, she should have liked it."

How To Clean Up Your Language

When we think a thought, we usually get a mental picture too. Since images evoke feelings and physical responses, it is important to watch what you are saying. Consider such phrases as, "I'm *sick* and *tired* of...," "I'm *scared* to death...," "I'm *afraid* I can't do...," "I'm just *sick* about not being able to do that," or even "I'm so happy I could *die.*" What kind of messages are you sending to yourself? You may not literally believe your boss is a *"pain* in the neck," but saying it may actually create the conditions in your body.

By the same token, it's important to watch the names you call your children, mate, and friends. When kids misbehave, for example, it's inappropriate to tell them they are "bad." What they did may be bad and you can say so, but by implying that they themselves are bad people, you will encourage a negative self-image, with a self-fulfilling dimension. "Dingbat," "turkey," and "dummy" are powerful words, and by using them consistently, you reinforce this inappropriate self-image in another person. Find positive, loving words instead of denigrating ones. I know a woman, for instance, who frequently called her husband "baby"—until she realized that one reason she spent so much time taking care of him was because she'd been reinforcing a variety of dependent behaviors.

When you think negatively, worry, awfulize, or absolutize, you create unpleasant emotions. These emotions rarely have anything to do with the actual event. Start now by noticing what you are saying to yourself. Write it down. Are there phrases you tend to use? Now is the time to stop and replace those thoughts with healthy ones.

Understanding Where Your Negative Thoughts Come From

Many of us have beliefs about ourselves and the world that create stress in our lives and may prevent us from living a fully satisfying life. As women, we are conditioned to believe that we must be perfect, and approved of by everyone, a totally impossible expectation which causes only unhappiness. Another misconception is expecting everything to go the way you planned or imagined it to be. This certainly sets you up for disappointment. Thinking others cause your unhappiness is a belief that puts the blame on everyone else, leaving you with no control over your emotions. Another assumption is that we cannot change old patterns.

Realizing that we respond to new situations in a way determined by our past experiences and self-perceptions, we can become aware of these ingrained beliefs and, then, change our current behavior.

Cathy, a thirty-year-old doctoral candidate, carries with her an "uneven" self-image; though it's often positive, some situations elicit an old negative image. In such cases she responds with conditioned behavior, rather than as the person she really is—a well-educated, intelligent woman. When she recently began working in an academic setting, she found herself making mistakes and feeling inadequate. When talking to her dean, for example, Cathy felt intimidated, became flustered, and was unable to articulate the questions and answers she had carefully formulated. This conditioned response to certain authority figures, Cathy recognized, stemmed from her belief during adolescence that she was a "dumb blonde," a self-image she had acquired when she had difficulty learning math. Her viewing herself in this way became a habit. Fortunately, Cathy could see her current behavior was based on old, incorrect stored information that resulted in her continuing to act in situations like the scared, "inadequate" girl in algebra class. Through reframing her thoughts and using affirmations and visualization, Cathy changed this behavior. She now has a very comfortable relationship with her dean, and although she may make mistakes, she realizes they are natural ones that come in the course of any working situation—not because she expects to make them or because she doesn't focus on what she's doing.

Often, we operate under the influence of old beliefs handed down to us by others or by an experience where we felt afraid, humiliated, or guilty. Aware of her poor self-image, Cathy could then break her pattern. Leslie, the unhappy secretary, responds negatively in general to people and situations. When she was young, her parents didn't give her the love and affection she needed. Being treated poorly became familiar to her, so she has continuously sought or created situations where she feels badly about herself. Leslie needs to appraise her situation and examine her beliefs about herself and others. She does a lot of absolutizing and expecting the worst. In addition to using affirmations and visualizations, she may also want to seek counseling to help her deal with her feelings and see how her past is influencing her present.

Understanding where our behaviors come from is not license to simply continue them, however, rationalizing that they occur because we did not get what we needed in earlier life or had a bad experience. Instead, recognizing patterns can help to change behavior for the better.

How To Stop Negative Self-Talk

To stop negative self-talk, listen to what you tell yourself. Carefully consider the situation. Is your self-talk related to fact or old beliefs? (Do you have a poor self-image? Do you always expect the worst? Do you usually feel that you never have enough time?) Ask yourself if the feeling is familiar. Is this what you always feel or think, or are you responding to the situation appropriately? Is there a basic irrational belief involved ("I'm not as smart as my co-worker," "I'll feel terrible if I don't type this just right")? Do you spend time and energy obsessing over a situation, trying to determine who's to blame? Or do you respond to the present needs of the situation? If you're behind on preparing a report, for example, consider the worst that can happen (you'll have to extend your deadline, feel ashamed that you didn't finish on time, be reprimanded by your boss). Then ponder the good things that can occur when you complete your work (you'll have a sense of satisfaction, get paid, receive the recognition you want). After going through this process, use an affirmation about the situation to support a healthy response: "I have the time, knowledge, and ability to finish this report," "I enjoy a challenge," or "I am learning to stay calm and relaxed when working under pressure."

FOOD FOR THOUGHT

Our mind stores past experiences, ideas, and beliefs, very much like a sophisticated bio-computer. But like any computer, it is only as good as the information that is put into it. You control what is stored, and it is therefore important to fill your memory bank with positive, healthful thoughts.

Five Steps To Using Affirmations To Reduce Stress

Words create pictures in your mind and your mind believes what it sees. You can therefore use positive self-talk, or affirmations, to create changes you desire, neutralizing old beliefs and irrational thoughts. French pharmacist Emile Coué, in the early part of this century, successfully treated stress-related disorders by having his patients repeat the phrase, "Every day in every way I am getting better and better," and other affirmations to achieve their desired goals. Affirmations can help you cope with stress on the job. Feeling overwhelmed by too much responsibility often leaves you drained emotionally and with little energy left over for anything else. If you have a big project, for example, that is weighing on you, using affirmations can actually help you create the conditions necessary to accomplish your task. Affirmations are statements that refer to any condition you wish to create—be it an attitude, emotion, or situation. They are like goals, and it is up to you to determine your goal. It may be getting to work on time, finishing a project by the deadline, becoming more organized on the job, improving your eating habits, being more patient with your children, falling asleep easily, overcoming a fear, or being more relaxed in general. Once you decide on the situation you wish to change or improve, you can structure your affirmations using the following guidelines:

1. USE THE PRESENT TENSE. State your desire as if it has already happened. Say "I am well-organized," rather than "I will get well-organized." Or say, "I am learning to be organized," or "I am setting up the conditions to be well-organized." If the affirmation is too far from reality, you will not relate to it.

2. USE THE PERSONAL. Always say "I" or use your name. For example, "I make time to regularly practice my relaxation."

3. USE THE POSITIVE. Don't say, "I will not lose my temper at work." The mind will form a picture of you blowing your top and reinforce the behavior. Instead, say something like, "I stay relaxed during work," or "My emotions are appropriately expressed," and picture yourself maintaining a balance at work. Note: I am not saying to suppress your feelings, but instead to be in touch with why you are angry and apt to blow up. Use affirmations to help yourself to relax and understand your behavior.

4. BE SPECIFIC. General affirmations are excellent and can be used to create conditions such as being relaxed, having enough time, staying focused. If you have a clear goal, however, state it. If you want to lose weight and your goal is 125 pounds, say this in your affirmation. If you want to lose five pounds, don't say ten and hope you will make the five. On the other hand, if you have a great deal of weight to lose, make a schedule with realistic mini-goals. In addition, always use visualization with your affirmations: see yourself at your desired weight. For example, take a picture of yourself and in

black marker draw over it how you want to look. See yourself as a thin person. Using affirmations will help you discover certain reasons for remaining overweight, such as a "fat" body image that you carry with you.

5. BE REALISTIC. Your goal should be reasonable. You may wish to increase your income from $20,000 to $30,000 a year, which is realistic. But if you start affirming that you will make $100,000 the following year, you may set yourself up for failure. If you do want to make $100,000 a year, establish it as a goal and work toward it, setting up short and long term goals to help achieve it.

For affirmations to work, you must repeat them. But it shouldn't be just rote recitation. Affirmations are an active process. You need to say them with emotion, energy, and belief, repeating them with feeling and conviction. See the desired goal and believe it can happen. Affirmations take time to work. I recommend using them daily. They can be said aloud or thought anytime—while traveling to your job, working, walking, exercising, or doing tasks such as washing the dishes. When I feel overloaded by responsibilities, I use, "I have an even flow of energy that sustains me throughout the day and night." Using this will keep you from burning out or getting hyper. Another one that takes pressure off is "I have the energy for all conditions I need to meet."

How To Make Affirmations A Part Of Your Day

Work with a few affirmations at a time, such as three or four, and stick with them. It's good to keep a record of them too. Take note of any changes that you notice. I can't say enough how important this is. Acknowledge your accomplishments no matter how small they may seem to you. Try any one or a combination of the following methods for using affirmations. Just ten minutes a day can make a big difference!

1. SAY AFFIRMATIONS BEFORE BED AND UPON AWAKENING. As you drift off to sleep or when you first wake up in the morning, you are in a less "conscious" state and open to suggestion. Try to put in positive information. Even if you don't use affirmations, you can set the tone for your day. For example, see yourself having a positive, productive one, accomplishing your goals, or feeling good at the end of the day.

2. USE AFFIRMATIONS WITH RELAXATION. Say your affirmations after doing your relaxation exercises or after meditation. Again, this is a time when your conscious mind is quieted and you are open to suggestion.

3. SAY AFFIRMATIONS ALOUD. Hearing affirmations reinforces the message. Be sure to listen to what you are saying.

4. TAPE-RECORD AFFIRMATIONS. Put affirmations on tape and play them back. You may want to put on a relaxation sequence followed by affirmations.

5. WRITE DOWN YOUR AFFIRMATIONS. This can establish a strong visual connection. Write them out ten or twenty times. In the morning, during the first half-hour you are awake is the most beneficial time to do this. When you first determine a new affirmation, write it on a page, then wait and see what comes up in response to the statement. If there is any resistance, even slight, write it down. As you record your affirmation with pen and paper, continue jotting down all your thoughts and feelings. Affirmations are not designed to simply override thoughts, but to help you become attuned to why you have certain negative thoughts. For example, I know someone whose affirmation was "I deserve to be wealthy." As she wrote this down, a flood of old family scripts came into her mind, such as "wealthy people aren't nice." Write your affirmations on cards, and put them up where you can see them.

6. REPEAT YOUR AFFIRMATION INTO THE MIRROR. Say your affirmation while looking in the mirror. Watching yourself and hearing your voice creates more rapid changes. How you really feel about the statement will be visible on your face. One technique is to look in the mirror and say that you love yourself, a difficult task for many people but an extremely powerful exercise. I recommend it.

7. USE AFFIRMATIONS BEFORE AN EVENT. Say affirmations before a presentation, test, audition, asking for a raise, or any stressful situation. This helps you overcome feelings of helplessness and instead gain control. Affirmations can be used in conjunction with mental rehearsal, a technique discussed in detail later in this chapter.

If you experience resistance to your statements in the form of tension or disagreement, pay attention. First determine what your feelings are. Are there negative beliefs associated with the goal that would keep you from attaining it? Explore these thoughts. Is there disagreement because the affirmation is so far removed from reality? If you are having difficulty falling asleep, for example, and use the affirmation "I fall asleep quickly and sleep through the night," it may need to be revised to "I am creating the conditions for falling asleep easily" or "I can fall asleep easily." Know that you are creating conditions for change, and affirm that you are open to letting go of any obstacles.

Remember that the situations or behaviors you are seeking to change may have been in existence for years and will not go away overnight. If, after a month, nothing has happened or you are still not getting the results you want, use a process of sorting through your goals to find out what's holding you back. Use the visualization techniques beginning on page 97 to help you. You may need to re-word your affirmation or develop a new one. Try breaking down your goal into smaller, more attainable ones. Go back to the paper where you wrote them down and look at the feelings that came up; they probably need to be explored further. Fine-tune your images.

Of course, it is not enough to simply say an affirmation; you have to follow through with action. If you affirm that you will weigh five pounds less, then exercise more and/or reduce your calories. Use the affirmation to help you attain your goal, but not in place of doing something about it.

Learning To Do Affirmation Exercises

1. FIND A COMFORTABLE POSITION, SITTING OR LYING DOWN. Close your eyes and focus inward.

2. SLOW YOUR BREATHING. Spend a few moments watching your breath. Slow it down, using a breathing technique from Chapter 2.

3. USE PROGRESSIVE RELAXATION. Start with your feet and go through your body, sensing and releasing each part: feet, legs, but-tocks, abdomen, etc. Feel your hands and feet, arms and legs, as being heavy.

4. REPEAT (SILENTLY OR ALOUD), "I AM CALM AND RELAXED." You may want to say the "I am" on the inhalation and the "calm and relaxed" on the exhalation. Say this three or four times.

5. USE A GENERAL AFFIRMATION. If you are working with a general affirmation, such as "everyday in every way I am getting better and better," or "I am filled with healthy energy," say it now. Repeat it three to four times.

6. USE YOUR CURRENT AFFIRMATIONS. Repeat them six to ten times. Remember not to use more than three or four.

7. REPEAT DEEP BREATHING AND SAYING CALMING AFFIRMATIONS. Go back to watching your breath, and affirm you are calm and relaxed several times.

8. AFFIRM YOUR RESULTS. Affirm that these desired changes will come about. You can say "this or something better will come about" or "I achieve my goals," or whatever you feel comfortable saying.

9. OPEN YOUR EYES AND STRETCH.

STRESSBUSTER:
SEVEN STEPS FOR CREATING POSITIVE ATTITUDES

1. Have a desire to make changes.
2. Identify what you want to change.
3. Clean up your negative self-talk.
4. Use visualization to help achieve your goals.
5. Use affirmations to help identify and change old patterns.
6. Trust the power of your inner mind to create pleasant things in your life.
7. Believe that it is possible to make changes.

   You have the power!

CREATIVE VISUALIZATION: A TOOL FOR CHANGE

Visualization is perhaps the most powerful tool we have to make changes in our lives, because whatever the mind thinks or imagines, the body feels. In autogenic training, for example, when you imagine that your hands are warm by visualizing the sun beaming down on them, they feel warm and blood flow is increased. Through creative visualization, you can use your imagination to create what you want in your life—and reduce stress. For example, you may choose to imagine yourself being more assertive at work, making more money, being more easygoing with your children. The choice is yours.

Let's say that you want be more assertive at work. To start, get into a relaxed state. Then see yourself calmly and clearly stating your ideas at a business meeting, or letting your boss know that you are happy to contribute but are unable to stay late every night under the current arrangements. Put in all the details, how you look, feel, and so forth. Through creative visualization, you're setting the conditions for these events to actually happen.

Visualization and guided imagery have been used for centuries to improve health, promote healing, and rehabilitate injuries. Therapists and health professionals instruct patients to visualize arthritic joints as smooth, knotted muscles as long and relaxed, tumors as dissolving, injured parts as functioning. Doctors Carl Simonton and Bernie Siegel have reported success using visualization in conjunction with chemotherapy in treating cancer patients. Studies have shown that practicing athletic skills with visualization can improve performance. Today, many Olympic athletes employ a combination of autogenics and visualization in their training programs. Visualization also can help you change old mental and physical patterns that are keeping you stressed and allow you to create new desired conditions.

Identify areas of your life that you find stressful. Then go about creating a clear picture of how you want these situations to look. If the project manager keeps overloading you, causing you to feel angry and put upon, see yourself telling her in a calm but assertive manner that you will be unable to attend to the new task until you finish other priorities. Put in all the details—including feeling good about yourself and your ability to state your needs without getting emotional. Also visualize yourself doing your work throughout the day with an even flow of energy, pacing yourself, and accomplishing your tasks.

Here's a little exercise that illustrates the power of imagery. Read through the following paragraph, and picture yourself doing what it says.

You are going into your kitchen, opening the refrigerator, and seeing a lemon. Take out the lemon, put it on the counter, take out a knife from your drawer, and cut open the lemon. Bring the lemon to your nose and smell it, then bring it to your lips and put your tongue on it.

What happened? Did you see the lemon? Did your mouth water when you tasted it? Did you have to swallow? When a thought comes into your mind, the mental images that are created signal the release of chemicals, which are sent to the cells, causing the body to respond. Simply imagining tasting a lemon can cause you to salivate! Because of this connection between thinking and responding, you can learn to use this normal everyday process as a tool for creating positive experiences in your life.

We constantly use our imagination throughout the day—from the mundane, such as thinking about what we'll have for dinner, to the more profound, including creatively solving problems at work or being insightful and sensitive in dealing with other people. Most of us get a mental picture or imagine a situation when we think of something. When you contemplate what you are going to wear to a meeting, for instance, you may get a picture of yourself in one of your outfits or have an image of a skirt you'd like to wear, which may remind you that it needs ironing. If you've misplaced something, you usually try to remember by "seeing" where you put it last. You mentally go over your actions.

Although we constantly use our imagination, Shakti Gawain, author of the best-selling book, *Creative Visualization,* points out that many of us use our power of visualization in negative and unconscious ways. As was mentioned earlier, most people carry around old negative beliefs about themselves that are self-limiting in terms of achieving their full potential. These unconscious beliefs lead you to expect limitation, difficulties, and problems. As you think, "I shouldn't ask for a promotion because I probably won't get it," "the market is too bad for me to find a better apartment," "I'm not going to knock myself out on this project because no one appreciates my work anyway," you get mental pictures. Some people think that if they expect the worst they won't be disappointed if they don't get what they want. Since the mind believes most of what it sees, your ability to visualize positive things in your life is extremely important. If you focus on the *worst* possibilities occurring, you can be sure you won't get the *best*.

Some women put these principles to work in their lives more readily than others. Recently one of my friends remarked that she couldn't believe that once again Sylvia had been offered a terrific new job opportunity out of the blue. I replied that it didn't surprise me one bit. She has always had a clear picture of herself successfully working in pleasant surroundings and making the money she needs. Sylvia's belief in abundance rather than deprivation permeates her work and personal life.

For some women it may take practice to creatively use their imagination. Before going on, practice using your visual powers with the following suggestions.

Close your eyes, and take a deep breath. Think of:

♦ A familiar place in which you feel comfortable—a favorite chair in your living room, your bed, a backyard hammock, a porch swing. Notice all the details: what is around you, the type of lighting, a favorite object.

♦ A pleasant moment that occurred within the last few days. Now observe your feelings, as well as the colors, textures, and sounds.

In these exercises you are drawing on your memory to help construct pictures. With creative visualization, you will draw on memory, in addition to letting your mind create desired states and conditions. You may conjure a relaxing place that is somewhere you have never been or has aspects of places you have seen or read about. By observing your imaginary environment, you are fine-tuning your ability to observe yourself in your daily life as well.

Now try this exercise:

♦ Visualize the last movie you saw. Observe yourself sitting in the seat. Are you comfortable? Are you alone or with someone? Are you eating popcorn? Can you smell it, or smell it in the theater? Are you having something to drink? How does it taste? What are you hearing? What is your emotional reaction to the movie?

In addition, you can imagine yourself in new roles and situations, drawing on images you know and applying them to yourself. You will visualize yourself as a supervisor or corporate chief. As you visualize, you will observe yourself and all the details.

How Relaxation And Visualization Work Together To Reduce Stress

Visualization is most successful when practiced in conjunction with relaxation. Start with a relaxation technique with which you are comfortable, then proceed with your visualization. Another good time to do visualization is just before you fall asleep and/or when you first awake in the morning. At both these times you are moving from sleep to waking and are open to suggestion. Put in your goals at night before you fall asleep. In the morning, the thought of seeing yourself that evening having completed all you had to do and feeling good about it is a nice way of starting the day. Any time at the office, you can close your eyes and imagine a beautiful place—a meadow, a beach—and take a mini-break, escaping to your mental getaway. Relaxation is most beneficial when it is associated with pleasurable feelings.

How To Use Visualization Successfully

To succeed at visualization you need to have a real *desire* for what you are visualizing. It is not enough to think you should change jobs, lose weight, or find a satisfying relationship. You need to be sure that is what you really want and have a clear sense of purpose. Make sure you are ready at all levels to change jobs. If you aren't or are uncertain, you may need to use visualization to find out why, asking for answers from deep within.

When your visualization manifests in your life, be able to *acknowledge and accept* it. Sometimes we get caught up in the process of pursuing rather than accepting. It is very important to acknowledge your accomplishments and your efforts. When you have met a goal, changed a behavior, or created a new condition, be sure to acknowledge that you have set down the conditions and followed through. Often when working on ourselves we only see how far we have to go rather than how much we've achieved.

You must *believe* in the possibility of your goal and that you have the power to attain it. You may not think, based upon past experiences, for example, that a promotion at work is possible. A negative response, such as a voice or a feeling that it can't happen, may sabotage your efforts, or falling asleep or the inability to hold the image may sidetrack your visualization. You will therefore have to identify your limitations and then determine if you have the power to make it happen. As you imagine yourself moving up the corporate ladder, *see* and *feel* all the details. Check out which higher position is appropriate for you. Pay attention to any resistances that come up.

A STRESS-SUCCESS STORY

When Roz, a legal secretary, was in her late thirties, with a daughter in high school, she enrolled in college and eventually earned both a bachelor's and law degree while working full time. At 51, Roz found she couldn't pass the bar exam. Twice, she became so nervous during the test, that she went completely blank, unable to recall the material she clearly knew. A friend suggested she work with me. I outlined a course of action that included fine-tuning her relaxation skills, using creative visualization to uncover any blocks that might be preventing her from passing, developing affirmations to support her intentions, and mental rehearsal to "program" herself to stay calm during the test. Outside our sessions, Roz practiced on her own using several relaxation tapes (see Appendix) and repeating affirmations.

This time during the bar review preparation course she found herself retaining more information, making more connections to the material, and feeling more self-assured. She became confident she was taking all the necessary steps to set the conditions for passing. Although she had periods of concern and nervousness, she used her tapes and affirmations and worked through them.

Roz called on the second day of the exam, excited and happy. She had survived the two days of testing and completed the essays—the part of the test that had caused her to go blank in the past. She reported that on the way to the exam she started to get nervous and listened to a relaxation tape. During her lunch breaks she did another one. When she noticed herself getting very tense and anxious, she stopped and did a count breathing. Roz didn't know how she did or if she passed, but she felt she had succeeded and was extremely proud of herself. During the four months that she had to wait for her results, she continued practicing relaxation. When the notification came that she had passed the bar, she knew what had made the difference.

Also tied to belief is *trust*. It takes time to learn to trust yourself. We are so accustomed to seeking answers outside ourselves, relying on experts and authorities. Yet, we actually have all the answers within ourselves. Often, however, looking inside and trusting ourselves is the hardest thing to do. To make creative visualization a part of your life and a regular tool for personal growth and stress reduction, it is helpful to have friends who use these techniques as well. They will be supportive in your efforts, and it will give you a common ground and perspective of how you approach your life. If creative visualization is new to you and your circle of friends, look for classes where you can learn not only techniques but meet others with similar interests. Holistic centers, meditation groups, and adult-education classes would be a good place to start. Often health-food stores list workshops and special classes, so check their bulletin boards. If you are unsure about your powers of visualization or would like some guidance, check "Resources" in the Appendix for audiocassette tapes.

Choosing A Creative Visualization Method

When working with images, you may visualize a goal you want to attain, rehearse something at which you wish to succeed, create a relaxing environment, use a "guided imagery," or ask for answers to a problem you have.

CREATING A RELAXING ENVIRONMENT. An effective method of reducing stress is to picture yourself in a pleasant environment, where you feel safe, peaceful, and relaxed. To do this, close your eyes and relax by focusing on your breathing. Then imagine yourself in a beautiful environment. It can be any place you would like to go: by a stream, in a forest, in a meadow, on a deserted beach. You want to explore your environment, noticing all the details. As you walk around, notice the colors, textures, sounds, smells, and temperature. How do you feel when you are there?

Many people like to imagine themselves at the beach. They can hear the ocean waves and the sound of the gulls, feel the sun beaming down on them, experience the texture of the sand as they walk, and smell the ocean air. On the other hand, if you don't like the hot sun, imagine yourself in the woods inside a cozy cabin with a large picture window and porch. Relax in a rocking chair, gazing at the beautiful scenery.

Creating your own special place is one of the best methods to begin practicing visualization. It helps increase your powers of visualization and your ability to relax, giving you a comforting place to travel to any time you wish. I have my own retreat in which I seek refuge: at a lake, surrounded by mountains, with a hot spring in which to soak. I mentally go there to be revived, relaxed, or nurtured. For a mini-break from a busy work day, sit back in your chair, close your eyes, take several deep breaths and spend a few minutes visualizing your special place.

ESTABLISHING A GOAL. It is difficult to accomplish something you can't imagine. Defining and visualizing your goals can set in motion the processes needed to realize them. Take Katy, for example. She had been on a diet program sponsored by her office and had lost weight, but she had reached a plateau and just couldn't seem to lose any more pounds, no matter how hard she tried. I suggested that she take a photograph of herself and then sketch over it the way she wanted to look. She also was to visualize herself at her desired weight. When she attempted to do this, she became very aware that there were certain emotional issues surrounding her appearance and weight. Katy learned to sort out these issues and some of her past experiences that led to her weight gain in the first place. Replacing them with a picture of herself thin, she lost weight in a gradual and healthy manner until she reached her desired goal—a goal that she has maintained.

You can choose any goal you wish to attain: getting a promotion, being more organized, having better health, gaining more energy, improving relationships, receiving a raise, garnering a better living situation. Choosing your goals will force you to think about or become more clear on what you want. So often, we limit ourselves by what we believe we deserve or by what we think is possible. Decide what you want and then set your goals. (See Chapter 8, for tips on goal setting.)

MENTAL REHEARSAL. When you perform a skill, you need concentration and a tension-free body to enable proper coordination. Some women, for example, have the talent or skill to play the piano or to swing a golf club but lack concentration or the ability to compete under pressure. Using relaxation improves your concentration and overall tension level. Practicing visualization can help overcome fears of failure and form a new self-image. A successful speaker, performer, or athlete is clear, focused, relaxed, and sensitive and responsive to her environment.

In mental rehearsal, you visualize yourself going through an event or activity at which you wish to perform well. You see yourself giving a speech at a conference, asking for a raise, perfecting your backhand, performing a violin solo. Visualizing not only improves your performance ability by practicing the skill correctly in your mind; it reinforces that you will play in a relaxed manner and decreases the nervousness that will interfere with your physical and mental ability.

You can mentally rehearse for anything. Carolyn, for example, was nervous about how she would do on her doctoral defense, so she used visualization to prepare for it. She visualized herself calmly and intelligently answering all the questions asked of her and supported the visualization with affirmations. As it turned out, Carolyn was so calm and self-assured that she caught her committee off guard. When using visualization, see yourself performing well in front of your greatest adversaries. You may want to picture yourself remaining calm and relaxed during a job interview, answering and asking pertinent questions.

Performers have found these techniques particularly beneficial. Amy, a music teacher, was concerned about an upcoming piano competition. She had a tendency to get nervous during a performance and was afraid of going blank and forgetting passages. Her fears were causing her a great deal of stress and had the potential to interfere with her performance. To deal with this problem, she used the following technique: Daily, she visualized herself before, during, and after her performance, seeing herself feeling calm, relaxed, and self-assured, putting in all the details she could. She saw the pleased responses of the judges, and she visualized herself after the concert feeling good about how well she had played. She also used affirmations, to affirm her ability to remain relaxed during the performance. On the day of the concert she did a general relaxation exercise. Amy was naturally somewhat nervous before her performance but not as much as she had been in the past, and she played well, getting through all the passages correctly. Very happy with her performance, she realized she had felt more in control while preparing for the recital and knew she would continue to use visualization to improve her performance ability.

In mental rehearsal it is vital to see yourself through the whole activity, start to finish. Tina, for example, had chronic back pain, but after using visualization, she could do more activities, like sit through a movie or a long dinner out, without being so bothered by her back. In the beginning, however, although she was able to go out after work, the next day she would be in pain. She hadn't followed through seeing herself getting up the next day and feeling good as well. Once Tina started visualizing being pain-free not only during the activity but the following few days, she was able to slowly increase her activities. The mind is very literal; it believes what it sees, so you must be very clear on what it is you want.

SETTING CONDITIONS YOU DESIRE. As I have said, your inner mind is extremely creative and powerful. You can use it to program what you want your life to be like. If you wish to awaken in the morning feeling refreshed instead of groggy, visualize it. See yourself waking up and feeling energetic, looking forward to the day. If you want to arrive at meetings on time and remain relaxed throughout their duration, visualize this with all the details. See yourself arriving on time, prepared, and breathing freely throughout the meeting.

GUIDED IMAGERY. Some visualization exercises are referred to as "guided imagery." Using guided imagery helps you tap into your own creative powers to change old beliefs, heal past wounds, solve problems, gain answers. Working with a therapist, audio tape, or on your own, you are guided through a structured exercise and fill in details with your imagination. For example, you may be told to see yourself walking down a path and meeting a person with whom you wish to talk.

In a technique called "inner child work," a person can go back and "repair" a painful memory or bad situation. She visualizes herself as an infant or young child and then interacts with that child, giving her the love she needs, or taking her out of a bad environment. When working with a therapist or guide, you may be asked what is taking place in your visualization, and it may be suggested where to take the images. Your creative mind will supply the images and direction you need to take. Invariably, if a client gets stuck in a visualization and I make a suggestion, she will know right away if it is appropriate or not; if it is not, she can get the images she needs.

SEEKING AND RECEIVING ANSWERS. If you feel stuck with a problem or decision and don't have the answers, or something is bothering you, ask yourself for help. You can get in touch with old beliefs, ideas, and emotions by letting your subconscious, or inner wisdom, guide you. As I said earlier, we all have the knowledge we need within ourselves. Most of us, however, don't rely on or trust our intuition. In making decisions, we gather all the facts and then look at them logically in hopes of making the correct choice. This works for decisions based upon logic, but as we all know very well, personal decisions are rarely based upon logical choices. You can learn to rely for guidance on your intuition or inner wisdom, which has the answers, rather than on your conscious mind, which usually doesn't.

In a relaxed state you can ask your inner wisdom to give you solutions in areas where you have questions. You can ask that it come to you in some form, word, idea, or image, while you are meditating or within the course of the day or evening. You may ask to get the answer in a dream while you are sleeping.

Some people like to consult what they call their "inner guide." In a relaxed state they imagine themselves in a pleasant environment and see their guide in some form: a wise woman, an old man, an animal, a bright light, and then engage in a dialogue with the guide.

Once you begin using imagery, you will find you are more attuned to inner communication, which takes place all the time, but to which most of us don't listen. When we focus inward, we have the opportunity to experience our feelings. This scares some people, so they avoid spending quiet time with themselves for fear they may discover something painful, which is too much to deal with. I believe, however, that we don't get in touch with more than we can emotionally handle. If you aren't ready to face a fear or other emotion, you will probably just fall asleep while trying to meditate. Not knowing, however, what we are carrying around within us, I feel, is much more detrimental than knowing it and accepting it. Whatever it is will affect you in some way even though you are not consciously aware of it. And you do have the potential to deal with it. When you encounter depression or any other emotion, feel it, acknowledge it, and then breathe into it. You can either see the depression lifting as you breathe in and out, or stay with the feeling, determining where it comes from. You always have a choice to utilize creatively any feeling or state of mind in which you find yourself.

Many times we encounter resistances on the way to attaining the goals we envision. We cannot concentrate, so we avoid practicing relaxation and visualization and look for distractions, or we visualize but no change occurs. Consultant Charles Lawrence, who uses visualization among other techniques to aid his clients' personal growth, recommends that you "make a friend of your resistance." When you meet resistance, sort through it and really get clear on what you want. Respect the resistance and let it guide you without forcing it.

Visualization is a powerful tool. Using visualization should not be something at which you work hard, though; it should be effortless. Put your goal out, give it positive energy, and let it go.

Don't worry, however, if you find it hard to get or hold on to images. It takes practice. Some people visualize and use images more easily than do others. Many people get auditory "images"; they hear words rather than see pictures. Others are good at recalling smells. Imagining pleasant smells, for example, is very beneficial. The more senses you use in a visualization, the more powerful the experience. Start by experimenting with what feels most comfortable.

STRESSBUSTER:
TEN TIPS FOR SUCCESSFUL CREATIVE VISUALIZATION

1. Have a clear goal. Take time to sort through it until it becomes clear.

2. See your goal in all its detail and visualize the outcome you desire. See yourself having completed your goal and feeling good about it.

3. Visualize in a relaxed state of mind. Do visualization with a relaxation exercise and/or before going to sleep and/or upon rising.

4. Have a strong desire to accomplish your goal.

5. Have the belief you can achieve your goal.

6. Focus often on your goal.

7. Use affirmations to support and enhance visualization.

8. Develop trust in yourself and your ability to use visualization for creative living.

9. Acknowledge your success.

10. Read or talk to other people about visualization, attend workshops, work with visualization audiotapes.

Visualization and affirmations are effective methods of helping you reduce stress in the workplace. Many women maintain ongoing unidentifiable stress that leaves them wondering why they are so worn out. You may be toiling in a dead-end job because other members of your family did, or because a boss reminds you of a very demanding family member which causes you to respond the way you did when you were young. Perhaps you simply haven't clearly defined what it is you really want, or you don't believe you can—or deserve—to have it. Practicing visualization can break down old patterns of thinking, feeling, and behaving that are keeping you from getting what you want. Use it to create the most healthful lifestyle you can imagine. Go through the steps necessary for setting clear goals in Chapter 8, and use visualization to help bring them about.

Chapter Five

WORKING ON THE BODY TO DECREASE STRESS

Cindy, a lawyer in a small New England town, has always found aerobic exercise to be an ideal method of relieving stress. For years, via dance classes and running, she has included exercise in her daily routine. Since becoming a mom (her son is now two), Cindy has found that an hour-and-a-half to two hours of volleyball or tennis (plus stretching and warm up) four times a week keeps her healthy, allows her to feel good about herself, and enables her to withstand the rigors of being a working mother. Her choice of activities permits her to socialize with other people and have a life apart from her family. Since time with her son and exercise are priorities, Cindy limits her office time and often works on cases after her son goes to bed.

THE POWER OF EXERCISE

In talking to numerous women about their exercise habits, I have been amazed by the commitment of many working women, especially mothers, to regular exercise. Time and again, they speak of how they fit exercise into their schedules. Many women I know take a long lunch hour and go to a nearby gym. June, an accountant, takes a ballet class daily. Elyse, a book editor, goes for an hour-long brisk walk through the park before heading to the office. Sandra, an art director, jogs to work and back. You may not, however, be able to take long enough lunches to accommodate an exercise class or modify your work schedule to meet your exercise needs as Cindy does. Therefore, in this chapter you will not only learn about the benefits of exercise but what kinds of activities you can fit into your busy schedule.

Our bodies require physical activity to function properly. Today perhaps even more than ever, we need to combat the stress of modern life and a sedentary lifestyle that contribute to heart disease, obesity, fatigue, muscular tension, and many joint and disc problems. In addition, working women want and need more in their lives than just work and home responsibilities. Exercise enables you to have enough energy for both work and play.

Aerobic, or endurance, exercise is a vital component of any stress-reduction program. As I've mentioned, the fight or flight response prepares the body for physical activity; yet this response rarely ends with such action. This is one area where exercise can make a difference. Regular endurance exercise helps to reduce the physical symptoms associated with immediate or chronic stress as well as to improve mood and fight depression and insomnia.

Aerobic exercise is any sustained activity that requires you to increase your use of oxygen by working the heart and lungs. Walking briskly, cycling, jogging, running, swimming, low-impact aerobics, and rollerskating are all good aerobic activities. Brisk walking, although it requires a longer period of time to be effective (forty to forty-five minutes), can be done anywhere, requires no equipment, and is less strain on the joints than jogging or running. Swimming is excellent, if available, because it places little strain on the joints and uses many muscle groups. Running in place or walking in water (with the water working as resistance) are wonderful means of exercise.

How much exercise do you need? Ideally, three days a week, for twenty to thirty minutes. To strengthen your cardiovascular system you need to raise your heart rate enough to reach what is called the "training effect" (see the target heart rate formula on page 104 to determine this). For successfully reducing stress, exercise should be rhythmic, continuous, and devoid of competition. Many sports, particularly those that are competitive, require skill and practice. If you are a high achiever and feel you need to do well or that you have to win, these sports activities may become an extension of your working life rather than a relaxing activity. Squash and handball are often very competitive, for example, and can add stress rather than reduce it depending on how you approach it. A strenuous set of tennis can be a means of dealing with your stress, or it can create more. Therefore, it's important to find an activity that you enjoy, which fits into your schedule and suits your personality and capabilities.

Benefits Of Regular Aerobic Exercise

We've been talking mostly about the benefits of exercise in terms of stress release. The obvious physical results of exercise include increased muscular strength and improved tone. Combined with a healthful diet, exercise can aid in weight loss. Diet alone is usually not enough to keep pounds off because your metabolism changes to accommodate the reduced intake and begins burning fewer calories. Exercise also helps to get your appetite under control. If you're exercising for weight loss, four to five times a week is best.

Practicing regular aerobic exercise over a period of time can have health benefits that range from simply feeling better to lowering the risk of heart disease (depending on how much you exercise). Regular aerobic exercise:

- Improves cardiovascular efficiency (the heart increases in size and strength and in the volume of blood pumped)
- Increases efficiency of oxygen utilization
- Lowers resting pulse rate
- Improves utilization of blood glucose
- Lowers level of blood fats (triglycerides and cholesterol)
- Helps reduce tension
- Increases metabolism
- Helps reduce body fat
- Increases energy and helps fight fatigue
- Improves physical ability and stamina
- Helps combat insomnia
- Improves alertness and concentration
- Enhances sense of well-being

- Helps reduce anxiety and depression
- Possibly decreases risk of heart disease

Determining Your Target Heart Rate

For exercise to be beneficial you need to increase your heart rate above its normal resting rate to what is called your target heart rate (the rate best for you) for at least 20 minutes. The easiest and most practical way to determine your target heart rate is to use the maximal heart-rate method. The intensity at which you wish to work out should be based upon your current fitness level and exercise goals. If you're in good shape, working at 70 or 80 percent of your maximal heart rate will improve your cardiovascular fitness. However, if you haven't exercised in a long while, are recovering from an illness or injury, or use medications regularly, you will want to lower your target heart rate starting at 60 or 65 percent of your maximal and build up. Going higher than 80 percent will cause strain and not improve fitness.

To find your maximal heart rate subtract your age from 220. Then multiply by the intensity at which you wish to work out. The formula looks like this:

Maximal HR × % of Intensity = Target HR

A thirty-five-year-old woman who wishes to exercise at 70% of her capacity would calculate:

185 (220 – 35 = 185) × .7 = 129.5

To get your 10-second target heart rate, divide target HR by 6 and round off to closest number.

129.5 ÷ 6 = 22

Through this easy-to-use formula, you can determine your approximate target heart rate, but also consider as guidelines the way you feel during exercise and your recovery rate afterward as well.

To measure your heart rate feel for your pulse by placing two or three fingers below your jawbone to the right of your adam's apple or over the artery near the center of your wrist. Using a second hand on your watch or clock, count the number of beats for fifteen seconds. Multiply this number by four to get your heart rate in beats per minute. Or count for six seconds and multiply by 10. Measure your heart rate before and after exercising and at least twice during your exercise period.

Moderation Is The Key

During the early 1970s, a fitness craze developed in America, beginning with jogging and running and followed by aerobic dancing, with classes springing up everywhere. Unfortunately, though, for women in particular, emphasis was often placed on the way fitness makes the body look, and resulted in a trend toward over-exercising for the purpose of attaining the sleek stature of fashion models. The price some people paid was multiple muscle and joint injury, not to mention the stress of keeping up with a strict exercise regimen. I taught with a marathon runner, for example, who had such a bad foot injury that she could hardly walk or teach her classes, but she refused to give up running every day.

Repetitious, high-impact aerobic exercises have been linked to back injuries, shin splints, and knee, ankle, and foot injuries. I know a young woman who suffers from chronic foot pain due to nerve entrapment in her feet, as a result of compulsive aerobic exercise. Fortunately, the trend today is moving toward exercise for the sake of good fitness, improved appearance, and stress relief. More emphasis is now being placed on activities less injurious than running, and which also fit more easily into busy schedules.

Low Impact Aerobics

The frequency of injuries from aerobic classes has spurred a movement toward low, or soft, impact aerobics. Low-impact aerobics uses marching, dancing, and walking combinations, rather than the jumping, hopping, and kicking components of its high-impact counterpart. One foot maintains contact with the floor at all times, reducing the stress to the joints. Arm movements are often added, which increase the cardiovascular workout. You can take low-impact aerobics classes, work out at home with an exercise videotape, or do your own moves to music.

"Going For The Burn"

Pain during exercise is a signal that something is wrong. Phrases such as "going for the burn" and "no gain without pain" are not only dangerous, they don't even make good sense. Going for the burn will not increase your strength. It simply indicates that your muscles can no longer get the fuel they need and are too tired to keep going. Yes, exercise needs to be a challenge, a workout, but it shouldn't be painful. If you push yourself to the point where you are too sore or tired or hurt to work out two days later, what is the point?

If you haven't exercised or used certain muscles in a while, you can expect mild muscle soreness about twenty-four hours after exercise. A gentle warm-up and some stretching will help alleviate the achiness. The next day repeat the warm-up and stretching, followed by your aerobic activity, just decrease it slightly, building back up when the soreness is gone.

Stretching And Warm-Ups

Any exercise regimen should combine aerobic exercise with stretching and a proper warm-up. Stretching aids in keeping the muscles flexible, which are stronger and more resilient than rigid ones. Flexibility is essential for a comfortable, tension-free body. Vigorous exercise hardens and tightens muscles, making them more susceptible to strain and injury. Gentle stretching helps guard against both the demands of exercise and of time. The loss of flexibility is not an inevitable part of aging. Although muscles do lose some elasticity as we age, it is our lifestyle that most greatly contributes to our loss of mobility.

Stretching is not necessarily a warm-up exercise, however, since it causes the muscles to contract. When stretching, be careful not to force your body into certain positions, and don't bounce. Bouncing makes the muscles tighten rather than release, increasing the risk of injury. Gently stretch your arms and legs and rotate your head after strenuous workouts.

Warm-up exercises are mandatory before embarking on any workout. The body needs to move through its full range of motion before doing strenuous exercise. (Warm-up exercises simply feel good too!) The good news for those who want to lose weight is that warmed-up muscles start burning fat sooner than cold muscles, which burn sugar (carbohydrates).

A good warm-up gently moves the joints and muscles in all directions without straining. Warming up increases blood supply, raises the temperature, and makes the muscles more pliable. Some experts believe that when gradually engaged, the motions you use during exercise are enough to prevent injuries. They suggest that if you plan to jog, for example, you can start by walking and build up to jogging. I, however, feel strongly that beginning with an overall warm-up is important, if for no other reasons than to help you feel comfortable during exercise and to help you move smoothly in a coordinated manner.

You can combine your stretching and warm-up. Doing the two allows you to gradually find out how your body feels before you work it and which areas may need more attention. You may discover, for example, that your right shoulder is a little stiff or that you slept in a different position and your neck is tight.

Always warm up the neck, shoulders, and low back; this is especially important before engaging in weight-bearing aerobic activity because the impact is felt in those joints. Begin the upper-body warm-up with a slow, small head circle, which gradually gets bigger. Then rotate the shoulders in both forward and backward directions, followed by circling the arms. Gently curl the spine; role the pelvis. Be sure to move slowly, gently, and with attention to the movements you are making. The slower you go, the more work you actually do, since moving fast often uses momentum rather than muscle action. In addition, going slowly forces you to use the correct muscles and move them from deep inside the muscle. (This warm-up can be done while sitting at your desk to provide a mini-break during the day.)

Many exercises entail taking hold of a body part with your hand and pulling it. Your stretch will be greater and will last longer, however, if you relax and soften into the joint rather than forcing it. After you have the release, you can repeat the stretch and pull if you wish.

STRESSBUSTER: STRETCHING TIPS

 ◆ Go slowly

 ◆ Warm up the muscle before you begin

 ◆ Relax into the stretch

 ◆ Don't bounce

 ◆ Don't force the movements

 ◆ Use breathing and relaxing to further your stretch

 ◆ Focus on the part you are moving

 ◆ Stretch every day for at least ten to fifteen minutes

 ◆ Breathe while stretching

Strengthening

Building strength and endurance are important aspects of exercise. Contracting the muscles develops strength; calisthenics, push-ups, sit-ups, and weight training build strength and increase muscle mass. Cycling, jumping rope, and running increase leg strength, while developing endurance, which is your muscles' ability to sustain an activity. Experts believe that strength training two days a week, along with weight-bearing aerobic exercise, can help decrease cholesterol levels and prevent osteoporosis caused by thinning bones.

Finding The Right Exercise Program

IT MUST BE SOMETHING YOU ENJOY. This seems self-evident, but some people view exercise only as a necessary evil. They feel that exercise should be difficult and lots of work. I've watched a few fitness classes where that was clearly the message. But exercise shouldn't be boring or taxing. I'm optimistic enough to believe that most people can find a physical activity they enjoy. Also, the more you work out and begin to feel good, the more you will like exercising. If you find an exercise class that's fun or a sport you like, you'll want to do it. It's as simple as that.

IT MUST BE SOMETHING YOU HAVE THE SKILLS FOR AND THAT YOU CAN FEEL COMFORTABLE WITH. Trying new activities and being open to new experiences is important, but for exercise to be stress-reducing it should not tax your abilities or cause you frustration. If you are a person who is not very coordinated, a jazz dance class might be too demanding and you might want to start with aerobic dance and work up.

IT MUST FIT INTO YOUR SCHEDULE. To maintain a regular exercise regimen, you should make sure it fits into your schedule and is convenient. Swimming might be your favorite exercise, but the amount of time it takes to get there, go swimming, and then shower, especially if the pool is open only at certain hours, will certainly be a factor. On the other hand, if it is something you really enjoy, you may want to adjust your schedule to accommodate it. Realistic planning is the key. Check out gyms, Y's, and exercise classes close to your job or on the way home that offer classes after work or during lunch hour.

IT MUST FIT INTO YOUR RESOURCES (FOR EXAMPLE, MONEY, AVAILABILITY, NEED FOR OTHER PEOPLE). When selecting an activity, think about the resources that it will require. If you play tennis, you need a partner and a court. This is often more difficult if you live in a large metropolitan area. Weight training will involve joining a gym or health club, or hiring a personal trainer.

Work Out At Home With Videocassettes

Exercising at home saves time and money. If you are a well-motivated person, you can maintain a regular exercise program at home. Yoga, body-awareness techniques, stretching, Tai Chi, low-impact aerobics, and calisthenics can all be done at home, before or after work. I have a client I see once a year, who lives in a rural area in the midwest that is limited in terms of exercise classes and health clubs. Before heading to her job, she works out every day with a videocassette for stretching, strengthening, and low-impact aerobic exercise.

Plan to exercise with a friend or co-worker at least once a week and share the cost of the videocassette. Try a Step Aerobic Program, starting off without the steps and then building up (see "Resources" in the Appendix for videocassettes). There are many commercial tapes—both bad and good—and cable TV stations also carry a variety of exercise programs. Before using a videocassette or following a televised exercise show, make sure that the instructor:

- Warms up the body slowly and gently
- Doesn't use a lot of bouncing, especially from a hanging or standing position
- Doesn't rush you through exercises
- Gives you a good overall workout
- Gives a warm-down after a strenuous workout

Find A Class

Almost anywhere you live (unless you live in the country) you can find an exercise class. Y's, hospitals, adult learning centers, continuing education programs, and health clubs all offer a wide range of activities, from traditional sports and exercise to yoga and martial arts, to body awareness techniques such as Alexander and Feldenkrais (discussed on page 118). Take a class after work or on your lunch hour, if it is close by. Lena, a clothing designer, takes a 7:30 A.M. yoga class before going to work and it really prepares her for the day.

I'm Too Busy To Exercise!

If you lead a busy life, you can't afford not to exercise. Without exercise, you will become more tense and fatigued rather than less. Here are a few tips on how to put more exercise into your life.

If you are too busy to take a class or join a gym, put on an upbeat record and dance around the house for twenty minutes before you leave for work or when you get home. It will give you more energy for your day or the rest of your evening. Move your arms as well as your legs. For movement ideas, watch exercise programs, or just try rock & roll dances from the Sixties, such as the twist, jerk, monkey, freddy, pony, and the swim.

Walk to work or walk part way. If you take the bus get off at an earlier stop. Or if you drive, park your car a greater distance from work and walk. It takes longer and will require that you wear running shoes or sneakers if you walk a distance, but you will be getting to work and exercising at the same time.

Rather than taking a mid-morning coffee break at work, take a short walk around the block. This will give you a boost of energy and make you feel better than a cup of coffee, which stimulates the stress response, or a donut or candy bar, which will pick you up and then let you down.

Combine exercise and being outdoors. Too many working women don't see the light of day. Getting outside is very important to your well-being: Sunlight is necessary for vitamin D absorption, but more important, it improves your general spirits, increases alertness, and may even boost the immune system. Take a twenty to thirty minute walk during your lunch hour. Bring your lunch and eat it after you walk. The exercise will decrease your appetite. In nice weather try to find a place outdoors to eat.

Climb the stairs at work, which will tone your legs and burn calories. Don't substitute this for regular aerobic exercise, however.

If you pick up your kids after school, exercise together, walk home or stop off at a park. It's better for them (than sitting in front of a TV) and for you.

Exercise Tips

1. SET REALISTIC GOALS. You must work up slowly. The goal for aerobic fitness may be twenty to thirty minutes three times a week, but a beginner must work up to that. A woman who is not physically fit should take about four to six weeks to build up to thirty minutes of vigorous exercise three times a week. If your goal is running two to three miles three times a week, start with brisk walking and gradually build to jogging slowly, each week increasing time and speed. I strongly believe that any exercise is good. If you only begin by walking twenty minutes three times a week, you have increased your activity. It may not give you cardiovascular fitness, but you will feel better while building up your fitness level. If you overestimate your capacities, you will just sabotage yourself.

2. TAKE A CLASS. Although it's convenient to exercise at home, joining a class can help to motivate you. If you have signed up and paid for a class, you are more likely to go. It's also a good way to socialize while doing something good for yourself. If you work for a large company, petition it to offer classes on the site during lunch or after work. Or get together with co-workers and form a class on your own. Ask for space at your place of work.

3. EXERCISE WITH A FRIEND. Exercising with someone else is a good motivator. You can take a class together or exercise at home.

One summer my sister and I agreed to swim regularly after work. Sometimes I would be tired and not feel like going, but she would call and we'd do it and I would feel revived. On the days when she was feeling too busy, I motivated her. It was a great help to both of us and we really benefitted from it.

4. SHARE AN ACTIVITY WITH YOUR MATE. It's fun to participate in a physical activity with your mate. You spend time together while sharing a common interest—and stay physically fit at the same time. Try a ballroom dance class. Fast partners' dances are a great way to exercise.

5. MAKE IT PART OF YOUR SCHEDULE. Don't wait until you feel like exercising. Plan it into your day, week.

6. SEE A PHYSICIAN BEFORE STARTING AN EXERCISE PROGRAM. You really shouldn't begin any exercise program without first seeing a doctor for a physical exam, but it's a must if you are overweight, have high blood pressure, or are over age forty. Once you begin exercising, should you experience dizziness, chest or arm pain, heart palpitations, or have difficulty catching your breath, see a doctor.

STRESSBUSTER: THE BODY'S NATURAL TRANQUILIZER
Fifteen to twenty minutes of mild exercise has been found to be as relaxing as taking a tranquilizer. Researchers believe this is because of endorphins, natural pain killers and mood elevating chemicals associated with happiness and well-being. Studies have found increased levels of endorphins in the bloodstream of long-distance runners, who report the "runner's high." Athletes have also been found to have increased levels of norepinephrine, which aids in nerve transmission.

Keep A Record

I'm a firm believer in making charts and keeping records. It helps you see progress and stay motivated. The hardest part of exercise, once you get started, is keeping up with it. Use the chart provided on page 113 to keep track of the amount of exercise you do and the time you do it; this will help you to see where you need to adjust your schedule if necessary.

◆ Put your chart where you can see it.

◆ Use the technique of visualization to help you attain your goals (Chapter 4). See yourself exercising and feeling good about it. Picture yourself at the end of the day, relaxed and proud of yourself for walking, going to an exercise class, or running.

◆ Be sure to acknowledge your progress. Too often we only focus on where we should be, rather than giving ourselves credit for where we are and what it took to get there. If you increase your exercise five minutes a day, congratulate yourself.

◆ Give yourself rewards. When meeting reasonable goals, treat yourself in some way.

EXERCISE DIARY

	Time of Day	Stretching	Strengthening	Aerobic
Monday				
Tuesday				
Wednesday				
Thursday				
Friday				
Saturday				
Sunday				

Make a phote-copy of this chart (you may want to enlarge it). Use the chart to keep track of your weekly exercise. Make several copies so you can reuse.

Preventing Stressful Conditions

Exercise can be very effective during different stages in a woman's life. Mild exercise can help reduce discomfort during menstruation. In addition, regular exercise has been found helpful in dealing with the tension and mood changes associated with menopause.

A major problem for women as they get older is thinning bones from calcium loss, which leaves them susceptible to fractures and

STRESSBUSTER: YOGA AND TAI CHI

Yoga and Tai Chi Ch'un provide the benefits of both relaxation and exercise. Yoga, developed in ancient India, is a means of joining the mind, body, and spirit. Breathing and meditation are part of the practice of yoga. The physical method most familiar to Westerners is Hatha yoga. Performed in a meditative frame of mind, it seeks harmony and inner calm. Hatha yoga is designed to release trapped body energy and tensions, using breathing and various physical positions called asanas. The positions, coordinated with breathing, relax the mind and the body, stimulate circulation, and stretch and tone the body. These positions resemble dance and stretching exercises and are an excellent means of physical activity, helping reduce stiffness and fatigue, improve posture, and increase well-being. Yoga is one of the best means of keeping the mind and body fit, especially if you are experiencing muscular problems as a result of stress.

Be sure to find a good teacher who warms you up properly and doesn't push too hard. You will need to experiment with which positions are comfortable for you—not all will be. Once you have learned the positions and sequences that are best for you, you can work on your own. You should practice three times a week. For stress reduction, do ten minutes of relaxation (breathing, progressive relaxation, etc.) before or after your exercises. Finding a nearby yoga class to take during lunch time is a splendid and refreshing way to decrease stress and re-energize for a busy afternoon. Or take a class after work to relieve the stressors of the day. There are also televised programs or videocassette tapes and instruction books.

Like yoga, Tai Chi uses deep breathing and trancelike concentration. Visitors to China can see people of all ages practicing Tai Chi outdoors in parks and yards. It is an excellent body conditioner, working all parts, especially developing strength in the legs. It improves coordination and concentration. Particularly beneficial for stress reduction is the emphasis on breathing while moving. You need no special equipment or very much space, and you can wear normal (loose) street clothes. As a full program of exercise, Tai Chi uses thirty-seven body movements, performed slowly, smoothly, and continuously, going from one movement to another while concentrating on breathing. To learn Tai Chi, look for classes at Y's, health clubs, or martial arts studios. For videotape suggestions, see the Appendix.

gives them a stooped appearance. What many women may not realize is that they begin losing bone mass during their thirties, but when
estrogen diminishes after menopause, the rate of bone loss increases and can result in osteoporosis. Moderate strengthening and calisthenics are believed to help prevent osteoporosis. Impact exercise
such as walking, jogging, tennis, and jump rope has been found to
prevent bone loss and can increase bone mass in younger women.
(Swimming, although an excellent exercise, may not help combat
osteoporosis.) Also necessary in the prevention of osteoporosis is an
adequate supply of calcium, through dairy products, sardines (with
bones), certain vegetables such as kale, broccoli, carrots, and cauli-
flower, and supplements. By the way, stress and the overconsump-
tion of refined sugar, coffee, high-fat foods, and alcohol are major
causes of calcium deficiencies.

HOW BODY AWARENESS TECHNIQUES
HELP RELIEVE STRESS

Exercising is not the only physical adaptation you can make to
improve the way you deal with stress and help eliminate the toll it
takes on your body. There are other techniques, some of which may
seem a bit similar to traditional exercise—because they engage the
muscles and require movement—but they work the body in very different ways. For example, though exercise can strengthen, tone, and
trim, it won't necessarily correct a swayed back, locked knees, or a
misaligned spine. In fact, you can exercise every day; yet if you have
postural imbalances, you could be using your muscles incorrectly,
and not developing the deep strength needed to maintain aligned
posture. Poor postural alignment can cause weakened muscle tone,
strain, and discomfort, as well as susceptibility to injuries. Therefore,
good posture is crucial not only for looking good but for feeling
good.

There is a group of body therapies that focus on the re-educa-
tion of habitual motor patterns. These patterns result from one or
more factors:

* our occupations, such as those that require continually sitting in
  front of a computer or working at a repetitive task.

+ injury and illness, in which imbalances are created because of weakness

+ the imitation of others

+ misinformed ideas about how we think our bodies should look, such as copying postures of fashion models; or

+ psychological elements such as fear or feelings of inferiority.

Body awareness methods, also referred to as body therapies, use a variety of techniques to help recognize and release accumulated muscle tension that interferes with posture, ease of motion, and sense of well-being. The most well-known of these systems are the Alexander Technique, Feldenkrais Method, Ideokinesis, Kinetic Awareness, Sensory Awareness, Bartenieff Fundamentals, and Body-Mind Centering.

When does body therapy take up where exercise left off? Take Marilyn, for example. A talented artist who works for a successful male art director, she often had difficulty speaking up for her ideas or receiving credit for her work. Her slumped posture reflected that of a timid ne'er-do-well, rather than that of a talented, successful careerwoman. Though she has a personal trainer, private yoga instructor, and regularly plays tennis, her physical exercise and activities were not improving her posture to her satisfaction. Her contracted and slightly rounded shoulders represented a body pattern of tightly holding herself in, giving her the appearance of a shy young girl. Marilyn's body reflected old feelings about herself and how she has dealt with authority figures. She began work on increasing her awareness of her body with a technique called Kinetic Awareness. Since practicing Kinetic Awareness, in addition to her other therapies, Marilyn's body has begun to change, her shoulders opening and expanding, her spine becoming lengthened and her stance wider. She has gained the self-confidence needed to assert herself on the job and in her personal relationships as well.

Although Marilyn had been in excellent physical condition before her Kinetic Awareness work, she, like many people with poor posture, had been negatively affected by a poor self-image. She benefitted greatly from body awareness techniques, just as do others who regularly practice these methods over a period of time. These are some of the benefits reported by Marilyn and other body awareness devotees:

- Increased physical and mental awareness
- Release of muscular tension
- Increased range and efficiency of movement
- Greater physical comfort
- Improved posture
- Enhanced self-image
- Increased sense of well-being
- Increased concentration
- Reduction of anxiety (especially with such techniques as Sensory Awareness, Kinetic Awareness, and Ideokinesis)

Why Does The Body Need Therapy?

The way we hold our bodies can contribute to—or actually cause—physical problems. Growing up and adapting to our environment causes a build-up of muscle tension that is consistently held and interferes with how our bodies function. Most of us hold excess tension in the body, especially the neck, shoulders, and low back, which at times can cause pain and discomfort. When an area is constantly contracted, or "held," the muscles and ligaments become hard and brittle, the joint becomes "frozen," and movement may feel stiff and awkward. Most detrimental of all, chronic muscle tension distorts our alignment and can cause strain and injury. Although the muscles can support imbalances for a while, if you engage in physical exercise, heavy lifting, or continuously working in one position, injury may occur. Emotional stress can compound this.

How Does Our Posture Go Awry?

Poor postural habits are learned early in our childhood and imitation is one of the most powerful contributors. Parents provide our early models as we learn to stand and walk. Later we may copy a favorite friend or admired figure or model. As women, we are constantly bombarded by the media with images of how we should look. In fact, we fall prey to fashion looks that are extremely detrimental to our bodies: the model slouch, with the pelvis curled forward and the shoulders rounded; the arched back, as seen in jean ads, which places strain on the lower back; and the sleek-legged look of wearing high-heeled shoes, which tighten the calves, hyper-extend the back, and throw the weight onto the balls of the feet.

Sitting is another culprit in the development of poor posture. As children, we are required to sit in school for long periods of time, which isn't healthful for our young bodies. During childhood, we learn to adapt to the discomfort of sitting still and condition ourselves to block out uncomfortable sensations. By the time we reach adulthood we don't notice the discomfort of slumping (which places great strain on the spine), or working all day in poor positions.

Postural habits are often exacerbated on the job, where we acquire additional troublesome postures as well. Typing, computer programming, writing, and assembly-line work, among other occupational demands, all reinforce holding and overusing the body in one position. Chairs that are too deep or curved cause strain on the spine and encourage the muscles to sag and weaken. Back muscles become over-tight and abdominals weak. Job pressures further contribute to tension patterns. See the section on designing a stress-free work environment in Chapter 9 for more on sitting.

Emotional tension adds its own component to the poor-posture scenario, so by the time a person is an adult she has often developed a wide range of poor physical habits.

How Do Body Awareness Techniques Work?

Body Awareness techniques teach you to pay more attention to your muscle patterns and how to release unnecessary tension. They use focused attention, slow movement, breathing, touch, imagery, and manipulation to help you improve your body alignment and usage. An Alexander teacher, for example, guides you through the better use of your body with touch and verbal directions. In Awareness Through Movement classes, a teacher of the Feldenkrais Method directs you through slow exercises designed to bring about neuromuscular changes. With Kinetic Awareness, you lie on a soft rubber ball, which gently massages the area and helps release tension as you slowly move the body part. Although the methods differ, what these techniques have in common is the attention paid to the body—in other words, "body awareness." By using focused attention to mentally sense the body or parts of the body while moving or at rest, tension can be released and the part will move with more freedom and comfort.

Are You A Candidate For Body Work?

Though everyone can benefit from body therapy, there are three main groups of people who find it very helpful. They are:

1. *Those who desire pain relief from physical problems such as low back pain, stiff neck and shoulders, and knee and foot injuries.* Most women who seek help from these techniques experience physical discomfort that is intensified by their job or personal life: emotionally stressed, they get pain elsewhere, or sitting all day with little or no exercise they run into problems. Usually something triggers the pain—you decide to exercise, or you lift something heavy and strain a muscle, or you have a fight with your husband or boss. For most people, emotional stress compounds the problem of already existing bad posture and poor sitting habits that have developed at work.

2. *Women who want to gain a greater understanding and control of their bodies.* Many women see physical awareness as vital to their personal development and growth. Because our emotions are expressed through our bodies, you can become more attuned to your emotional states by becoming aware of your body. Conflicts at work may get translated into a pulled neck muscle or strained back. Poor posture may be a result of holding onto a body posture of a parent, a response to an emotional trauma, or an outdated body image. These techniques allow you greater access to recognizing the relationship between your emotions and their physical expression and increases your ability to recognize, respond, and express physical and mental tension appropriately.

3. *Performers who want to improve their musical, theatrical, or dance performance.* Performers are keenly aware of how stiff muscles interfere with any performance. They need to be aware of bodily habits and free of muscular tensions. These techniques have begun to appear as basic training in many performing arts curricula, especially in dance.

Although the goal of body awareness training is not stress reduction per se, one of its results is the quieting and centering of the mind. Kinetic Awareness, Sensory Awareness, and Ideokinesis, for example, have a meditative quality, and individuals who practice these techniques report benefits often attributed to relaxation and meditation. For information on finding a practitioner in your area, see the Appendix.

Seven Ways You Can Practice Body Awareness

The following are body awareness tips that can be practiced on your own. Remember, it's difficult to change your posture—the way you always do something is what feels normal. Before going on, try this: Clasp your hands with your fingers intertwined. Notice which thumb is on top, which index finger. Now open your hands, and change the position by reversing the thumb and fingers. How does this feel? Hold it a moment, and notice the response you have. Most people feel very uncomfortable in this unfamiliar position. Similarly, new, correct postures, because they are unfamiliar, won't necessarily feel good at first.

1. INCREASE YOUR AWARENESS OF HOW YOU USE YOUR BODY. Correcting alignment is a twofold process: You must first become aware of tense muscles and parts of the body that are held out of alignment, and then you need to learn to release them and bring them into balance. To do this, you have to be conscious of your body throughout the day, not just during a few minutes of exercise. If you are in the habit of standing on one leg all the time, check your posture when waiting in lines, for the bus, and so on. If you tense and raise your shoulders, lift them to your ears and lower them several times a day, feeling the release. When they creep back up, do it again. Through repetition, your body will re-learn the correct, relaxed position.

2. MOVE FREQUENTLY. Never stay in one position for any length of time. Your body is meant to move! Change positions, so that your body doesn't become accustomed to one stance. Just because a position isn't uncomfortable doesn't mean it is good for you.

The best thing you can do for a tight or stiff body part is to move it. While sitting at your desk, gently roll your neck, rotate your shoulders, move your spine, stretch your calves. Very slowly move your shoulder, for example, in all the directions it can go; when you finish, it should be more released and easier to move.

3. IMPROVE THE WAY YOU SIT AND STAND. Do you slump down in your chair, never sitting upright? Or do you sit with your legs crossed and body curled to the side? Do you always stand on one leg, putting all your weight on that part, or lock your knees for balance?

In sitting and standing, you want to achieve a sense of lengthening. Imagine the head as a helium balloon floating on top of the spine, or use the image of a puppet being pulled upward with a string (running through the center of your head). Think of your neck moving upward from the back of the spine and your chin moving slightly downward. When seated, sit squarely in your chair, with your back straight—the muscles should be released, though, not held. To find your centered position, rock gently back and forth until you feel balanced over your sitz bones (the bones you sit on). For more information on correct sitting/working positions, see Chapter 9.

When standing, keep your feet about shoulder width and your knees relaxed. To find a balanced position, slowly shift your weight forward and backward. Discover the point where the weight is centered between the balls of the foot and the heel and is being carried through the center of the ankles.

Many women lock their knees. They put excess effort into their knees and press backward. To find out if you lock, try this, standing sideways in front of a mirror: Bend your knees, then slowly straighten, stop when your knees are relaxed but straight. Then see if your knees want to push back farther. If you lock your knees, being straight will feel like the knees are still bent. You can use this exercise to break the habit: Bend the knees, then slowly come to straight, hold. Then let your knees slowly push backward into the locked position. Feeling your knees push backward is the key. The more you do this the more you will become aware of the locking. Practice letting the legs stay straight for longer periods of time before releasing them back to how you "wear" them. When striving for a relaxed stance, be sure not to simply bend your knees (and hold them), which is as stressful as always locking them.

Here are some "directions" from the Alexander Technique to use for aligned standing. Let your neck be free on top of your shoulders. Widen your back and hips (imagine the area between your shoulder blades and buttocks opening). Let the spine lengthen upward from the tailbone, relax the hips, and release the legs into the ground. Do not lift or hold upward, though; these are not movements but rather a conscious release of the muscles. When using the image of lifting the spine upward, let the hips release downward.

Another way to achieve a balanced posture is to encourage a lift up the front of the body and a release down the back. To do this draw your right hand up, starting at the pubic bone, and move it up to slightly above your head. As you do this, feel a gentle lift in your torso (this is more of an action than that used in the previous exercises). Leave your hand there with your shoulders relaxed or dropped. Then repeat with the other arm. Both arms will be in front of your body (like a ballet dancer). Keep the lift in the front. Next imagine the spine releasing downward into the heels. Then, drop the arms. Raise your shoulders up toward the ears and release them, while keeping the lift in front and releasing down the back. Another way to encourage the action is to place your hand on your abdomen and lift upward while pressing down with the other hand on the lower back. To reinforce the release in the back, a nice image is of a waterfall running down your back, ending in pools by your feet. Experiment with images that work for you.

Ocassionally when standing, distribute your weight evenly on both legs. If you work a job where you must stand for a long time, relieve pressure by putting one leg a bit higher and changing legs.

4. WATCH HOW YOU CARRY A PURSE, BRIEFCASE, AND SHOPPING BAGS. Carrying a heavy handbag, shoulderbag, or briefcase every day definitely distorts the body's alignment. Adding extra weight to one shoulder or arm throws the body off center, pulling it out of alignment and putting excess pressure on one side. Adding to the problem, some women contract their shoulder to hold the bag in place. This can cause tense shoulder muscles, neck strain, and/or uneven shoulder height. The ideal is to balance the weight evenly, for example, using a sling bag across the body, a "fanny pack," or a backpack. If you must carry a heavy shoulderbag, change shoulders frequently. Better yet, minimize the weight you carry: Use a lightweight bag and limit the contents to essentials. When you carry a shopping bag or tote, let it swing free. If your arm muscles contract to hold it, it's too heavy. When carrying groceries or other shopping bags, distribute the contents evenly into two bags, one for each hand.

5. NOTICE THE AMOUNT OF ENERGY YOU USE IN YOUR DAILY LIFE. Do you expend the same amount of energy lifting your coffee cup as you do lifting a heavy file? When you write, how much pressure do

you use to hold the pen or pencil? How much to hold the paper? Throughout our day, most of us exert more energy than is necessary, which tires us and adds excess tension.

Observe yourself to see how much energy you are expending. If you can't tell how much effort you use, or don't know how to release the tension, try putting more tension into the engaged body part and then letting it go. Here's how: Put your right hand in your lap, fingers relaxed. Put a tiny amount of tension into your hand (without making a fist). Just use a little. Feel it and let it go. Now try a lot of tension; feel the difference. Let it go. Between the two is a large range. Now try a medium amount of tension. You can become very attuned to how much energy you exert and develop your own scale, using effort and then releasing it. Practicing progressive relaxation (as described in Chapter 4) will also help you recognize the amount of muscular tension.

6. BE SURE TO BREATHE PROPERLY. Throughout the day, check that you are breathing correctly and not holding your breath. Sitting in the proper position does little good if you still hold your breath. But sitting and standing correctly will make it easier and encourage you to breathe.

7. WEAR COMFORTABLE CLOTHING. Some people wear such tight or stiff clothes that they look—and feel—uncomfortable and constrained. To look stylish and feel great, try clothes that are both attractive and comfortable. Avoid garments that restrict freedom of movement. If you walk a lot or stand on your feet all day, wear low-heeled shoes, preferably those with rubber soles. Today you can find attractive flats with lower heels.

As you begin to incorporate regular exercise and body awareness into your day-to-day life, you'll find that your efforts will be worth it. Both will help you combat the effects of stress. Some body awareness exercises are described in Chapter 10. Practicing the back, neck and shoulder, and jaw exercises will not only improve your comfort on the job but increase your concentration as well. You may find yourself tired in the beginning from exercising (and fitting it into your busy schedule), but you will soon adjust and find yourself better able to cope with life's stressors.

Chapter Six

NUTRITION: YOUR FIRST LINE OF DEFENSE IN THE FIGHT AGAINST STRESS

Peggy, 28, a legal secretary, allows herself about forty-five minutes to get ready for work in the morning. She makes a cup of coffee, showers, dresses and does her makeup, and straightens up a little if there's time. Her husband leaves earlier and usually picks up a fast-food breakfast on the way to his job. Peggy eats a donut or danish and drinks another cup of coffee as she drives to the office. By 11 o'clock she often feels draggy and needs more coffee. Sometimes she has a snack. For lunch, she usually munches on a sandwich while sitting at her desk, trying to catch up on some work. Sometimes when she's behind she rushes through her lunch and suffers with an upset stomach an hour later. In the afternoon Peggy almost always indulges in another mug of java, and occasionally someone brings in cakes or cookies from home. By then she really craves sweets, to help "ease" her end-of-the-day irritability and stress. When she and her husband get home from work, both are tired, especially Peggy, and she often doesn't want to cook. They'll order Chinese food, pizza, or go to a fast-food restaurant. Lately, Peggy has become concerned about her weight; both she and her husband have gained several pounds. Yet since she's low on energy and not feeling in the best of health, Peggy wonders if it would be smart to diet right now.

In Peggy's case, her diet, more than job stress, is the culprit behind her fatigue and grouchiness: The excess caffeine and sugar she consumes stimulate her adrenal glands, triggering a stress response. Her stomachaches come from rushing through her lunches. And because of her large intake of empty calories, she isn't getting proper nutrition to fuel her body. She's too tired to prepare healthful meals and therefore perpetuates the cycle.

Peggy's story isn't unusual and may sound familiar. What's wrong with a routine of a danish for breakfast, a sandwich for lunch, and a fast-food dinner? Plenty. Having a nutritionally sound diet is your first defense against the negative effects of the stress response.

Poor concentration, restlessness, irritability, low energy, hyperactivity, allergies, frequent colds, earaches, and food cravings have all been linked to a poor diet. There is now overwhelming evidence to suggest that diet affects your long-term health and susceptibility to illness and certain diseases, including colon, breast, uterine, rectal, and lung cancers, heart disease, diabetes, and high blood pressure, as well as osteoarthritis, gallstones, and hemorrhoids. This information isn't new. For some time the American Heart Association and the National Cancer Institute have been promoting the importance of eating whole grains and fresh foods and vegetables for better health. Yet many who have suffered a heart attack and are told to change their diet and increase exercise to prevent another attack or surgery continue with their old habits. Why? Time, habit, and availability.

I'm always fascinated and somewhat mesmerized when I go into a large supermarket to see the rows and rows of packaged, processed foods, full of sugar and preservatives, with little food value. The amount is staggering! Sadly, these items with very little or no nutritional value seem to be as popular as ever—maybe even more so as technology improves their "look" and their packaging, while making them more "convenient" than ever.

Although many of our choices are governed by convenience, we are also drawn to what we think tastes good. That cup of coffee or glass of wine with dinner that you can't do without, that danish for breakfast every day, the frozen yogurt you go out for every afternoon on your break, those M&Ms you crave from the vending machine, are all taste habits. Women who try to give up soda, dessert, or coffee often find themselves "addicted" to the taste and are amazed at how hooked they really are. However, once they have stopped for a period of time, and replaced the "addiction" with a healthier substitute, most women no longer crave the thing they gave up.

One of the problems in changing our eating habits is that we feel we are being deprived when we can't have coffee or sodas or candy bars. It's therefore a good idea to eliminate difficult cravings one at a time. Make sure you treat yourself with tasty—but healthful—foods that compensate for your missing "fix." Focus on the positive; knowing that you are improving your health can help you to persevere. (And, of course, once you improve your eating habits, you may feel a little smug that you're now "food-smart," but don't act self-righteous around your friends or become a diet watchdog, because you'll certainly turn people off from healthful eating and make people resent you.)

Time is at a premium among all working women and certainly factors into your ability to maintain a balanced diet. Granted, it may seem easier to stop at Burger King or pick up a frozen dinner on your way home from work, but healthful eating doesn't have to be too time-restrictive or unappealing. Although a nutritious diet does take more time, with increased awareness and planning you can prepare well-balanced meals, which, in return, will give you increased energy and stamina. This chapter is designed to help you improve your eating habits by providing information, healthy choices, and ideas for overcoming some of the stumbling blocks.

Fifteen Ways To Develop A Nutritionally Sound Diet

1. DEVELOP EATING WISDOM. There is often a great disparity between what our appetite tells us and what our body really needs. If you crave potato chips or sweets, it doesn't necessarily mean that you need them or that you have any food deficiencies. *The poorer your diet, in fact, the more cravings you will have for sugar, refined foods, caffeine, and alcohol.* We crave foods because of emotional reasons, social pressures, allergies, and poor eating habits. You need to be aware of the types of foods you crave and when. Consider a more healthy choice that you can substitute. Changing takes time, and habits are hard to break.

If you want something crunchy and salty during the day, and carrot sticks don't satisfy you yet, try some nuts. They are high in fat like potato chips, but are nutritious. Take crudites to work so that you won't be tempted to head to the office vending machine when you want a snack. After work, before dinner, dip carrots into some spicy mustard or a mixture of yogurt and herbs. The more nutritious the food you eat, the more your body will begin to want it—and so will your taste buds. It may be hard to imagine, but you can reach a point where you crave fruits and vegetables as much as junk food. It just takes time.

2. EAT A VARIETY OF FOODS. The body needs a variety of vitamins, minerals, amino acids, certain fatty acids, and calories from carbohydrates, protein, and fat. We need different combinations to make up our nutritional requirements. An optimal diet consists of fresh foods that are high in complex carbohydrates and fiber, low in fat, salt and sugar, and moderate in protein.

Some women eat the same foods for breakfast and lunch every day. Oatmeal or yogurt with a nut mix on top are healthful choices, but try to vary them with other nutritious selections, to ensure that you're meeting your body's needs. Also, if you eat a certain food daily, you may develop a sensitivity to it, which increases your craving for it.

The "Food Guide Pyramid" recommends: 6 to 11 servings daily of grains (whole grains if possible)—bread, cereal, rice, pasta; 3 to 5 servings of vegetables; 2 to 4 servings of fruit (preferably fresh); 2 to 3 servings of meat, poultry, fish, dry beans, eggs, nuts; 2 to 3 servings of milk, yogurt, cheese; and to use fats, oils, and sweets sparingly.

If you're dieting, take special care in choosing your foods. Reduce foods that are high in fats, oils, and sugar; cut down on alcoholic beverages.

3. EAT MORE COMPLEX CARBOHYDRATES. Carbohydrates are our best source of fuel. Ideally 50 to 60 percent of our diet should come from complex carbohydrates: fresh fruits, vegetables, legumes, and whole grains. These provide the important vitamins, minerals, and fiber your body needs. Adding more complex carbohydrates will actually decrease your calories and improve your energy level. On the other hand, simple carbohydrates, such as refined sugar, white flour, and alcohol, which are high in calories and low in food value, should be limited.

Dietary fiber, which is found in whole-grain breads and cereals, dry beans and peas, and vegetables and fruits, is an important aspect of our diet. It provides the bulk we need to maintain healthy bowel function. Eating high-fiber foods can help reduce symptoms of chronic constipation and hemorrhoids, which are often associated with stress.

Fruits and vegetables actively protect against cancer and other diseases found among women, and should be eaten daily, preferably two to three servings of fruit and three to four servings of vegetables. When increasing your carbohydrates, don't worry about getting enough protein. Most Americans tend to consume about twice as much protein as necessary. In fact, excess protein has been found to deplete calcium, which is so important for women's bones. Combining grains and legumes will give you a complete protein that is high in fiber and low in fat. Legumes, including tofu, whole grains, low-fat dairy products, nuts, and seeds, are good replacements for red meat.

4. REDUCE FAT CONSUMPTION. The body needs a small amount of essential fatty acid each day (the equivalent of one tablespoon of vegetable oil). The recommended percent of fat in your total daily calories is 20 to 25, far lower than what most of us get. In fact, according to health writer Jane Brody, the average American consumes eight times the necessary amount of fat per day. That's enough to clog anyone's arteries! And it's not just men who are having heart attacks these days.

Fat is the major culprit in the development of most health problems, and fatty foods must be avoided. Don't be fooled, by the way, with packages labeled "cholesterol free." That doesn't mean the product isn't loaded with fat and calories! In addition, fat contains more calories than any other nutrient, so if you're watching your weight, look out. (See "Eating Lean" on page 135 for tips on avoiding fat.)

Check labels; most packaged foods list fat content. Remember, visible fat, such as butter, salad dressing, and fat on meat, is only a part of the fat we eat. The remainder is "hidden" in food: egg yolks, nuts, avocados, whole milk and cheese products, and meat fiber. To reduce your fat intake, eat fewer foods consisting of saturated fat, which is found in animal protein, dairy products, and coconut and palm oils. Saturated fats increase cholesterol levels. For your cooking and salad dressings, use small amounts of polyunsaturated oils, such as safflower, sunflower, soybean, and sesame, and monosaturated oils, olive, canola, almond, avocado, and peanut, which come from vegetable sources. These oils are healthier, especially those that are cold pressed. Margarine, although a vegetable source, has been artificially saturated, or hydrogenated, and is not a healthful choice unless your history of heart disease either personally or in your family, prevents the use of butter.

STRESSBUSTER: CALCULATING YOUR DAILY FAT INTAKE

To calculate 25 percent of your total calories in grams of fat, multiply your total daily caloric intake by .25 and divide the result by .9. Out of a daily intake of 2,000 calories for example, only 55.5 grams should come from fat.

---

5. REDUCE SUGAR INTAKE. The body has absolutely no nutritional need for refined sugar. All the energy we need can be easily obtained from fruits, grains, and other carbohydrates. Sugar contains no nutrients and can actually rob you of vitamins since it takes calcium, B vitamins, and magnesium to metabolize sugar. Too much sugar in the diet has been linked to certain types of diabetes, hypoglycemia, glucose intolerance, osteoporosis, and arthritis.

When you start reading labels on foods, you will find that most all of our packaged foods contain sugar, from soups to crackers. Catsup, salad dressing, commercial peanut butter, cereal, canned fruits, frozen dinners, and luncheon meats, generally have added sugar, which can also be listed as corn syrup, fructose, dextrose, and sucrose. Some products contain more than one! Even baby food contains sugar, so that we start developing this taste habit at an early age.

Since sugar is a taste habit, you can modify it. Replace processed desserts, cookies, and cakes with dried or fresh fruits. In some supermarkets, fruit markets, and in health food stores, you can buy a wide range of cookies and snacks made with fruit juices and rice and malt syrups. Products containing natural sugars usually use the sweetener sparingly in proportion to the other ingredients. Jams and jellies consisting of fruit only are available everywhere. Frozen-fruit bars are a better choice than ice-cream bars, in terms of sugar, fat, and calories. You can treat yourself without having to resort to refined sugar.

6. LIMIT SALT. As adults we need about one-fifth of a teaspoon of salt a day for the body to function. The average American woman, however, consumes more than she needs—about two to two-and-a-half teaspoons a day. Excess salt overworks the kidneys, contributes to water retention and potassium loss, and has been implicated in high blood pressure and hypertension. Processed foods contain large

amounts of salt. Replace frozen, packaged, or canned products with fresh foods. Again, check labels; salt sources include monosodium glutamate (MSG), sodium nitrate, sodium benzoate, sodium bicarbonate, disodium phosphate, and baking soda.

7. REDUCE CAFFEINE CONSUMPTION. That jolt you get from a cup of coffee or a coca-cola can be wearing down your adrenal glands and stressing your body. Insomnia, restlessness, headaches, ringing in the ears (tinnitus), a racing heartbeat and tenderness in the breasts, have been associated with excess caffeine. If you drink coffee or tea, try to limit yourself to one or two cups a day. Many women like to have a cup or two in the morning to get started and then have decaf the rest of the day or evening. If your office kitchen doesn't provide decaf, lobby for it or bring in your own. Should you decide to cut down on coffee or give it up altogether, you may have to deal with the effects of caffeine addiction. If you stop completely, be prepared for a few days of headaches. A way to kick the coffee habit is to withdraw slowly by mixing half decaffeinated coffee with your regular as you cut down. Herbal teas are a good substitute but may taste weak in the beginning.

Coffee, which has the greatest amount of caffeine, is a diuretic and washes out important water-soluble vitamins C and B, and stresses the kidneys. If you take vitamins and are a coffee drinker, don't take them together.

Just how much caffeine is in certain beverages? The following are the approximate amounts of caffeine in:

> Coffee—90-120 mg. per cup (not mug)
> Tea—42-100 mg. per cup
> Coca-Cola Classic— 64.7 per can
> Dr. Pepper— 60.9 per can
> Mountain Dew—54.7 per can
> Pepsi—43.1 per can

8. LIMIT CHEMICAL ADDITIVES. Chemicals are added to foods to improve their appearance and to prevent spoilage. The long-term effects are not certain, but many nutritionists believe they should be avoided. Some have been shown to be carcinogenic (cancer-causing) in research studies. Others cause immediate side effects; monosodium glutamate (MSG), in particular, can cause headaches and dizziness in some people. Limit or avoid such chemicals as BHT,

BHA, MSG, nitrates and nitrites, artificial colors, phosphates, and sodium bisulfite. Additives considered safe by the Center for Science in the Public Interest include: sorbitol, monodiglycerides, sodium benzoate, EDTH, caraganan, citric acid, ascorbic acid, glycerin, vegetable gums, lactic acid, and polysorbate.

9. EAT WHOLE FOODS. A whole food has no part removed and has not been chemically altered. Whole foods nourish the body because of the amount of vitamins, minerals, proteins, fats, and enzymes they contain. Foods labelled as "refined" have been processed in such a way that the basic nutrients and fiber have been removed. If a food is enriched, it just means the nutrients have been processed out with a few put back in. To make white bread, for example, the outer layer of bran and wheat germ, which provide bulk and B vitamins, is removed. Then the remaining grain, primarily starch, is bleached with a chemical and a few vitamins are added back, "enriching" it. Commercial whole wheat breads often have chemicals added to them but are closer to being a whole food than is white bread.

10. EAT HEALTHFUL SNACKS. We all snack for many reasons, including hunger. Snacks are fine; what's important is to get into the habit of eating healthful snacks. Bananas, raisins, and frozen fruit can satisfy your sweet tooth. Nut mixes, almonds, sunflower seeds, and popcorn (good with a little garlic and cayenne pepper or veggie salt) are easily transportable to work and can satisfy those munchie cravings. If your office has a microwave, make low-fat microwave popcorn. For a special treat, spread a banana with cashew butter and roll in crushed nuts.

11. DRINK PLENTY OF WATER. We've all heard this one, even when we were young. The body must have water to regulate circulation and digestion, remove impurities, cleanse itself, and nourish the skin. Daily, we require four to six pints of fluid, which we get from food and drinks, but a portion needs to come from pure water. To determine how much you need a day, use the ratio of one ounce of water for every two pounds of body weight.

If you find "plain" water boring, try this. Fill a pitcher with water and add a few fresh orange slices. Refrigerate. Or, instead of orange, add cucumber slices from home-grown fresh-picked cukes (don't use grocery-store cukes, which have a waxy, bitter coating!). Or add a few sprigs of fresh mint to water and "steep" in the fridge. At work, keep a bottle of water by your desk or in the office refrigerator.

12. EAT IN A RELAXED ATMOSPHERE. Sit down to eat, even if you are only having a snack. Concentrate on eating. This is especially important for dieters. The snack you had while working in the kitchen, or the breakfast you ate while getting ready for work, may not seem like much, but you will get the same amount of calories sitting or standing, so sit and enjoy it (and digest it). If you're eating with someone else, encourage pleasant conversation. Meals are not the time to discuss problems. You won't be able to digest your food properly.

13. EAT SLOWLY AND CHEW YOUR FOOD THOROUGHLY. I think all of us need to hear this one over and over again. We often gulp our food, taking large bites, then running off to work, a meeting, to pick up our kids—and we wonder why we have upset stomachs or gas! Eating too quickly also can interfere with proper absorption. Give yourself time to let your food settle and be absorbed before jumping up and rushing off.

14. EAT BREAKFAST. Start the day with a healthy breakfast, and at work you'll be more alert, have more energy, and won't be craving coffee or sweets at 11:00 A.M. You don't have to eat a big breakfast. Whole-grain cereals with fruit and low-fat milk or yogurt, or whole-grain bread, muffins, or waffles with nut butter are good choices. Whole grains keep your blood sugar stable. Avoid sweet rolls, donuts, and sugared cereals. If you're hungry before lunch, have handy a piece of fruit—bananas are filling and satisfying—or some shelled sunflower seeds.

15. EAT SMALLER MEALS MORE FREQUENTLY. Many experts feel that it is better to eat smaller meals along with healthful snacks rather than three big meals. Since most of us snack anyway, it makes sense to reduce the size of meals and make our snacks healthier.

How Stress Causes Poor Eating Habits—And Vice Versa

For many women, eating is a means of coping with stress. To soothe anger, disappointment, or loneliness, we overeat—particularly processed foods. Many of us crave sugar when we're feeling lonely and depressed: We eat large meals to comfort ourselves, or we eat out of anger, to release pent-up energy or to avoid feeling the anger. This just leaves the over-indulger feeling worse because of the sugar, fats, and chemical additives the snacks contain. It also sets up a pattern of eating junk food, since these foods intensify cravings for them. This poor coping method then adds the secondary problem of weight gain.

We are a nation of women obsessed with weight, appearance, and fitness. Women are constantly told by the media that being skinny is the ideal. This has led to the cycle of going on food binges and purges, which is seen in so many young women. If you think you have a problem with eating, and have found that switching to a healthier diet and using relaxation techniques aren't helping, seek professional help. Sometimes food cravings are related to food sensitivities, and you may need to be tested for this by a nutritionist or allergist.

STRESSBUSTER: DIET VS. DIETING

Don't confuse dieting with diet. Watching your weight does not guarantee that you are eating healthfully. Eating healthfully means eating a variety of whole foods, using sugar and salt in moderation, and choosing foods that are low in fat. Many weight plans endorse processed foods—frozen meals and desserts high in salt, sugar, and added chemicals. Nutrasweet and diet sodas should be consumed in moderation or not at all.

Fitting Healthy Eating Into Your Life

Almost everyone's diet can use improvement. Using the information in this chapter, look carefully at your eating habits. Are your habits less healthful than you'd like them to be? Are you eating too much sugar, fats, or processed and convenience foods? Is coffee your main source of fuel rather than the proper nutrients? Looking back now at how Peggy might make changes should help you come up with some ideas for yourself.

Instead of eating a donut or danish en route to work, Peggy needs to get up a bit earlier to fix and eat a healthy breakfast. Since she is used to a small, sweet breakfast, eggs probably won't appeal to her. Instead she can choose a whole-grain cereal with a banana and low-fat milk one day, whole wheat toast and a small amount of nut butter and fruit-sweetened jam another, and whole-grain toaster waffles with butter, fruit-sweetened jam, or honey, a piece of fruit

and a glass of skim milk the next. These breakfasts are quick and filling, and require little preparation.

Peggy needs to take a snack to the office—fruit, raisins, or
nuts—for the 11 A.M. munchies, especially if she is going to have a
late lunch. If Peggy desires a sandwich for lunch, sliced turkey (or
another lean meat) on whole wheat (with mustard instead of mayo)
and lettuce and tomato is a good choice. A vegetable accompaniment—salad (without mayo) or carrot sticks, for example—provides
necessary vitamins and can be nibbled on all afternoon. She should
leave her desk, even for a sandwich, and eat slowly.

For more nutritious evening meals, Peggy needs to plan ahead,
choosing several selections for the week and shopping ahead for
food. She can use the meal plans and recipes beginning on page 137
for guidelines and may want to invest in cookbooks with easy-to-
prepare meals. To save time and energy on the evening she goes
shopping, she and her husband may want to take out Chinese food,
ordering lean choices with vegetables. When dining out, they should
avoid fast food, choosing restaurants where they can make healthy
choices. To further alleviate stress, Peggy needs to ask her husband
for help with the dishes, cooking, shopping, and so forth.

Peggy needs to make these changes in her eating habits before
she starts a reducing diet. Restricting her calories may leave her feeling deprived, sending her back to her old habits. In addition, the
more vegetables and whole grains she eats, the better her chances
of losing weight—and she will be establishing lasting habits.

The busier you are, the more crucial it is that you eat healthfully. The "catch 22" is that it takes some thinking and planning
ahead—but you can work this into your schedule if you try. You'll
find it is well worth it. Giving up your junk food habits may be tricky
at first, but you'll be surprised how your tastes will change. And the
occasional cheese cake or chocolate mousse you have as a special
treat will taste that much better!

YOUR GUIDE TO SHOPPING LEAN

Pre-Shopping Tips:

◆ Plan meals ahead and make a list of the foods you need

◆ Pick well-balanced choices—think low fat

◆ Eat before you shop; you will buy more if you're hungry

Shopping Tips:

♦ Buy a variety of fruits and vegetables. Buy enough so that you can use them as snacks as well as with meals.

♦ Some stores have already cut up vegetables. Although they cost more, you can take them to work for snacks or with lunch, or to help save time in preparing meals.

♦ Choose low-fat or nonfat dairy products—low-fat or skim milk instead of whole; low-fat yogurt; cottage cheese; etc.

♦ Select fish, chicken, or lean cuts of meat. Many stores now carry ground turkey as an alternative to ground beef or pork. When buying red meat, look for leaner cuts; "select" meats are lower in fat than "prime" or "choice." Cut back on bacon and sausage that contain high amounts of fat as well as preservatives. Turkey bacon is available in some stores. Buy tuna in water, not oil (see recipes on page 141, for tuna salad variations).

♦ Read the labels carefully!

YOUR GUIDE TO EATING LEAN

Fat-Reducing Tips:

♦ Trim off as much fat as possible from meat; remove skin from poultry.

♦ Use non-stick pans.

♦ Cook or sauté with vegetable broths or skimmed chicken stock. This adds flavor as well as cuts down on fat content. Make chicken broth from chicken bones and giblets (if you have them). Add some onion, carrots, and celery tops.

♦ Add garlic, onions, and fresh herbs and spices instead of fat. Flavor salads with lemon juice or vinegar.

Cooking Methods:

♦ Steaming. This is an excellent method of cooking fresh vegetables without fat. It also retains the vitamins better than boiling

and leaves them tasting better. Use a steamer or colander to
hold vegetables in the pot, add a little water, and cover.

◆ Microwaving. There has been controversy over whether
microwaving destroys the vitamins in food. The answers aren't
in, but for now it seems a fast way to cook and without adding
fat.

◆ Broiling. Broil chicken and fish with herbs and spices, thereby
reducing oil and retaining flavor.

◆ Stir frying. This method uses less oil than frying. Use a little oil
and cook vegetables for a short time constantly moving the pan
(or purchase a wok).

◆ Crock-Pot. This is not only an excellent low-fat cooking
method, it's easy and timesaving too. Put vegetables and water
in the crock-pot before leaving for work, set on low, and when
you get home soup or stew will be ready. (See recipe on page
145.)

◆ Braising. Good for meats that need longer cooking times to
become tender, braising is used for brisket, bottom round, and
chuck roast. Brown meat first in a small amount of oil or its
own fat, and then simmer in a covered pan with a little liquid.
You can do this with vegetables that you want to cook a little
longer without adding oil.

WEEKLY MENU SUGGESTIONS

(* indicates recipes included beginning on page 140)

Monday

Breakfast
>   Bowl of sliced bananas, sprinkled with cinnamon, and skim
>   milk (or glass of skim milk)
>   Whole wheat or multi-grain toaster waffle(s) with fruit-sweet-
>   ened jam and/or nut butter

Lunch (From deli or restaurant or make yourself)
>   Tuna Salad* or sandwich

Green salad
Rye crackers
Orange

Snack
Sparkling water
Raw almonds or sunflower seeds

Pre-dinner snack
Carrot sticks with mustard dip

Dinner
Quick Chicken*
Herb Potatoes*
Steamed broccoli
Whole-grain bread or dinner roll

Dessert or snack
Low-fat fruit-sweetened cookies

Tuesday

Breakfast
Orange juice
Two poached eggs on English muffins with tomato slices

Lunch (From deli or restaurant)
Sliced turkey breast with lettuce and tomato on whole wheat
Cole slaw
Fresh fruit salad or grapes

Snack
Small bag of air-popped popcorn, carrot sticks, or small amount
of dried fruit

Pre-dinner snack
Celery sticks

Dinner
Crock Pot Soup*
Green salad or spinach salad
Whole wheat bread or rolls

Dessert or Snack
Low-fat yogurt

Wednesday

Breakfast
>   Low sugar/low-fat granola with fresh fruit and skim, rice or soy milk, or plain yogurt

Lunch
>   Crock Pot Soup with beans (leftover)
>   Whole wheat bread or roll
>   Pear

or
>   Vegetarian pita pocket sandwich with cheese, tomato, carrot, and bean sprouts

Snack
>   Low-fat yogurt or box of raisins

Pre-dinner snack
>   Cucumber slices with herb salt substitute

Dinner
>   Grilled Fish*
>   Rice
>   Steamed green beans with sesame seeds
>   Multi-grain bread

Snack
>   Low-fat fruit-sweetened cookies
>   Apple juice

Thursday

Breakfast
>   Almond butter and fruit-sweetened jam on whole wheat toast, rice cake or muffin
>   Apple
>   Skim milk

Lunch (From deli or restaurant or homemade)
>   Egg Salad sandwich with lettuce on whole wheat bread*
>   Green salad with carrots and tomato
>   Orange

Snack
>   Raw sunflower seeds or trail mix
>   Fruit juice-sweetened sparkling water

Pre-dinner snack
    Carrot sticks
Dinner
    Easy and Tasty Pasta Sauce*
    Green salad and/or Corn and Black Bean Salad *
Dessert or Snack
    Frozen fruit bar

Friday

Breakfast
    Instant oatmeal with pecans and cinnamon, with skim or soy
    milk
    Apple
Lunch
    Lentil or split pea soup
    Greek salad with feta cheese
    Pita bread
Snack
    Banana and decaf coffee or small box of raisins
Dinner
    Take out Chinese (chicken and vegetables) or eat out
Dessert
    Rice or soy ice cream or fruit sorbet

Saturday

Breakfast
    Whole-grain pancakes with sliced bananas or baked apple
    Skim milk
Lunch
    Grilled low-fat cheese on whole wheat with tomato, or tofu
    spread with lettuce on whole wheat
    Carrot and celery sticks
Dinner
    Sole Delight*
    Couscous
    Vegetable
    Whole-grain roll

Snack
    Popcorn with garlic salt

Sunday

Breakfast
    Shredded wheat or other low sugar cereal with sliced fruit and
    skim, rice, or soy milk
or
    Orange juice
    Scrambed eggs or egg substitue
    Grilled tomato slices with herb seasoning or lemon pepper
    Whole wheat toast

Lunch
    Zucchini with Summer Stuffing*
    Lettuce and carrot sticks
    Whole grain bread
    Blueberries or melon (in season)

Dinner
    Whole chicken (rubbed with garlic and rosemary) roasted with
    carrots, pearl onions, red or new potatoes, and zucchini strips
    Mixed field greens salad with balsamic vinegar dressing
    Nine grain rolls

Snack or dessert
    Apple Crisp

NOTE: These menu suggestions follow standard nutritional guidelines.
They include one serving (of the recommended 2 to 3 daily servings)
of dairy, which has been found by some health professionals to
cause, for some individuals, a variety of problems, including allergic
reactions. You may, therefore, want to restrict your dairy intake,
replacing it with soy and rice products. Be sure to take a calcium sup-
plement and eat broccoli and leafy green vegetables for necessary
calcium. Also balance the amount of wheat products you eat with a
variety of grains, including rye, corn, oats, millet, barley, and rice.

RECIPES

The following recipes are ways to prepare healthful dishes quickly—
that taste good too! Make enough at night to have leftovers for lunch,

or add to a dish the next evening. For example, what's left of the baked whole chicken can be used in stir fry with vegetables the next night.

Perking Up Your Lunch Time Salads

Use mayonnaise sparingly; try the reduced-calorie, lower fat ones, preferably those made from cold-pressed oil with no preservatives, if possible. Flavor with lemon, mustard, capers, vegetables, herbs, and spices.

TUNA SALAD   Bored with tuna salad? Try this variation, instead of using high-fat mayonnaise. To solid white or chunk tuna in water, add the following to taste:

lemon juice

spicy mustard, Dijon, or others

drop of olive oil, if tuna salad is dry

capers

fresh Greek or Spanish olives

fresh red pepper, pimento, or sweet Italian peppers

carrot shavings (optional)

Take this to work in a plastic container with lettuce or in a whole wheat pita.

EGG SALAD   If you find egg salad a little gooey, try this variation, which is heavy on vegetables. To two eggs add:

red and green peppers in medium-sized chunks

a little green onion, onion salt, or dried onion

reduced-fat mayonnaise and spicy mustard to taste

pepper to taste

Serve with leafy green lettuce on whole wheat bread or pita. If dieting or watching your wheat intake, have with bed of lettuce and rye crackers (take in plastic container).

CRAB SALAD

2 crab sticks, sliced

1 hard-boiled egg

1/4 avocado cut in pieces

sliced celery (1/2 to 1 stalk to suit taste)
season with a little onion, lemon juice, and cayenne pepper
mayonnaise to taste
Serve on lettuce with rye crackers or whole wheat bread.

Quick And Tasty Chicken Breast Dishes

My mom is a whiz with chicken breasts. She always keeps frozen skinless breasts on hand and can thaw them quickly. Here are some of her variations. They are all low in fat, as well as low-cal. She browns the breasts in a little olive oil and then uses chicken broth to sauté breasts and vegetables. You can also put chicken in the broiler.

SPICY CHICKEN   Coat chicken with Dijon mustard and then roll in whole wheat cracker crumbs. Brown in a little oil in a skillet or under the broiler.

ORANGE CHICKEN   Sauté chicken breasts in a small amount of olive oil. Then add fresh lemon and orange juice, and orange slices. If you want a thick sauce, add a little cornstarch or flour. You can also add a small amount of white wine to the sauce.

CHICKEN AND PEPPERS   Brown chicken in a little olive oil and then turn down the heat and add chicken broth. Sauté sliced red and green peppers in chicken broth or cook peppers in microwave and mix with chicken. Add fresh basil to chicken broth and cook another minute. Serve chicken breast topped with broth, peppers, and basil. Brown rice or couscous (very easy to make) make a nice side dish topped with the vegetables as well. (Hint: If you don't have fresh basil, use a little dried. You can make your own dried basil: buy fresh basil and hang it up to dry; it will be fresher than the commercially packaged basil.)

QUICK CHICK   Spread chicken with mustard, spicy brown or Dijon, lemon juice, and basil or other herbs. Put under broiler. I like to leave some skin on (and bones) for flavor while cooking but take it off before eating. Steamed broccoli and herb potatoes make a good accompaniment with whole-grain bread.

Herb Potatoes

Steam small red potatoes until tender. Put in a baking dish (or reuse a disposable aluminum container), and sprinkle with a little olive oil, pepper, and rosemary and/or parsley. Broil while you are broiling chicken or fish.

NOTE: Steam broccoli or other vegetable in the same pan as you did the potatoes, while you broil meat and potatoes.

Yummy Bean Ideas

Beans are a great protein substitute for red meat. Here are a couple of tasty recipes that are healthful too.

APRIL'S BEAN SUPPER
    1 can of beans: black beans, kidney beans, or garbanzos
    2 tablespoons olive oil
    2-3 cloves chopped garlic
    1 yellow or Spanish onion, diced
    1 tomato diced
    2 tablespoons cooking wine
    1 red or green pepper diced (optional)
    1 cup brown rice
    1/2 teaspoon tumeric
    salt and pepper to taste
    While rice is cooking, sauté 2 cloves garlic, onion, in olive oil until transparent, add peppers, followed by the tomatoes. Add the can of drained beans. Cook until mixture thickens, add wine and stir. If you love garlic, add the third clove (finely minced). Serve with brown rice seasoned with tumeric (added while cooking).

CORN AND BLACK BEAN SALAD
    1 can black beans
    4 ears of corn, cooked and kernels cut off (can substitute 1 cup
        frozen corn kernels)
    1 red pepper, chopped

4 stalks celery, chopped

3 tablespoons cilantro, chopped (optional)

3 scallions, chopped

1 tablespoon olive or canola oil

1 teaspoon balsamic vinegar

1 teaspoon Dijon mustard

1 teaspoon honey

salt and pepper to taste

Mix all vegetables in bowl. Make a mustard-vinaigrette with oil, vinegar, mustard, honey, salt, and pepper. Stir into vegetable mixture and combine well. Served on a bed of lettuce, this tasty salad goes well with chicken or fish or makes a meal when combined with whole wheat bread and a green salad. (Serves four.)

Tasty Fish Dishes

SOLE DELIGHT

4 pieces filet of sole or flounder

2 tablespoons olive oil

2 tablespoons frozen orange juice concentrate

1 tablespoon fresh lemon juice

3 tablespoons water

3 tablespoons pine nuts

3 tablespoons golden raisins

fresh parsley

While broiling fish, in a saucepan, at medium heat, stir in olive oil, orange juice, and lemon juice. Add pinenuts, raisins, parsley to taste, and water. (Increase ingredients amounts according to how many pieces of fish you're serving.) Pour sauce over broiled fish (don't overcook), and accompanying couscous. Garnish with lemon slices and parsley sprigs.

QUICK FISH Fix as in "Quick chick," page 142. Using a filet—salmon, tuna, swordfish, snapper—spread fish with spicy mustard, lemon juice, and dill. Cook in broiler (turning fish at least once) until done. You can add capers for extra flavor, or make a sauce of more mustard, a little butter, and lemon juice to put on before serving. Make sauce in microwave or sauce pan.

Zucchini With Summer Stuffing

4 large zucchini

1 cup corn kernels

1 medium onion, chopped fine

1 tablespoon olive oil

4 scallions, chopped fine

1/2 - 3/4 cup low-fat ricotta cheese

1/2 cup grated Parmesan cheese

salt and pepper to taste

Cook zucchini in boiling water for 5-10 minutes, until a sharp knife pierces to center easily. Remove from water and place in ice water to cool. Slice lengthwise and scoop out centers, leaving a sturdy shell. Chop scooped zucchini and set aside. Sauté onion in oil until transparent. Add chopped squash, and cook until liquid is cooked off. Cool, then blend with ricotta, scallions, and half of Parmesan. Season with salt and pepper. Return mixture to zucchini shells and top with grated cheese. Bake on cookie sheet at 350 degrees for 35-45 minutes, until heated through. This also makes a nice side dish for chicken breasts or a light supper with salad. (Serves four.)

Crock-Pot Soup

You can let this cook while you are at work. Set on low. It will take eight hours to become really flavorful. This recipe uses no oil, and there's no chance of it burning. Wash vegetables the night before and assemble in the morning. If you have a microwave and wish to eat when you first get home, cook beans and zucchini in the microwave; otherwise, add them to the soup during the last hour of cooking.

1 can plum tomatoes and juice

3 stalks celery, sliced

3 carrots, sliced

1 medium onion, sliced

beans (chickpeas, navy, or kidney)

green beans or other veggies, zucchini, spinach (optional)

basil, thyme, oregano

Place tomatoes, celery, carrots, and onion in crock-pot; add water to cover. Simmer all day. Add extras during the last hour of cooking—spinach, zucchini, beans, and spices.

Easy Pasta Sauce

1 tablespoon olive oil

1 to 2 tablespoons chopped onion

1 tablespoon grated carrot

1 tablespoon chopped green pepper (optional)

2 cloves of garlic cut in half

1 28-ounce can of Italian peeled tomatoes (Progresso or Italian brand if possible)

Fresh basil to taste

Sauté onions until golden in a small amount of olive oil; add garlic halves, carrots, and peppers. Cook another minute. (Peppers and carrots cut acidity of tomatoes.) Add tomatoes, cooking over medium heat. Stir occasionally and mash garlic cloves. Cooking time is about 45 minutes, although you can let it cook for longer or shorter. Toward end of cooking add basil and a little parsley. Put over any kind of pasta. While the sauce is cooking, make a green salad. You will also have time to fix lunch for the next day or take a moment to relax.

VARIATIONS: Sauté zucchini and serve on spaghetti with sauce, or broil a chicken breast and serve with sauce and spaghetti, zucchini or eggplant on the side.

Salad Tips

Buy several kinds of lettuces, such as romaine, red leaf, butter, and spinach. Wash well, dry and put in a sealed plastic container. Use during the week for salad, adding other vegetables as you wish. Add toasted sesame, pumpkin, or sunflower seeds to salad for taste and nutriments.

Chapter Seven

HOW ASSERTIVENESS CAN LEAD TO STRESS REDUCTION

How many times have you felt frustrated because someone took advantage of you, spoke out for something you wanted, or pushed ahead in line without your complaining? Haven't you been taught to be polite, to not make waves, or that to complain will only make the situation worse? Women are conditioned to be considerate, unselfish, and put others' needs first. Always putting other people's desires ahead of your own, however, is not healthy behavior. When you constantly fail to get your needs met, it becomes extremely stressful. In fact, many people who develop stress-related symptoms are found to have few assertiveness skills.

Linda is such a person. In the midst of buying a catering business from her friend Nancy, Linda is very enthusiastic about the opportunity and looking forward to it. There are many details about the transaction, however, with which she is unhappy. But she hasn't been able to bring them up with her friend because of Nancy's own predicament: Her husband got a job in another city, and although it is a good promotion for him, Nancy regrets having to give up her business and leave friends and family. Linda knows she is going through a difficult time and doesn't want to make things worse for her by discussing details that might cause conflict. On the other hand, she has some real concerns that need to be addressed. This situation has put a strain on their relationship, and Linda's frustration causes her either to say nothing or to blow up. Her stomach has been frequently upset as well.

Does this sound familiar? Have you ever had feelings similar to Linda's? Try taking the following assertiveness test, if you're still uncertain as to your own degree of assertiveness.

Think about how you respond to the following scenarios:

TEST YOUR ASSERTIVENESS

Work

When one of the staff was out sick, you took up the slack. Now since your boss has seen that you can get the work done, you are being given more and more assignments. You respond by:

_____

_____

You've been given a project to complete. You enjoy the challenge, but you're finding that you are not given time during work hours to spend on it and are expected to do it on your own. You decide to:

_____

_____

Service

A friend recommends a hair salon, saying that the stylist is wonderful and doing the best and latest looks. But when you go, the hair stylist tells you what he wants to do and you have serious reservations. You would:

_____

You ordered a rare hamburger and it came well done, which you don't like. You would:

_____

Personal

Your mother calls and tells you she is having a family dinner and expects you to come. You have tickets to a play. You would:

_____

_____

Your husband yells at your child in public when she misbehaves. You believe this is destructive to your child's self-esteem and that her behavior doesn't merit your husband's reaction, but you know if you criticize his actions, he will become even angrier. You decide to broach the subject during a private moment, but when you try, your husband downplays your concerns and changes the subject. You react by:

_____

_____

Friends

When you and your friend Rachel go to the movies, she is always late and you end up sitting so close you get a stiff neck. You:

_____

_____

You arrive at a friend's dinner party and discover that she has prepared veal, which you normally do not wish to eat out of principle. You would:

_____

_____

Look at the answers you've just written and then read the rest of the chapter. When you get to the end, go back and answer the questions again, seeing where you can be more assertive.

_____

Assertiveness involves standing up for your personal rights and expressing your thoughts, feelings, and beliefs in direct, honest, and appropriate ways. You should be able to state your needs without making the other person feel degraded, dominated, or humiliated.

Assertiveness encompasses not only stating your needs but also expressing your personal likes and dislikes, talking about yourself openly, accepting compliments, asking for clarification, disagreeing with another's opinion, and saying no.

Think over the past week: Was there a time you got involved doing something you didn't want to do? Did you want to volunteer a suggestion at a business meeting but were hesitant to speak up? Were you criticized unfairly by your boss and didn't know how to handle it? Did you want to do something with a co-worker but didn't speak up? Does anything stand out? What happened and who were you with? Do you remember what you said, how you felt, and how they responded? How did it end? Were you happy with the results or left feeling frustrated?

As women, we often find that learning to ask directly for what we want is one of our hardest lessons. Since childhood, I was well-trained to state indirectly what I desired so as to appear polite, or to say nothing for fear of seeming greedy and self-centered. Fortunately, I live with a man, my fiancé, who cannot stand it when I don't ask directly for what I want. As a matter of fact, it drives him crazy. There are many times when asserting myself feels rude or inconsiderate, but I am learning to do so more often. I've found that the more I ask for what I want, the better I feel about myself. Another thing I've learned from my fiancé is that asking for what you want doesn't mean you'll always get it. The other person has feelings, ideas, and thoughts of his or her own that may conflict with yours. You need to let others know where you stand so they can make their own decision, or you can compromise based on both your stated needs. But you'll certainly never get your needs met if you don't assert them; your self-esteem will also be increased when you ask for what you want. Certainly, this takes practice.

Assertiveness training can help you reduce stress by teaching you to stand up for your rights without being aggressive. Assertive communication is based upon the assumption that you are the best judge of your thoughts, feelings, and desires and therefore the best advocate for expressing your opinion.

I've learned that my own earlier inability to speak up for what I want stems from several things: the way I feel about myself, my training from childhood, and my desire to avoid conflict of any sort. My experience is not unusual. For generations, women have been taught to sit back and be supportive of men's opinions rather than form their own. Over the last twenty years, these beliefs have gradually begun to change. Of course, some women—and many men—have not really changed their thinking in this direction. The socialization of women, beginning in childhood, still goes on—but fortunately not to the degree it was ingrained in society during the Fifties, when I was growing up. Women's old roles almost guaranteed low self-esteem and feelings of intellectual inferiority. Remember in junior high, when the most popular girls were the ditsiest? In many families, girls are still taught that they have to be perfect and not make mistakes. Other idealized, outdated views of women are that they should be selfless, flexible, responsive to others, and put others' needs first. Assertiveness is not a feminine trait, we are told. Women have been given the message that it is rude to interrupt others or to disagree with someone older or in a position of higher authority, to accept a compliment, to compliment oneself, to end a conversation started by another person, or to use statements starting with "I," "I think," or "I feel."

It's one thing to acknowledge that women are conditioned to be selfless and put others first, but understanding it in practice and letting go of these old habits is another matter. Think about this scenario. You and a male colleague plan a business lunch. You'd like to eat at a cafe with a large salad selection but you chose the restaurant last time and you want to be accommodating. So you say you don't care, even though you do. Since you haven't communicated what you want, your colleague suggests a hamburger joint. Even though you're trying to avoid eating red meat, you say fine, but resent his choice and begin withdrawing. Afterwards, you complain about the food and say that you greatly prefer light fare for lunch. Sound familiar? This is called "passive aggressive" behavior. We all experience variations of this scene, but if it is a habit, it needs to be broken.

How To Recognize Assertive And Non-Assertive Behavior

The first step toward becoming more assertive is to understand what assertive behavior is and to recognize its patterns. Everybody can be assertive in some situations and passive or aggressive in others. You may be assertive with a co-worker, but not with your haircutter. Or you may be able to ask for what you need from your boss but become aggressive with your spouse. Certain situations will trigger specific behaviors, and being aware of them helps you to gain more confidence and skill in saying what you really mean and getting what you want. Becoming assertive takes practice; you will have to overcome patterns of behavior based upon perhaps a lifetime of beliefs about yourself and what society thinks you should be.

Read through the following styles of behavior and determine if you tend to use one style more than the others. It is important to be familiar with them so you know when you are using each.

NON-ASSERTIVE OR PASSIVE BEHAVIOR. When you behave passively, you fail to express your true feelings, thoughts, and beliefs, thereby permitting others to violate your rights. Or you express your thoughts and feelings in such a self-effacing manner as to indicate that they don't count and that others can easily disregard them. The message you send is that you aren't important and can be manipulated. You're saying the other person takes priority. When you send this message, you don't get rewarded for being a selfless, nice person; instead you simply get taken advantage of.

Take Alex, a photographer's assistant, for example. She continually assumes her boss will see she is overloaded and therefore make adjustments. Not wishing to upset the busy photographer, she is unable to tell him of her need for help, and ends up working through her lunch hour and staying late. And still the work piles up. Alex, anxious and stressed out, blames her boss and directs all her anger at him, but never confronts him with her feelings. As long as she passively accepts her work load, however, her boss will continue to overburden her.

Passive behavior means that in addition to exhibiting a lack of respect for your own needs, you show a subtle lack of respect for another person's ability to take responsibility for and handle his or her own problems and disappointments. Too often, we are concerned about the other person's reaction, fearing what he or she might feel, assuming we know what it will be. In our culture, we are afraid of unpleasant emotions and cannot seem to tolerate conflict. The goal of passive behavior is to avoid conflict at any cost. We appease others so we (and the other person) won't have to feel badly.

We often choose this behavior because we believe we are being nice, or because we mistakenly think we are being helpful, or we want to be liked and may be afraid of the consequences of speaking up. Actually, non-assertive behavior may result in a decrease of anxiety in the short term, but in the long run, it causes your anger and frustration to build up, your self-esteem to drop, and a loss of respect from others.

AGGRESSIVE BEHAVIOR. When you express your needs in a way that subsequently violates the rights and feelings of others, you're behaving aggressively. This manner of expression makes others feel either patronized, inconsequential, disapproved of, or stupid. The message is, This is what I want and your needs don't count. In aggressive behavior the goal is to dominate or win. Winning is ensured by humiliating, belittling, or overpowering others so they become weaker and less able to express or defend themselves.

Often we react aggressively because we feel powerless and threatened. Aggression becomes an overreaction to feelings of vulnerability. Linda, in our example, sometimes responds aggressively when dealing with Nancy, because she feels she has no control over the situation. Aggressive responses can also be a reaction to a past emotional experience. The current situation triggers old emotions, which cause you to respond inappropriately to the present experience. Some people are aggressive because they think it is the only way to get across their ideas. Their poor communication skills prevent their being taken seriously, so they resort to aggression to express themselves. If this behavior succeeds, it is reinforced and they continue to use it.

The immediate consequences of aggression are an emotional release and gaining a sense of power. In the long run, though, aggression keeps you from having close personal relations by driving people away. It keeps you on guard and constantly wound up, thereby increasing physical stress.

Very often women respond passively to situations and then reach the point where they feel pushed and helpless and respond aggressively. They don't really know how to assert themselves or understand what being assertive means.

PERSONAL ASSERTIVENESS SCALE

Take time to go through each of the following situations; think about where you tend to be non-assertive. Rate how comfortable you are in each instance, using this scale:

1: comfortable   2: mildly uncomfortable
3: moderately uncomfortable   4: very uncomfortable

1. Asking for Help

Boss:____   Co-Worker:____   Spouse:____   Children:____

Family:____   Friends:____   Service Person:____

2. Saying No

Boss:____   Co-Worker:____   Spouse:____   Children:____

Family:____   Friends:____   Service Person:____

3. Expressing a Difference of Opinion

Boss:____   Co-Worker:____   Spouse:____   Children:____

Family:____   Friends:____   Service Person:____

4. Responding To Criticism

Boss:____   Co-Worker:____   Spouse:____   Children:____

Family:____   Friends:____   Service Person:____

5. Expressing Negative Feelings

Boss:____   Co-Worker:____   Spouse:____   Children:____

Family:____   Friends:____   Service Person:____

6. Expressing Positive Feelings

Boss:____   Co-Worker:____   Spouse:____   Children:____

Family:____   Friends:____   Service Person:____

7. Receiving Negative Feelings

Boss:____   Co-Worker:____   Spouse:____   Children:____

Family:____   Friends:____   Service Person:____

8. Receiving Positive Feelings

Boss:____   Co-Worker:____   Spouse:____   Children:____

Family:____   Friends:____   Service Person:____

9. Making A Request

| Boss:____ | Co-Worker:____ | Spouse:____ | Children:____ |
| Family:____ | Friends:____ | Service Person:____ | |

10. Asking Questions

| Boss:____ | Co-Worker:____ | Spouse:____ | Children:____ |
| Family:____ | Friends:____ | Service Person:____ | |

11. Asking For Service

| Boss:____ | Co-Worker:____ | Spouse:____ | Children:____ |
| Family:____ | Friends:____ | Service Person:____ | |

12. Asking For Favors

| Boss:____ | Co-Worker:____ | Spouse:____ | Children:____ |
| Family:____ | Friends:____ | Service Person:____ | |

13. Speaking Up About Something That Annoys You

| Boss:____ | Co-Worker:____ | Spouse:____ | Children:____ |
| Family:____ | Friends:____ | Service Person:____ | |

14. Other _____

| Boss:____ | Co-Worker:____ | Spouse:____ | Children:____ |
| Family:____ | Friends:____ | Service Person:____ | |

Use this exercise to help you identify situations where you are not assertive. This will aid you in making changes. You may want to start with one area that appears less emotionally charged and, as you gain confidence, gradually become more assertive in a variety of situations.

Test Your Beliefs About Assertiveness

Assertive behavior is direct and honest. The basic message is: This is what I think, this is what I feel, or this is how I see the situation or problem. It is expressed with respect for the other person and his or her opinions. When you are assertive, you respect both yourself and others. In behaving in this manner you get respect as well. It sounds simple, doesn't it?

Most of us have irrational beliefs about assertiveness and its consequences that keep us from standing up for ourselves. Although logically you may understand these beliefs are unfounded, they may be very much a part of your emotional makeup. Here are some of them:

1. If I assert myself, others will get mad at me.

2. If I assert myself and people do become angry, I will feel terrible and it will be awful.

3. I'm afraid if I'm open with someone and say no, I will hurt that person's feelings (even though I want people to be open with me).

4. I am responsible for another person's feelings if I hurt him or her by being assertive.

5. If someone has a legitimate request, I should do it because if I don't he or she will think that I'm not a nice person and won't like me anymore.

6. People who are assertive are cold and alienating, so if I'm assertive, people won't like me.

7. I should avoid asking questions or making statements that will make me look ignorant or stupid.

As you read through this list, what was your response? Did you find any of the statements familiar? One of the major themes is that of wishing to be liked and avoiding having people become angry at us. We all tend to believe that the effects of assertiveness will be negative and will cause conflict. Yet assertive people are *not* insensitive to others' feelings; they simply know how to state their feelings while still showing concern for the other person. Being assertive only enriches a relationship.

Go through the list again and think about the statements. Are you really responsible for other people's feelings, and are they that fragile? Will you fall apart when someone does get angry? You do have the right to refuse even legitimate requests, and you can't please everyone all the time. Again, logically understanding your rights and actually asserting them are two different things and it will take practice before you become comfortable with them. (There are some excellent books that delve into this subject in detail; see the "Reading List" in the Appendix for recommendations.) Some women do not believe they have the right to ask for what they want, a belief that is deeply ingrained in the psyche. Following is a list of rights that has been compiled from several sources and experts in the field of assertiveness. These are the rights all of us have, and if yours aren't being addressed, you need to look at why. Go through the Bill of Rights. Do you agree with these? Are there some with which you have problems? Think about each right and put it into context with specific situations. What stands out and why?

BILL OF RIGHTS

- You have the right to express your thoughts, feelings, and opinions.
- You have the right to say NO without feeling guilty.
- You have the right to not have to justify yourself to others.
- You have the right to ask for what you want.
- You have the right to ask for help.
- You have the right to get what you pay for.
- You have the right to make mistakes.
- You have the right to be listened to.
- You have the right to put yourself first.
- You have the right to change your mind.
- You have the right to ignore the advice of others.
- You have the right to not take responsibility for others' feelings, needs, and wishes.
- You have the right to be alone.
- You have the right to choose to be assertive or passive.

What Are Your Problem Areas?

Think about what the most difficult areas are in your life. To jog your memory, go back to page 154 and look at the situations in which you were non-assertive.

Get an overall picture of what kinds of feelings you have in different situations and with different people. Write them down. Your boss may make you feel inadequate, your family may make you feel guilty, your husband, helpless, and so on. You will react differently based upon how you feel at the time—about yourself and how the other person makes you feel. Are you consistent? If you assert yourself in some situations, you can transfer those skills to people and situations where you find it more difficult to express yourself.

Go through these steps:

1. Review the Bill of Rights.
2. Write out the situations where you are not assertive.
3. List three situations that you will want to change in the near future.
4. Pick one from your list and go through the following exercise.

Describe the situation:

_____

_____

How do you usually respond in this kind of situation?

_____

_____

What are your thoughts and feelings in this situation?

_____

_____

What do you think the other person is feeling?

_____

_____

What is your goal? What do you want to change?

_____

_____

What are the consequences if you follow through?

Positive _____

Negative _____

What would be a positive affirmation around this goal?

_____

_____

After going through this exercise, mentally rehearse your ideal scenario (explained in Chapter 4). Put in all the details. See yourself remaining calm, breathing deeply, and expressing your feelings and your request clearly and audibly, using eye contact.

Your body language is an important aspect of assertiveness. If you're stating your requests while looking down at the floor and speaking in a quiet voice, you're not being assertive. Stand up straight, look the person in the eye, and speak clearly. Don't whine or be apologetic. Most of us tend to apologize when asking for something we have every right to get.

When you express your feelings, use what are called "I" statements. Claim your feelings; say "I feel hurt" rather than "you hurt me." Use "I" statements rather than stating someone else's opinion, like "Most people in this situation would feel hurt," or "Cindy said she would have felt hurt by that." Without blaming, state why you are upset: "I feel hurt when I don't feel I'm being listened to," rather than "I feel hurt because you never listen."

Once you have stated your request or feelings, listen to what the other person has to say. Listening requires attention and putting aside your feelings and ideas on the subject while you focus on what the speaker is experiencing. Ask for clarification or more information and then acknowledge that you heard what he or she was saying.

For example, if speaking up in meetings is an area you have identified as difficult, go through all the above steps. Think about how you usually respond, what your thoughts are, how you would rather behave, and so on. Write out the ideas you want to present. Identify both what you want to say and how you want to say it. Then use visualization to mentally rehearse your idealized scenario. See yourself calm and relaxed, breathing easily, sitting tall in your chair, making eye contact, and using "I" statements to present your ideas. Follow through by seeing yourself after the meeting, feeling good about how you handled yourself. You may want to visualize yourself talking to a friend or colleague about how well it went. Also practice stating your ideas in more familiar situations, noticing your thoughts, feelings, and behavior.

If you want to take charge in a meeting because you are frustrated that nothing ever seems to get accomplished—a few individuals focus on their narrow concerns, or go off on unrelated tangents, or there is too much socializing and little focus on what needs to be done—plan ahead. Think about ways of bringing the focus back and then mentally rehearse them. If someone gets off track, acknowledge the contribution and firmly suggest that he or she stick to the topic, such as, "Your ideas are very good, Tom (or that is a really interesting aside), but let's stay with this aspect before we address other concerns." You may want to remind participants at the start of the meeting that there is limited time with much to do and enlist their support in staying focused. When it does go off track you can remind them. When presented assertively (respecting the other individual), rather than aggressively, you will get the response you are looking for and the respect you are seeking.

In working with women, I have found that lack of assertiveness is a major component in their stress and that learning assertiveness skills is essential to stress reduction, especially in the workplace. Women must learn both that it is acceptable to express their needs and how to do it in an appropriate manner.

Start now by paying attention to your behavior; it may take a while to identify all the different situations in which you are passive, aggressive, or assertive. As you become more aware of your thoughts, feelings, and actions, the easier it will be to put assertive behavior into practice. Keep in mind that change is a gradual process. There will be many times you aren't even aware of your passive behavior until after the fact. When you are assertive, take note of how it makes you feel. Once it becomes part of your usual behavior, you'll recognize how much more in control you are. Remember, it is lack of control that is most associated with the stress response. You can't control your boss, husband, or mother, but you can control the way you respond to them—and that is an essential element in any stress-reducing plan.

Chapter Eight

GOAL PLANNING AND TIME MANAGEMENT

Tools for Fighting Stress and Moving Ahead

Ellie, 30, keeps in dead-end jobs. In the beginning each appears to be an interesting place to work—a television station, a production company, a talent agency—but in each her position turns out to be at the bottom of the totem pole, where she is relegated to being a gofer, answering phones, running errands. None utilizes her talents or challenges her, and she doesn't have the patience to wait years before moving up. Instead, she quits, trying out the next job that looks glamorous on paper but is dull in reality. She constantly complains about her situation to friends and vows to get a better job, but the same thing always seems to happen. Ellie doesn't have a sharp picture of what she wants and what her talents are; therefore, she has not formed any clear-cut goals. Until she does, she will probably remain stuck, wondering why others have all the luck.

GOAL PLANNING TO ELIMINATE STRESSORS

In reality, successful people don't just happen to become successful, they plan for it. In fact, there's a saying: Great men have purposes, while others have wishes. Ellie has wishes about what she'd like her career to be. Formulating clear goals gives a sense of purpose and direction, helping you realize your ambitions while improving the quality of day-to-day activities. Not having goals, on the other hand, leads to poor planning and prevents effective time management, both of which can leave you feeling overwhelmed and stressed or directionless and bored.

As a working woman, you will want to balance short- and long-term goals in both your professional and personal life. Setting goals not only enables you to achieve the success you want, but helps reduce stress by allowing you to manage your time and energy. And once you prioritize your goals, you can tackle them one at a time, which will lead you to a better organized schedule.

Take time to think through and clarify your goals. Are they *appropriate* and *realistic?* Can you picture yourself attaining them? Your goals must be achievable, but don't underestimate your abilities. Obviously, becoming the CEO of General Motors or another major corporation will not be a realistic goal if you are currently working in a clerical pool of a small company. Attaining management level within your company, however, or owning your own business may be a very realistic goal.

In addition, your goals should be under your *control.* You must be able to make them happen yourself. This is not to say that others won't be involved while you meet the necessary challenges, but you mustn't be dependent on someone else to realize your goal. If you want to make more money, for example, set the conditions to do so. This may involve changing jobs, adding more responsibility to your current job, or asking for a raise. But don't wait for your boss to recognize your productivity or contributions and therefore reward you with a raise. Likewise, don't wait for someone to recommend you for a job you want. Instead, set up an appointment to discuss your contributions to the company and the raise you seek; or send out your resumé and solicit a new position.

Make your goal *specific* and *concrete.* Katrina, 29, who recently earned a master's degree in clinical social work, set her goal of working in the out-patient psychiatric clinic of a renowned metropolitan hospital. Her first job out of school, providing psychotherapy and social services in a large hospital, is the first step toward reaching this goal. Being clear on what she wanted helped Katrina set the conditions needed to realize it and has kept her focused on what she must continue to do.

A goal must be *measurable*. If reducing your stress level is your goal, you will need to identify specifically how stress is affecting you and what you can do to relieve it. Using positive terms, write down how you want to be, and see yourself functioning in the way you desire. Then determine the steps you need to take to reach that goal: for example, communicate better with your supervisor, start an exercise class, spend more time with friends, practice relaxation on the job. Each month evaluate your progress.

Your goal should also be a *challenge*. Often we set our sights too low because we don't think we deserve to attain certain things or we are afraid we might not succeed. We let our current situation limit our aspirations. An aerobics instructor may want to increase her class volume and add private clients over the next six months or year. But her long-term goal might be higher—developing a program that is used at other studios and gyms, teaching other instructors, making a video, or opening her own studio.

When setting goals, focus on what you want to do, rather than on what you don't wish to continue doing. Visualize your goal as already happening. If you want to move from a secretarial position to office manager, for example, see yourself at your new position. Use affirmations to help augment this goal. Refer to Chapter 4 on using visualization and affirmations to achieve your goals.

Remember, you must have a strong desire to meet your goal and believe you can make it happen. This will provide you with the energy to realize your goal. We can all think of things we wish would happen, but without a belief in our ability to make it a reality, aspirations go no further than wishes and fantasies.

TRULY SUCCESSFUL PEOPLE HAVE THESE QUALITIES

1. A belief in themselves and their abilities
2. Valued goals and ideals
3. A sense of well-being
4. Lots of energy and good health
5. Loving relationships
6. Personal satisfaction

(The material through page 166 is based on the technique developed by Brian Tracy in his "Psychology of Success Series.")

Define Your Goals

When considering your goals:

1. List the things that are most important in your life.
2. Ask yourself what makes you feel good about yourself.
3. Think about what you would do if money were no object.

The purpose of this exercise is to free your imagination and help create a picture in your mind of what you really want. Using question one to guide you, think about your life's purpose or mission. Your purpose may be something like have a healthy life full of satisfying relationships and work opportunities, or feeling productive and respected, being satisfied that you've enriched others' lives, or feeling you've contributed to your field. Use your purpose along with your answers to question one to guide you in setting your goals.

Write out goals for the different categories that follow on page 165. If you're reading this book on your way to work, in a waiting room, or before falling asleep, think through your answers to the questions as you read, but be sure to find time to write out your goals later. Studies show that the success rate for people who write down their goals is ninety times higher than for those who do not! Keep your goals and affirmations to support them in a notebook or purchase a nice journal.

Once you have written down your goals, think about how you will benefit from them. Where will you be, what will it look like? Are your goals general or specific? Let's say you wrote down these goals: Working on a stimulating project in connection with your job, gaining more professional recognition, taking a vacation, improving your relationship with your husband, and increasing your physical strength.

Now you need to get specific on each goal's details: Clarify the role you wish to play on the project, the extent of your involvement, the hours you wish to put in. Pick one goal and use it as you go through "Ten Steps to Attaining Your Goals" to see how this process works using your journal to write the answers. By going through them you will learn what steps to take to get started on the project, improve your relationship and gain strength.

DEFINING MY GOALS

Write goals for:

1. Work/Career

_____

_____

2. Lifestyle

_____

_____

3. Personal/Personal Growth

_____

_____

4. Relationships

_____

_____

5. Health

_____

_____

Ten Steps To Attaining Your Goals

The more steps you take in clarifying your goal, the sooner it will become a reality. For each of your important long-term goals, go through the following:

1.WRITE OUT YOUR GOAL. This establishes a strong visual connection to it. Keep your goals in a notebook or journal so you can refer to them. Write out a description of how you want your life to look.

2. IDENTIFY THE KNOWLEDGE, SKILLS, AND TOOLS YOU NEED TO ATTAIN YOUR GOALS. Do you need any special skills or knowledge to reach your goal? Write out what it will take.

3. IDENTIFY WHAT COULD STAND IN YOUR WAY. What can get in the way of your achieving this goal? Look at old beliefs and limitations, lack of self-esteem.

4. IDENTIFY ANY PEOPLE WHO CAN CONTRIBUTE TO YOUR GOAL. Who can directly contribute to your goal or support you in attaining your goal?

5. MAP OUT YOUR STEPS. A goal should be broken down into smaller goals. After going through the above steps, make a detailed plan of action. For a goal that will take a year or two, you should have a plan for today, three months from now, six months, and so on.

6. SET A TIME FRAME. After establishing a plan of action, estimate how long it will take to implement each step, and set an approximate date to accomplish your goal.

7. SEE YOUR GOAL AS HAPPENING. Using the visualization and affirmation techniques in Chapter 4, concentrate on your goal.

8. REVIEW YOUR GOAL. Look in your notebook at your written goals. You can visualize your goals while practicing relaxation, upon falling asleep or waking, or during a break at work.

9. RECOGNIZE YOUR ACCOMPLISHMENTS. When you have made progress toward your goal, acknowledge it. If you have completed a training course, put together a resumé, or contacted a friend in the field, acknowledge that you are working toward your goal.

10. MAKE A COMMITMENT. Don't establish goals you are not prepared to meet either emotionally or physically.

How would you like to be remembered? Think about it. Take time to write it out, putting in details about your work history, satisfying relationships, where you live, the things you enjoy, and so on. This will incorporate your purpose or mission and the realization of your chosen goals. Remember, your goals should be based on what you truly value, not what society values or what you think women are supposed to accomplish today. If being in your current job allows you the time and energy to do the things you really want to do, don't feel pressured to get a promotion or work your way up the corporate ladder, which may take you away from the hobbies or leisure activities you enjoy. A good test is to ask yourself if you can visualize yourself in your current position in five years, ten years, and so on.

STRESSBUSTER: MAKING YOUR DREAMS COME TRUE

I know a very successful woman named Sandra, who, instead of making New Year's resolutions, writes out her goals each New Year's Eve. She inscribes them on a piece of parchment paper, rolls it up like a scroll, and ties it with a ribbon. In a relaxed state she visualizes each goal coming true. During the year Sandra looks at the scroll at least once and again the following New Year's Eve. Yearly, having accomplished her goals, she gains the satisfaction of seeing them and knowing she has succeeded.

Set Short-Term Goals As Steps To Long-Term Success

You will need to set long- and short-term goals. Write out goals for five years, three years, one year, and six months. Some of your short-term goals will be steps toward long-term ones. You may change and revise your goals over time. Each particular goal should guide you, aiding in your personal and professional growth. If one of your long-term goals is to have a summer house, for example, determine how long it will take to save the money and the steps to accomplish this. If you think it will take three years, for instance, you could save for a down payment by working harder and increasing your number of clients. You'll have to determine how many clients you'll need and how to get them. After three years you'll have the down payment because you started speaking at meetings and luncheons, writing for newsletters, and doing more networking. But, let's say, an opportunity arises to buy into a successful business. You decide to put the house on hold, plan a short vacation, and pursue the new business. If you hadn't had the original goal, you wouldn't have put things in place necessary for making the business happen. Now you have an opportunity to continue furthering your career and eventually obtaining your summer home if you choose.

What happens when you don't succeed? All of us wish for some things we never get. The following are reasons for failing to get what you want:

1. An inadequate self-image
2. The inability to use the mind's resourcefulness
3. Not having set clear goals
4. Unrealistic goals
5. Lack of persistence

Ellie, bored with her various jobs, fits the bill described above. She has failed to identify what she wants, nor has she used her resources to improve her life. Self-esteem issues may be clouding her image of what she is good at and impeding her efforts. Instead, she daydreams of an exciting job and having the things she wants. Without taking the steps outlined in this chapter, Ellie can expect to remain stressed and bored on the job and disappointed in herself.

Setting goals, as you will see in the next section on time management, is part of the process of becoming organized. As a busy woman, you are bound to find appealing the idea of getting organized and managing your time better. Now is the time to get started, put these ideas to use, and approach your goals.

ORGANIZING YOUR TIME
AND DE-STRESSING YOUR LIFE

"I don't have the time." "There aren't enough hours in the day!" "Where will I find the time?" How often do you find yourself making these pronouncements? Effective time management won't add hours to your day, but it will make the ones you have more productive. When dealing with stress, one of the best investments you can make is to use your time wisely. If you're unorganized, you can't be as productive as you'd like to be. Being disorganized will leave you feeling overwhelmed and out of control.

Lee, 48, a day-care teacher and supervisor, feels as if she's always running from one thing to the next, never catching her breath. She usually worries about what she has to do next, rather than concentrating on what she's working on at the moment. Because she needs to earn more money, Lee recently began taking classes at the local college to qualify for a better paying job. The most lucrative positions in her field are district supervisors; yet at the moment Lee is unable to supervise her own school properly. Typically, an unexpected "crisis" occurs, distracting her from important tasks. Yesterday, on the way to her college class, she realized that, having been sidetracked trying to catch an escaped pet rabbit, she'd failed to reorder the center's depleted supplies. Also in her haste to leave, she had forgotten her course notes. Often, rather than attending to her priorities, she spends her time responding to other workers' problems and needs. After work, when she's socializing with friends, Lee finds she can't relax because she's so distracted. She wonders how other women manage to work, run errands, fix dinner, and have a social life, without feeling pressured.

To decrease her stress level, Lee needs to organize her life based upon her goals, priorities, and daily responsibilities, and then plan out daily, weekly, and monthly activities. If Lee wants to put her projects into action, for example, she must understand how she spends her time at work. To do this, she needs to keep track of her daily activities. You can't organize your time until you know how you use it now. The chart on page 170 is designed to give you this information.

Using the chart, color in (with magic marker, colored pencil, or crayon) the amount of time spent on working, sleeping, eating, shopping, cleaning, relaxing, exercising, leisure activities, and socializing. Use a different color for each item so you will get a visual picture. This may take a while but it will give you a good idea of how you spend your time. You may be surprised at how little you relax or how often you shop, or discover that you really do have an active social life. This will give you an overview. Then get more specific by looking at how you spend your time within each of these categories.

HOW DO YOU SPEND YOUR DAY?

Determine what colors you will use to designate each activity and then fill in the chart putting in time spent working, sleeping, eating, relaxing, socializing, etc. For example, red for work, blue for sleep, green for eating, yellow for exercising, purple for relaxing, white for leisure and so on.

Time	Monday	Tuesday	Wednesday	Thursday	Friday	Saturday	Sunday
6:00 am							
7:00 am							
8:00 am							
9:00 am							
10:00 am							
11:00 am							
Noon							
1:00 pm							
2:00 pm							
3:00 pm							
4:00 pm							
5:00 pm							
6:00 pm							
7:00 pm							
8:00 pm							
9:00 pm							
10:00 pm							
11:00 pm							
Midnight							

Another exercise helpful in determining effective time usage is to separate and examine the types of activities upon which you spend your energy at work. This will allow you to decide if you should continue allotting your time in this way. Start by writing in a small notebook (that's always with you) all your activities over the course of three days. Divide your workday into morning and afternoon. Put in productive work, low priority, phone calls, meetings, socializing, and so on. Lee, for instance, will find that much of her day is wasted responding to other people's emergencies rather than dealing with her own priorities. After she sets her goals and lists priorities, she may need to discuss with the staff her plans for the future, letting them know she will expect them to take more responsibility because she won't be constantly available to solve their problems.

Be sure to take time to actually write out your schedule and complete the charts. If you feel pressured and overloaded, it's even more important, and should help you find ways to improve how you use that precious resource—time.

Let's say that you have written out goals, organized projects, and gained a sense of your time expenditures. That will leave you with planning your month, week, and days, for which you'll need an appointment book. There are many good ones, such as the Week-at-a-Glance, Day-at-a-Glance, Day-Runner, and Filofax systems, which you can get in stationery stores. In addition to my appointment book I make a list of what I have to do each day.

For making lists, I like to use large index cards. I learned their value while working in a hospital, when I was constantly moving from my office to meetings and patients' rooms. I noticed that some staff members were always consulting their white cards, which contained patient information and appointment times. Although we were provided with a general overall schedule, it was very beneficial to have notes on what I was doing each hour. Every morning before I left the house, I wrote down the things I had to do, therefore arriving ready to do them. I found I was better at keeping track of appointments because all I had to do was glance down and my day was there.

Constantly carry your book with you, which will enable you to make plans easily—for dinner, meetings, social events, and so on. You can use this book to refer to when making your lists. If you normally have a fairly routine day, you may not need to compile a list, but simply take along your appointment book. I've found list-making to be tension-reducing. If you compile your lists the day before, you can go to sleep knowing you will be organized for the next day, without worrying if you're going to remember everything. Do you trust yourself to remember all the calls you need to make during your work day? To order needed supplies? To pick up the cleaning after work? Or to buy everything you need at the grocery store on your way home? Also it is very satisfying to cross off what you've accomplished.

When scheduling your day, be realistic about what you can accomplish. Don't put in so many items that you must always be hurrying. Build time into your schedule for interruptions, unscheduled events, and problems. If you don't, you'll be frustrated by the interruption and fail to attend to it as well, then feel rushed to catch up. Arrange your activities to make the best use of your time. Don't run to the tenth floor twice in one day if possible (unless you're doing it for the exercise); schedule errands that are on your way home, or to save time, try to do them during less crowded off-hours. Be sure to schedule time to relax. Often we attend only to the demands of job and home, putting off exercise and relaxation.

Differentiate between high and low priorities. Some things can be put off. You may want to reevaluate your priorities. You might find you have too many and that you must decide what is really important and worthwhile and what is not. I remember Patty, an outpatient at the hospital who was committed to keeping her house immaculately clean. Since she worked as an elementary school teacher, had a daughter, and was coping with a physical ailment, the time and energy she spent doing housecleaning was not a good investment. She thought a fastidiously tidy home was necessary because of her upbringing and the old "shoulds and should nots" she carried with her. Patty had to reevaluate her attitudes toward her house and what it represented to her. It has not been easy, but she has begun to see that cleaning leaves her feeling fatigued, achy, and unable to do a good job at work or spend time with her husband. Therefore, she's made some adjustments.

Similarly you will need to prioritize your projects; obviously, some will be more important and may have built-in deadlines. For example, while I was writing this book, another project came up that I thought had to be addressed immediately, causing me to feel stressed and overwhelmed. Once I prioritized my work, acknowledging that I had a publishing deadline to meet, I could happily continue writing the book, knowing the other project could wait until I was finished.

STRESSBUSTER: GET ORGANIZED

Lack of proper organization and planning is one of the most basic forms of self-generated work stress. Being organized will help you feel more in control and help you better carry out your responsibilities. The time you put into getting organized is an important investment into your well-being and sense of satisfaction on the job.

Many women I know pride themselves on their spontaneity and flexibility, and resist planning and scheduling. Organizing your time in these ways, however, doesn't mean that you have to be rigid and adhere to a strict schedule or that every minute should be planned— it shouldn't. Instead, you should be flexible and spontaneous in using your time, letting your goals and priorities guide you. It's probably better to have lunch with the friend that unexpectedly called, instead of working through lunch to finish a project. The break will refresh you and give you the energy to keep going. Planning enables you to make such decisions, not be at the mercy of your demands.

My friend Merry, a college professor, would never make plans for any social activities on the weekends. She always had something she had to do hanging over her—an article to write, papers to grade—and she couldn't seem to get it done during the week. Often when we spoke, she would fret that she hadn't accomplished anything the past weekend. Feeling burned out, she couldn't concentrate and watched TV instead, or friends dropped by and she decided to go out with them. So she was behind and couldn't make plans for the following weekend even though she wanted to go to the concert or out to dinner. Her commitments seemed to be running her life, rather than being directed by her. Had she set priorities and become more organized, she would have found time in her schedule for social activities as well as her work. Planning isn't very time-consuming, and as you do it more often, it will become part of your thinking process. If you haven't been making plans before, it should take a few months before it feels comfortable.

Merry said that she didn't like to plan because it made her feel trapped—but the truth was that she was a procrastinator. Although she had the intention to work each weekend, she put it off. Two things that will keep you from using your time wisely are procrastination and indecisiveness. Here are some of the reasons for procrastination:

1. Lack of a deadline
2. The deadline is too far away
3. Lack of motivation
4. Fear of failure or other consequences.

As a master's thesis advisor, I certainly have an opportunity to observe procrastination. Granted, all my students work and go to school and have difficulty finding time to write. But what seems to be true most often is that the students' attitudes and beliefs keep them from doing the work. Most of them do the initial research, project, or performance without problems. It is at the writing stage that they begin to experience difficulties. For some, putting their own ideas on paper is frightening. They are afraid they don't know enough or they won't sound professional or they will be challenged and embarrassed. This holds true for many professional situations within which women find themselves. Fear of criticism keeps them from formally presenting their ideas at a meeting, preparing for a seminar, getting out a report. Taking the time to work on a thesis often seems to be a sacrifice for many women, and they feel deprived and want a distraction. But what happens is, they feel the thesis hanging over them the whole time they are not working on it, so they don't really enjoy themselves anyway. How often have you put off working on a project, only to feel guilty and distracted while you weren't doing it?

There is an expectation that finishing one goal means having to accomplish another. Some students feel that receiving a master's degree (or attaining a similar goal) means that they have to find a better job, get their life together, make decisions they are not ready to make, so therefore they procrastinate. Goals sometimes need reevaluating. Maybe after finishing one of your short-term goals you decide you need a break or are happy where you are—which is fine. Enjoying yourself can be a goal as well! Remember your goal belongs only to you and can be revised at any time.

If you have difficulty making decisions and tend to procrastinate, you may want to seek help to examine some of the attitudes that keep you from moving forward. Using the techniques in this book should enable you to take more responsibility for and control of your life. Modifying your time expenditures requires self-knowledge, planning, and understanding the benefits of managing the hours in your day.

Remember, many of the little problems and annoyances that add up and insidiously induce the stress response can be avoided by goal planning and time management. Probably nowhere is the old adage more true—an ounce of prevention is worth a pound of cure!

Chapter Nine

HIGH STRESS IN THE WORKPLACE

How To Avoid "Burnout"

Cindy has had it with her boss. She's always prided herself on her efficiency and sense of responsibility, but as the assistant to a TV production company executive, she is constantly trying to catch up with her work. She usually finds herself skipping lunch or gulping down a sandwich at her desk to finish up a project in time. The most frustrating part is that as soon as she finishes one report, her boss loads her down with three or four more assignments—in addition to her usual, daily tasks. It seems the harder she works, the more he pushes. Making things more complicated, having so many projects to finish causes her to lose concentration on the task at hand, resulting in her making more mistakes than usual. Every time she tries to broach the subject with her boss, he commends her on her work before she has the chance to say what's bothering her. In the meantime, she's been losing weight, has been suffering with headaches, and frequently wakes up in the middle of the night, unable to go back to sleep. After a few days of this, sleeplessness begins to take its toll and she has to call in sick and spend the day in bed—a pattern that is happening more and more often.

Patricia, a secretary for a wealthy businessman, is at her wit's end. All she can think about are negatives—her loneliness, her boredom, the crises in the world. Since her boss is constantly out of town, she has plenty of time to dwell on her problems. The most demanding part of her day is typing the list of phone messages she's taken and getting the numbers right—but lately she's even had trouble doing that. When she considers her college degree in English, she regrets not having been trained at a skill that could garner her more challenging work. Overqualified for her secretarial position, she never has to solve problems on the job, so she just frets over the things she doesn't like about her life. On top of everything, she has gotten into the habit of eating sweets and snacks—just to pass the time—and has put on ten pounds. Patricia also has trouble getting to work on time, frequently takes extra-long lunches, and often leaves early.

HOW STRESS OVERLOAD EQUALS BURNOUT

Although Cindy and Patricia don't seem to have much in common, each is suffering from unrelieved job stress, or burnout. Their jobs and attitudes may be as different as night and day, but they actually have many similarities. In both cases, their jobs are not meeting their expectations; emotionally, they feel overwhelmed and pessimistic about their positions; and their work is beginning to suffer from the situation, as is their health.

"Burnout" is a term used to describe the emotional, mental, and physical exhaustion experienced by many working women. A negative experience characterized by problems, discomfort, and dysfunction in the workplace, it involves feelings, attitudes, motives, and expectations concerning all aspects of a job and the work environment.

Women are at particularly high risk for work burnout for many reasons. They often toil at high-stress, low-paying jobs, receiving little feedback from supervisors, and for many, once they leave their paid position, more work awaits them at home.

Burnout is manifested in a variety of ways. You may feel physically exhausted and suffer from low energy, fatigue, headaches, nausea, and/or aches and pains. You may be catching colds frequently and finding yourself accident-prone. Like Cindy, you may experience headaches and insomnia. Emotional exhaustion may leave you with feelings of helplessness, hopelessness, and depression. You may find yourself crying more easily and unable to cope with even small upsets. Mental exhaustion can manifest in negative attitudes toward yourself, your job, and your life. Like Patricia, you may find yourself getting to work late and leaving early, watching the clock, taking extended breaks, and having difficulty concentrating. Although both men and women can become burnt out, women must also cope with additional gender-related stress, which I'll discuss on page 181.

Almost everyone experiences some form of burnout from time to time. For example, the natural excitement you have for a new job wears off, and as you begin to experience work stressors, you feel less positive and enthusiastic. It is prolonged and excessive stress that causes real difficulties, however, and leaves you with a variety of stress-related symptoms. Although there is no one definition for burnout, there are common sources, including being overloaded, having inadequate direction or supervision, being underqualified or overqualified, not being clear on responsibilities, having no sense of future, experiencing conflicts, being under-utilized, and having no sense of accomplishment and/or feedback.

How To Recognize Work-Related Stress

The first step toward eliminating job stress is recognizing that it exists. Women often deny that there is a problem meeting all their demands, especially since the myth of the "superwoman" has proliferated in our society. Many women see it as a weakness that they can't do it all. Others, such as Patricia, don't recognize that the underutilization of their capabilities can provoke an ongoing stress response. They feel guilty or blame themselves for their inability to find a fulfilling job.

If you aren't quite sure about your own situation, it's a good idea to make a list of all the things that bother you about your job. This can help you identify the actual sources of your stress. Go through the Sources of Work Stress Checklist on page 179; are you experiencing many on the list?

The next step is to understand how these stressors affect you. Think about any stress symptoms you've been exhibiting (headaches, stomachaches, constant fatigue, et cetera, as identified on the Stress Symptoms Checklist in Chapter 1). "Symptoms of Work-Related Stress" on page 180 lists a number of specific responses to

SOURCES OF WORK STRESS CHECKLIST

Check the sources of stress that are applicable to your situation:

❑ Too much to do and not enough time to do it
❑ Burdened with new responsibilities while still trying to finish old ones
❑ Job interferes with personal life
❑ A difficult commute
❑ Must work during lunch, at home, on weekends
❑ Have too much work to do a good job
❑ Never get compliments or reward for work well done
❑ Get frequent criticism from boss
❑ Make little progress at work
❑ Don't feel accepted or appreciated by others at work
❑ See little opportunity for growth or advancement
❑ Popularity and politics seem to count for more than good work
❑ Never get any feedback—good or bad—from supervisor
❑ Unsure of job's responsibilities
❑ Do not get clear instructions about tasks
❑ Feel underqualified for job's tasks
❑ Feel overqualified for job's demands
❑ Most of work is routine and unchallenging
❑ Little or no contact with other people during work
❑ Too little work to do
❑ Your values differ from those with whom you work
❑ Experience little meaning in work
❑ Get no support from co-workers
❑ Feel like a fish out of water
❑ Don't get enough information to carry out tasks
❑ Lack the authority to carry out responsibilities fully
❑ Unable to solve problems assigned by supervisor
❑ Can't make a difference in regard to work policies
❑ Feel trapped
❑ Can't overcome certain restrictions or requirements involved in problem-solving
❑ Don't understand how performance is evaluated

SYMPTOMS OF WORK-RELATED STRESS CHECKLIST

Check all the symptoms that apply to you:

❏ Feel continually negative, futile, depressed
❏ Have trouble making decisions
❏ Less efficient than in the past
❏ Quality of work has deteriorated
❏ Feel depleted spiritually, emotionally, and physically
❏ Catch colds and viruses frequently
❏ Eating habits have changed (eating more or less)
❏ Loss of interest in sex
❏ Drinking more coffee, sodas, or tea
❏ Smoking more cigarettes
❏ Drinking more heavily
❏ Using drugs
❏ Increased forgetfulness
❏ Frequent boredom
❏ Feel emotionally numb in regard to others
❏ Strained relationship with boss, co-workers, friends, family
❏ Lack of concentration
❏ Free-floating sense of dissatisfaction
❏ Only reason to go to work is for paycheck
❏ Frequent moodiness, irritability, impatience
❏ Little or no enthusiasm for job
❏ Feel continually tired, even after much sleep
❏ Constantly feel frustrated
❏ Desire to withdraw from work's demands

---

work stress. For each stressor, think about how it makes you feel (angry, resentful, frustrated, and so on). Once you finish, try to connect any of the physical or emotional symptoms to specific causes and situations. Too much to do and not enough time to do it may leave you with knots in your stomach, or a clenched jaw that can lead to headaches. Too little work may cause you to feel bored, unable to concentrate, and susceptible to colds and flu. You should be able to see a pattern emerge here. Sometimes we may try to deny that things are bothering us, but until we look honestly and rationally at a bad situation, we cannot change it. Once you see it in black and white, it's time to make a resolution to do something about it. This is where you begin to gain control. After going through this process, make a list of the things you *do* like about your job.

The Impact Of Gender-Related Stress On Women

Despite all the information, books, and political activism on equality, women continue to face inequity in the workplace. Women are often undervalued, underpaid, and underappreciated. Sometimes blatant and sometimes quite subtle, the effects of discrimination are the same. Reports show that professional women, when compared to professional men, experience four times as much job tedium. Women report that they have less freedom, autonomy, influence, variety, and challenge in their work, and report fewer opportunities for self-expression. Dealing with more pressures in the work environment, women tend to overextend themselves in response to other people's demands.

National statistics show that women working in the same profession as men are paid less than their male counterparts. Positions traditionally held by women, such as secretaries, sales clerks, waitresses, teachers, librarians, and nurses, are lower-paid than traditional male jobs, and a majority of these jobs are the more stressful. Seventy percent of women aged 25 to 34 work in a stereotypical "job ghetto." In fact, 55 percent of these women hold sales, clerical, and service jobs (as of 1990). In 1989, the median income for these jobs were $6,990, $13,542, and $5,487, respectively. Even in occupations dominated by women, according to a recent study, men earn more than women and are more likely to achieve supervisory positions. Also, women move much slower up the corporate ladder than men, and are given tenure less often. A report issued by the Older Women's League in 1991 stated that although middle-aged and older women make up an increasing portion of the work force, they are paid substantially less than men their age, reach their peak earnings a decade earlier than men, and are still largely segregated in traditional women's jobs. In 1989, the median annual earnings of women 45 to 54 years of age was $20,466, or 59 percent of the $34,684 median earnings of men their age. And while men 35 to 44 years of age earned 30 percent more than men ten years younger, women in the same age group earned only 8 percent more than women ten years their junior. The report was based on data from the Labor Department, Census Bureau, and other agencies.

When affected by these statistics personally, your ordinary job stresses are exacerbated. Single mothers who hold down full-time jobs in traditionally female areas can barely make ends meet with their salaries. Frequently, women who work as hard or harder than their male colleagues aren't compensated with raises, appropriate salaries, or bonuses. It's been said that "women have to work twice as hard as men to be considered half as good." The bottom line is that if you're in such a position, it's even more essential that you follow the advice given in this chapter. If you are the sole woman in your office, for example, seek support from a women's group or hotline. It's important not to feel isolated; you are not alone: thousands of other women are in the same boat.

Another serious problem women encounter in the workplace is sexual harassment, which consists of any repeated and unwanted sexual attention (verbal or physical). This ranges from suggestive looks, jokes, and innuendos to explicit propositions and touching. Although men can be sexually harassed, women are harassed more often than men and suffer more serious effects, such as anger, inability to concentrate, reduced job effectiveness, sleeplessness and low self-esteem.

Sexual harassment has been so pervasive that many women until recently have assumed that it was something they must accept as part of working in a "man's world." Women themselves are often blamed for sexual harassment, with male supervisors responding with "the woman asked for it," or the offender claiming she should find it flattering. Women often feel that they did something wrong, that if they had just acted differently it wouldn't have happened. It causes them to question themselves rather than the offender.

The Anita Hill case made it all too clear where women stand in the eyes of many of our nation's lawmakers and politicians. Fortunately, however, a recent Supreme Court decision indicates a change of thinking on this position. The decision determined that there needn't be proof that a woman's long-term psychological health or ability to function on the job must be affected in order for sexual harassment to be an issue.

It's important to understand that, like rape, sexual harassment is about power and control, not sex. This form of harassment makes women feel vulnerable and powerless and keeps them in positions of weakness. Silence, tears, or pleas make a woman look helpless and only encourage the offender. The more controlled and powerful you act the better. Say no, and let the offender know you mean it. Send clear signals.

Again, it's essential to face the problem head on, rather than denying it exists. Try to make changes; inform your harasser that his attentions are unwanted. Remember that *any* unwanted attention can be a form of sexual harassment and it is up to you to decide what is inappropriate.

If the harassment continues, voice your complaints to the harasser's supervisor. If the harasser is the supervisor, confront him about the problem in a calm, rational way—just as you would any other work-related problem. Should his behavior continue, don't allow this stressful situation to get the better of you. More and more companies are implementing anti-sexual harassment policies that ensure confidential investigations into such allegations. Look into your office's policy on the issue. Educate your office. Have someone come in and talk about sexual harassment. If necessary, transfer out of your department or find another job. More and more women are seeking resolution in the courts. Plan your strategy clearly and calmly before taking action. Should you report the problem to the appropriate channels, be prepared to deal with a possibly stressful investigation, perhaps even privacy-invading publicity.

Strategies For Change

Let's look at Cindy's and Patricia's situations and see how they can be addressed. For Cindy, identifying the problem—that her work load is too great and her boss is ignoring the situation—is mandatory. Cindy then must analyze her needs: completing one task before starting another, feeling a sense of accomplishment, and so on. She should look at her interaction with her boss and understand why she is unable to stand up for herself. Assertiveness training as described in Chapter 7 should help.

After identifying the problem and clarifying her needs (preferably in writing), Cindy should make an appointment to speak to her boss about the situation. Keeping the appointment is vital, and she should set the goal to discuss her problem and not get sidetracked.

During the meeting, she should state her concerns clearly and in a straightforward manner. In advance, she should have devised some solutions—planning ahead and prioritizing projects, hiring an intern to help her with clerical tasks—and should present them to her boss. She needs to get feedback on his expectations. He may not have clearly thought them through himself. After he and Cindy come to an agreement, she should reiterate their decision and clarify any vague points. Then it is up to Cindy to make sure her boss sticks to their mutual conclusions. If he backslides, she should assert herself, and if necessary make another appointment to speak to him and come up with a mutually acceptable plan.

In her situation, Patricia has basically three choices: She can continue on, feeling helpless and frustrated; she can stay in her job and use it to support outside activities in which she's interested; or she can look for another job or career that is more stimulating. If Patricia decides she's not ready for a job change, she can put her energies elsewhere, since they're not much needed at work. She needs to shift her attitude, though, by looking at her job's positive qualities and seeing how she can utilize them. Patricia can use her time outside of work in constructive ways—taking classes, exercising, getting involved in a hobby, developing more satisfying interpersonal relationships, doing volunteer work. She needs to engage in activities that help foster a positive self-image. As an interim step, she can investigate other avenues—via classes, volunteer work, perfecting a skill—that could lead to a new career. If she thinks it's time for a change, she may want to start part-time college or technical school classes, while still working at her job.

Apply some of the techniques recommended for Cindy and Patricia to your own situation. The following strategies should help you begin to deal effectively with job stress:

1. GET ORGANIZED. For busy working women, organization is a must. Being overwhelmed at work often comes from poor organization and time management. Are you spending extra time trying to find that file or phone number, or can't remember where you put the information you need? The more organized you are the more control you will have.

2. SET GOALS. Use your career goals to guide you on the job. This will help you set priorities. If you have a specific career objective and the job you're in feels like a dead end, take steps to change jobs or get training. Once you've identified sources of job stress,

establish goals that will enable you to change your situation. Break goals down into small steps that you can do bit by bit. For self-motivation, give yourself little rewards after each adjustment or accomplishment.

3. DEVELOP ASSERTIVENESS SKILLS. Being assertive is a major career asset as well as a means of coping with job stress. Women can't afford to be passive or aggressive on the job. Many sources of stress can be eliminated by being assertive and clarifying responsibilities, setting limits and asking for feedback. For many women, however, assertiveness doesn't come easy and will take practice. Refer to Chapter 7 for assertiveness skills. You may want to take a seminar and/or read one of the books listed in the Appendix on this subject.

4. CHANGE YOUR THINKING. Sometimes you need to change your thinking in certain ways. If you're feeling overwhelmed, for example, put your job into perspective. A client of mine was complaining about feeling overwhelmed by work responsibilities when I pointed out that in actuality she had less of a work load than she had had in the past. When she was able to look at her schedule she realized she could handle it. She had gotten in the habit of responding to all work demands by feeling overwhelmed. By reframing her thinking she was able to do her work and feel comfortable with it.

Step back and look at what is bothering you. A more detached attitude can help you accomplish goals without feeling overwrought about your ability to succeed. Once you remove yourself emotionally from the problem, you can focus your energies on solving it. Differentiate between the issues. Don't let negative attitudes such as feelings of being trapped or blaming others for your problems prevent you from doing a good job or reaching your goal. Remember, you do have choices and you are in control of your own fate.

5. TAKE BREAKS. During the day, be sure to take breaks. Get up and walk around. Vary your activities. Too many women work through lunch, eating at their desks. Take a lunch break away from your desk, even if it means simply finding an empty office or desk. The next section (beginning on page 188) will give more specific suggestions on break-taking and stress-proofing the work environment.

6. LIMIT OVERTIME. We all occasionally must work overtime to meet deadlines, but it shouldn't become a habit, especially if you work a 9-to-5 job. Workaholism is habit-forming, just as the name implies. Here, setting priorities again comes into play. A few extra dollars in overtime may not be worth the mayhem that working long

hours several days a week causes. Many of us find we've been conditioned by the work ethic to believe that we're being lazy if we don't stay after-hours and give a job all we've got. "You have to work hard to succeed" is a much-quoted axiom. This is not always true, however. In reality, it's better to know when to quit working and to give yourself a break. Overworked employees are usually the least effective ones; burnout causes a decrease in creative thinking as well as in efficiency.

Many women feel they have no choice but to agree to overwork and overtime. They fear that if they don't they will lose their job. To prevent being continually asked to work overtime by your boss, you will have to learn to say "no" to certain extra demands. This can be done in such a way that your supervisor understands it is in the company's best interest that you are not overworked. Evaluate your work load as compared to your job description; determine when demands seem excessive.

7. DON'T TAKE WORK HOME WITH YOU. The quickest way to burn out is to be constantly working or thinking about work. Separate work and home. If possible don't take work home, or at least limit it. You will think more clearly and be more productive if you schedule time for rest and recreation once you leave the office.

8. FIND ENJOYABLE OUTSIDE ACTIVITIES. It's important to get involved in other activities that have nothing whatsoever to do with your occupation. For example, if your work involves interacting with many people all day long, find a hobby that you can do alone. If your job is a solitary one, spend your spare time with other people doing social activities. Involve your family in planned get-togethers, if you have children. Should your work be more demanding than usual, give yourself small luxuries—like a massage or simply time alone with a rented video movie. Use your off-time to take classes or foster outside interests and skills. Study a foreign language, take a cooking course, learn assertiveness skills. Read books to improve your health and well-being.

You need time to unwind from work before going on to other activities. Exercise after work, or alternate exercise and relaxation. If you find you continually worry about work problems once you get home, use relaxation or visualization to break the cycle.

The time you spend before work is just as important as your 9-to-5 routine. If your schedule is such that you grab a cup of coffee and rush off to a traffic jam to get to work on time, reorganize your day. Go to bed an hour earlier, so that you can wake up an hour sooner. Eat a nutritious breakfast, and read an inspirational or educational book. Take an extra half-hour to walk to work, or use this time to exercise or do a relaxation session. You'll be surprised at the difference it makes when you set a pleasant tone for your day. You'll find yourself much more energized to meet your job's demands.

9. CULTIVATE YOUR RELATIONSHIPS. Studies show that one of the best predictors of job satisfaction is meaningful interpersonal relationships. Close relationships help alleviate work stress. Conversely, difficulties in a significant relationship increase feelings of stress in the workplace. It is important to feel you have friends and family with whom you can talk about your problems, share your joys and sorrow, who care about you and your feelings and will be there for you if things go wrong. Make time to be with friends and loved ones. If you are married or in a long-term relationship, make special time to spend together.

Identifying your sources of work stress and applying these techniques will pay off. As you begin to practice relaxation techniques described in this book, you will also find that staying relaxed in work situations will reduce your job stress and give you more energy to tackle related problems.

How To Handle The Double Whammy Of Working And Being A Mom

Being a working mother creates extra pressure on the job. If you have young children, you probably experience guilt at leaving them in someone else's hands or not being home when they return from school. It's even harder if your job is not fulfilling. The guilt women experience, however, comes in part from what our society or our upbringing has conditioned us to feel. The model of the woman staying home and caring for the children was set up by societies long outdated and have been passed down and perpetuated. Not many families —probably a bare minimum—live the life-style portrayed in the TV shows of the Fifties and Sixties.

Women who work do have more satisfying lives, and your child's world, in the hands of nurturing, responsible caregivers, will broaden as well. Your goal is to lovingly raise a child who is independent and self-sufficient and feels loved and cared for—something you can accomplish as a working mother. I won't tell you not to feel guilty, but do look at the advantages of being separated part of the day from your child and at the positive benefits he or she gains from spending time with others. Worry and guilt will only have a negative effect on how you function on the job. Also, if you feel guilty, you will eventually pass along negative feelings to your children.

On the other hand, it is not irresponsible to take a day off should your child become ill. Be honest with your employer; if you discuss your family's needs honestly, you'll feel better. Politicians have made "family values" a platform in recent years. Study your local representatives' viewpoints closely and vote for those who favor family-oriented policies, such as guaranteed parental leave from work. Support women who run for office and who value working women's rights. Organize a group of concerned parents to lobby for your children's and your own needs.

DESIGNING A STRESS-FREE WORK ENVIRONMENT

In addition to the mental and emotional stressors working women incur, there are other sources of stress on the job—aspects of your workplace's physical environment. For example, do you use a computer terminal or typewriter daily? Are you a clerical worker, data entry clerk, journalist, writer, airline reservation clerk, or directory assistance operator? If you answer "yes" to any of these, particularly in the area of clerical work, your office environment may be causing you stress. Researchers for the federal government, according to a spokesperson for the National Association of Working Women, now consider clerical work society's most stressful occupation because of its continual use of computers. Constantly using a video display terminal (VDT) has been deemed more stressful work than operating as an air traffic controller or a high-level executive. Women tend to sit in poorly designed chairs and work at tables that are either too low or too high. Working for long periods of time without changing positions or taking breaks, women may be unaware of how dramatically their bodies and energy levels are being affected. Often, they are required to meet quotas, while their keyboards are monitored and their trips to the bathroom counted. If you sit all day, work in one position, and do repetitive tasks, you will probably benefit by adapting your work space to better meet your needs.

Potential health hazards within the workplace, including complaints of physical problems, muscle strain, and fatigue, were overlooked for the most part until the recent computer age. With VDTs, more and more women began to complain of eyestrain, neck and shoulder pain, backaches, headaches, wrist and hand problems, and carpal tunnel syndrome (numbness and pain in the hand and wrist). These work-related symptoms can range from mild to serious, often leaving a woman unable to function in daily activity without pain.

Because the computer allows us to work faster and more efficiently, you may spend your entire day in the same position, hitting the keys, making thousands of strokes an hour. Although we all agree that the computer simplifies our work, and most of us can't imagine how we managed without it, the result can be that you work too long in the same position, which can cause painful and incapacitating conditions often referred to as overuse syndrome, or repetitive strain injury (RSI). Women employed as weavers, sculptors, painters, seamstresses, and musicians, who use repetitive motions in their professions, are also at risk for overuse disorders. One of my clients works in a factory and has painful carpal tunnel syndrome from twisting lids onto jars.

The hand and wrist are particularly susceptible to strain because the tendon in the wrist forms a tight band through which the nerves must pass from the arm into the hand. When the muscles in the arm and hand are overused (especially at an angle or with a torsion), this band swells and constricts the nerves, causing pain and numbness. Women who suffer from carpal tunnel syndrome may end up unable to lift a package or their kids, hold a teacup, or do normal everyday tasks. Less severe symptoms may or may not develop into serious disorders but need to be addressed immediately.

In a hospital clinic where I worked, two of the three clerical staff members experienced carpal tunnel pain. One was in constant pain and the other wore a brace (which keeps the wrist aligned) daily. To relieve their pain, I suggested they adjust the height of the computer, purchase a padded wrist pad (allowing a computer operator to type without bending the wrist, which causes strain), and use a footrest. Such techniques helped these women; they were simple solutions, but neither woman had asked the director or anyone else for help. They felt they had no recourse as they were used to having their needs ignored by the men in their office.

Veronica, a writer who was receiving medical treatment for carpal tunnel syndrome, made an interesting point about her ailment. She told me she had no problems until she started using a computer. She had not only typed all day before getting her computer but was a pianist and practiced when she wasn't typing, so she certainly was using her hands and wrists. In both activities, she noted, she was pressing down on the keys and then releasing—the way the muscles are designed to work. Upon hitting the computer keys, however, there is little give, enabling the typist to go faster, hit harder, and hold the fingers stiffer. Another difference is that with a typewriter, hitting the keys is interspersed with putting in paper, setting margins, and correcting errors.

Working at a computer or typewriter causes strain on other muscles as well, especially in the neck and shoulders. All the women I have seen with carpal tunnel syndrome have considerable tension in their neck and shoulders. Muscle spasms, painful in and of themselves, cause the muscles to shorten and compress the discs in the neck, which can lead to interference with blood and nerve supply. Therefore not only are the wrist and hand affected, but the arms and neck and shoulders as well.

Even if you are not at a keyboard all day, you may be experiencing neck, shoulder, and low-back strain from the chair you use and the positions in which you work. Sitting and working for prolonged periods of time in a fixed position can lead to serious stress on your body.

Step 1: Adjust Your Environment To Fit Your Needs

To relieve physical stress, adjust your chair, workspace, and lighting to fit your body's needs—not vice versa. The place to begin is with your chair. Many of you will be spending most of the day sitting, and you must be able to do so comfortably and at the proper distance from your work. The ideal chair should adjust to the height you desire and support your back. Unfortunately, many chairs are not adjustable and don't come close to fitting your body. Chair designers, who are often men, seem unable to design a chair that fits the bodies of women. Since every person's body is different, one would assume that office chairs would be made adjustable. Though such chairs are available, they are quite costly; a good chair will run from $300 to $1000, and many companies aren't willing to spend the money, even though it will save in the long run (preventing work absences due to back injuries, strain, and fatigue). But just as my co-workers did, you can modify your environment.

Your chair should be padded but firm, and support the curve of your back. If your chair is not adjustable, use a pillow. I find that most chairs are uncomfortable, so I carry a small pillow wherever I go. If you have a regular chair you use, leave your pillow there or attach it to the chair; you can buy pillows for office chairs that tie on or attach with elastic straps. If a pillow won't fit on the type of chair you have, try to find another one. Let your boss or office manager know the necessity of proper fit in the workplace. You wouldn't (I hope) sleep eight hours on a poor mattress and expect to feel good in the morning. You shouldn't work eight hours sitting in an uncomfortable chair. Some offices may not have any better alternatives or the resources to buy a good chair, so you will have to do what you can by adding pillows and moving frequently. See the Appendix for where to buy orthopedic pillows.

The height of your chair will depend on the kind of work you do: Typing and writing require a different height than if you're operating a computer. When using a computer keyboard, your arms should form a 90-degree angle so you type with a flat wrist. The angle of your upper arm to your lower arm should be between 70 and 90 degrees. When writing, phoning, or doing other tasks, let the arms rest on your work surface, arm rest, or lap to take strain off the shoulders. If you type, write, or read, your desk should be higher than the one you would use for a computer terminal. When typing, your arms should be angled slightly upward with your upper arms relaxed from the shoulders and eyes more downward. When seated, your feet should be flat on the floor; if they are not when you have adjusted to your desk height, buy or construct (out of a few pieces of wood) a footrest.

Ideally, your chair seat should tip forward or backward, depending on your type of work. If you work at a computer terminal, the seat should tilt slightly backward for proper lumbar support. Some people, however, like to be positioned slightly forward. When writing and reading, the seat should tilt slightly forward as you lean toward your work. Again, this is assuming you can adjust your seat. If you can't and find that your legs get tired, a small, thin, soft pillow (you can make one to meet your needs or find an old one that has lost its shape) can be used in the front or back of your chair. You should have a chair that rolls on casters so you can move around your workspace rather than having to twist or reach.

If you have an unadjustable chair that is too low, place a flat pillow in the seat to raise yourself, or check with other departments to find a chair. Someone else may have one that is too high and want to trade. If yours is too high and you work at a typewriter or terminal, raise the terminal.

The neck is another area that becomes easily strained during your work day. Watch the positions you get into. Too often I see people leaning forward with their necks stuck out, placing strain on the joints, muscles, and ligaments all the way down the back. When using the computer, your head should be straight ahead and you should look down with your eyes (at about a 15-degree angle). Have the screen at a comfortable distance from your eyes. When typing, look down at a greater angle, but again use your eyes and not your head to see your work. When reading and writing, pay attention to the angle of your neck: make sure it isn't tucked under, causing a double chin, or craned forward. Don't hold your head with your hand resting on your chin, since this position strains your neck. Although your head should be straight, avoid holding it in a stiff position. Frequently and freely move it and your shoulders. (Two books in the Appendix offer diagrams and detailed information on adjusting your computer to your needs.)

One of the worst things for your neck is talking on the phone. We tend to hold the phone by tilting the neck and raising the shoulder, straining and distorting both. Be aware of your position when using the phone, keeping your neck straight, shoulder dropped, and switching sides often. Try using a speaker-phone or a headphone-style phone receiver for long conversations or when you must take notes.

When concentrating on your work, it's easy to forget about your body and thus unconsciously assume poor body positions. Throughout the day, shift positions. Crossing the legs at the ankle is better than crossing one leg over the other at the knee; however, if you do cross one leg over the other, change positions and don't twist the body. Watch twisting your spine to one side, sitting on one hip, and twisting your legs under you. In one of my classes a young woman always sat with her legs completely twisted together. She went into this position every time she sat down and stayed that way throughout class. I was amazed by her ability to do it; it must have started when she was a child. It seemed a means of self-protection (she also crossed her arms in front of her), as if she were trying to disappear by making herself smaller. I often thought about what kind of physical problems she would incur later in life from sitting that way. The reason I'm mentioning this is that what feels comfortable and "natural" isn't necessarily correct or healthy. Look back to Chapter 5 for more on body awareness.

To help prevent hand and wrist pain, take breaks and gently move your hands and fingers in all directions. For relieving pressure, try this: Take hold of your right hand with the left one and gently pull to open the joint. Keep the hand straight and in line with your arm (don't bend and pull). Repeat with the left hand.

To relieve eyestrain, change focus often. Look away from the computer screen, paper, or book, and focus on an object across the room. You can strengthen muscles by closing your eyes and looking up and down, side to side, then circling in both directions. Rest your eyes by closing them and cupping your hands over your eyes. If you see colors, your eyes are strained.

Unfortunately, most of us can do little about the lighting or heating where we work. Many offices are lit with bright and harsh fluorescent lighting, which can cause fatigue and eyestrain. If possible, lower the overhead lights and use a desk or floor lamp instead. Try full-spectrum light bulbs; although more costly, these bulbs should lessen eyestrain and fatigue. If you work in a place that tends to be cold, keep a sweater around. Being cold causes your muscles to contract and further adds to tension.

Step 2: Create A Pleasant Environment And Atmosphere

Most women spend eight hours or more at the workplace every day. A drab, impersonal work area will influence how you feel. Brighten up your space, add pictures, plants, posters. Bring in fresh or dried flowers. Even if it is just a small space, try to personalize it.

Too many women work in offices with no natural ventilation. Without proper ventilation to counteract the effects of cigarette smoke, dust, vapors from chemicals, and overcrowding, symptoms of "office sickness" can occur. This syndrome's symptoms include sinus congestion, itchy and burning eyes, dry throat, headaches, and fatigue. Plants and bowls of water can help increase humidity. Air filters improve air quality, and if you are in a small space, you can bring your own. Plants will improve air quality too.

Your boss or supervisor may be reluctant at first to aid you in your quest to upgrade your work environment. Once you do make changes, the positive proof of an increase in your productivity, energy level—and cheerfulness—may be all you need to convince your company to implement more employee-based policies. Enlist your co-workers; have them read this chapter if they need more information. Together, petition for a more humane workplace—you deserve the best!

Step 3: Move Around

It won't matter how well you've adapted your work environment if you stay in one position for too long. Any fixed position, no matter how balanced, becomes stressful after a while. Therefore, it's extremely important to get up and move around. My friend Tricia, for example, has a chronic back condition but can work during the day as long as she moves frequently. She has terrible difficulty sitting still, and long movies are hard on her. During her work day, however, she gets up to retrieve files, goes to meetings in other rooms, and takes breaks, even if just to get a drink of water.

Taking breaks often is harder when you work at a computer all day; the majority of your work is in front of you and you can sit and type for hours on end. You will simply have to find ways of moving and stretching. Every so often, circle your head and neck, roll your shoulders, arch and curl your back. Stand up even for a moment to stretch. Walk around your space. It's important to take your eyes away from the screen to give them a break as well. For maximum work performance, take a break for a couple of minutes every hour, and a 15-minute break every couple of hours.

After reading this chapter, you're probably saying to yourself, "No wonder I'm so stressed out!" It's true, the traditional workplace is not exactly user-friendly, but by following the suggestions here, you *can* begin to alleviate job-related stress. Used in conjunction with relaxation exercises and the other stress-reduction techniques in the book, these tools will help to prevent burnout.

STRESSBUSTER: SEVEN WAYS TO DE-STRESS YOUR WORKSPACE

Arrange Your Workspace to Meet Your Needs

* Adjust your chair to fit your body
* Adjust the height of your chair and table
* Arrange your work materials to the best advantage
* Use back supports, wrist supports, and footrests when necessary

Sit in a Balanced Position

* Use your chair to support your back
* Sit in a balanced position with your weight evenly distributed
* Reduce slumping, craning forward, twisting to one side, and sudden twisting

Move Often

* Move your neck and shoulders (see Chapter 10 for neck, shoulder, and other exercises you can do at work)
* Rotate activities if possible; make phone calls, type, file
* Get up from your chair; stretch or walk around

Take Breaks

* Take a break from your work; socialize, go to the water fountain or bathroom
* Get outside during lunch if possible; take a quick walk. If you bring your lunch eat it away from your desk. Go out for fresh air, if even for five minutes

Take Mini-Relaxation Breaks

* Look away from your task
* Close your eyes
* Take a few deep breaths
* Do a quick overall progressive relaxation
* Focus on any part that is particularly tense; breathe into it, move it slowly

Develop Awareness

- The more attuned you are to your body the better able you will be to take care of it
- Pay attention to how you use your body while sitting and standing
- Notice how your body feels; look for physical signs of muscle tension
- Move often

Develop a Positive Attitude Toward Work

- Reframe your attitude toward work

Chapter Ten

RX AND EXERCISES FOR STRESS-RELATED PROBLEMS

Although most of us don't want to hear it, the way we live our lives contributes to how we feel. Overall, physical complaints such as headaches, backaches, and ulcers are less likely to be related to organic or structural causes than to the types of jobs we have, the way we use our bodies, the foods we eat, the amount of exercise we get, and, most important, what we worry about.

All of us experience mild symptoms of stress that signal we are overextended, such as an occasional headache, upset stomach, or a cold or flu, and we accept this as a normal part of everyday life. When stress goes unabated—you are overloaded at work and at home, you are experiencing stress in an intimate relationship, your extended family is placing extra burdens on you—the body lets you know with physical problems that interfere with your functioning. Eliminating these more serious complaints demands extra time and attention.

The following methods have been found effective by physicians and health-care professionals in preventing and eliminating stress-related physical problems, as well as diminishing the effects of organic and structural problems when tension is a factor. In this chapter, you will find relaxation exercises proven successful for each complaint, as well as therapeutic exercises that work directly on the tight muscles. Some of the suggestions in this chapter can be practiced on the job, but most will require time outside the workplace.

These methods are not designed to replace medical care. Physical symptoms triggered by physiological causes need to be addressed. If you experience any ongoing problem, consult a doctor. The exercises in this book support but should not be substituted for prescribed care.

FOOD FOR THOUGHT

Psychiatrist Walter Menninger, MD, of the Menninger Foundation, is one of many doctors who believes there is a clear relationship between stress and the aches and pains of everyday life. "A chronic backache," he has remarked, "may signal the load is getting too heavy; the ulcer may suggest dealing with a situation you can't stomach."

EASING NECK/SHOULDER DISCOMFORT

You're sitting at your desk, it's 5:00 P.M., and you're getting ready to leave work to make a 6 P.M. appointment. In runs your boss, with an emergency project that will take at least an hour, if not more, to finish. To top it off, you had already successfully completed one rush job during your lunch hour. You notice that your head is pounding, your neck and shoulders are in spasms, and your jaw is tensed. Worst of all, this is not the first time you've felt this way. Does this sound familiar?

Under stress you knit your brow, clench your jaw, tighten your neck, and raise your shoulders. In fact, in the first two or three seconds of an emotional upset, the muscles around the eyes, mouth, and jaw almost always tighten. Clench your jaw tightly and notice what happens. Clenching tightens not only the jaw muscles, but tenses the muscles on the side of your neck as well. Notice your forehead. Does it feel smooth and relaxed? The muscle in your forehead (frontalis) is a good gauge of the tension you experience throughout your body.

Not surprisingly, the muscles in the neck and shoulders have been referred to as the "tension triangle," with the shoulders as the base and the forehead, the top. Excess muscle tension from poor posture or as a response to stressful events can cause headaches and stiff neck and shoulders—which restrict movement and are uncomfortable. Muscle spasms and pain are the ways your body tells you to stop, slow down, breathe, and move. To reduce tension in your neck and shoulders, moving is imperative. Gentle stretching lengthens the muscles, warms them up, and increases blood flow. At work, you can do simple circling movements while seated; also be sure to get up, stretch, and move around. Regular practice of the following neck and shoulder exercises will help relieve and prevent pain and spasms.

Neck And Shoulder Exercises

These exercises are designed to release tension and increase mobility and range of motion. You should feel better after doing them. The Kinetic Awareness exercises help release frozen muscle patterns, and when practiced regularly can create permanent changes. They will help you become aware of any holding you may have and remind you to release it. The range-of-motion exercises loosen you up, increase circulation, and help you feel better, but benefits tend to be more temporary. You need to do both. The Kinetic Awareness exercises can be done before or after a relaxation exercise or in place of one. Use the range-of-motion exercises as part of your regular daily regimen, or as a break on the job.

Should you feel pain when practicing these exercises, make the movement smaller and slower. Movement promotes healing and should feel good. Experiment until you find the movement that is comfortable for you, even if you are hardly moving. You will probably feel stiffness as you move and that's okay. Work through it gently. Some people hear popping sounds or what they describe as crunching. Putting tension into an area causes it to lose its elasticity and become brittle. When tight ligaments move over bones, you hear and feel popping noises. The more you move, the less you will experience this.

STRESSBUSTER:
SIX TIPS FOR EASING NECK AND SHOULDER PAIN

1. Practice neck and shoulder exercises daily.

2. At work move your neck and shoulders regularly.

3. Watch the positions you work in, typing, reading, and especially talking on the phone; keep your neck and shoulders aligned.

4. Take breaks, move around, walk if only for a few minutes.

5. Watch what you carry. Heavy bags will tighten your shoulder and neck muscles.

6. Maintain a regular exercise routine such as walking, swimming, yoga or T'ai Chi.

Kinetic Awareness:
Slow Movement For Positive Changes

RELEASING THE NECK. The movement should be extremely slow, slower than you may have imagined you could move. The slower you move, the deeper the release. You should spend at least ten minutes or longer for best results. Do these exercises lying down with your head flat on the floor. If you have a pronounced curve or if you feel a strain, put a flat pillow under your neck.

1. Scan your neck and shoulders, notice the amount of curve, the relation of your shoulders to your ears, any feelings of stiffness, or pulling.

2. Slow down your breathing.

3. Very slowly, move your head to the right. Go only as far as is comfortable. Move back to center. Repeat to the left. Notice how far you were able to go without effort.

4. Move slowly side to side, paying attention to your breathing and all the sensations in your neck for about three to four minutes (longer if you can). Notice as you move:

   ◆ Any holding (tension) in your neck

- ◆ If the movement is jerky or smooth
- ◆ How much effort it takes to move slowly
- ◆ If both sides feel the same

5. Move your head up and down. Nod slightly forward (down) and up toward the ceiling without strain for two to three minutes; this should be a very small movement. Lengthen rather than tighten.

6. Alternate moving side to side and up and down. Continue this action for three to four minutes.

7. Move side to side, gradually making the side-to-side movement smaller and smaller until you come to center.

8. Move in a very small circle. Make a movement like the hands of a clock, go clockwise and counterclockwise.

9. Bring your head to center, and notice how your neck and shoulders feel compared to when you first started.

NOTE: You can do exercises 6 through 9 on a soft rubber ball (approximately 5 inches in diameter). Place the ball in the curve of your neck or at the base of your skull. Use if there is no pain.

RELEASING THE SHOULDERS. Approach this exercise as if you have never moved your shoulder joint before and are exploring for the first time what it feels like and what it can do. Again, go slowly and use little effort. Initiate the movement in your shoulder rather than moving the shoulder with your arm. Take as long as you can to do this exercise. The longer you do it, the more release you will have.

1. Move your right shoulder in all the directions it can go. Notice:
   - ◆ The effort it takes
   - ◆ The quality of movement—smooth or jerky

2. Repeat on the left.

3. Move both shoulders together.

4. Move your right arm in all directions it can go. Repeat on the left.

5. Move both arms together.

SHOULDER STRETCH. This is designed to release the muscles between your shoulder blades.

1. Lie down with arms extended to side, shoulder height.
2. Very slowly lift right hand off floor and toward the left arm.
3. When your arm is across your chest, fingers touching your left arm, roll your shoulder and head toward the left arm. Keep your head and left side on the floor; your shoulder and shoulder blade will lift off as you roll toward the left. Do not let the hips come off the floor.
4. Hold and feel the stretch in your shoulder blade.
5. Roll back, leading with your shoulder, open arm to side, bring head center.
6. Repeat with the left arm.

Freeing Your Neck And Shoulders with Range Of Motion Exercises

NECK AND SHOULDER SEQUENCE. These exercises can be done sitting or standing. All movements should be slow, small, and without effort for best results. (They are not done as slowly as the Kinetic Awareness exercises.) Repeat all movements at least *four* times.

The Neck
1. Move your head side to side (position your head straight forward).
   a. Continue moving side to side but each time you move, gradually lift your chin until you reach the base of the neck. Move back to center.
2. Circle your head (small circles clockwise and counterclockwise). Do not let your head drop too far backward.
3. Tilt your head side to side (ear toward shoulder).
   a. Tilt head to right and hold in that position while you lift your left shoulder up and down. Bring your head back to center. Repeat other side. Return to center.
   b. Move your head forward and hold; lift both shoulders up and down.

4. Lift your chin upward and downward (small movement)

   a. Curl forward, moving each vertebra separately, going over a few vertebrae at a time and coming up. If seated, curl over as far as you can go.

   b. Arch spine upward and backward. Start mid-back. Do not collapse head backward.

Shoulders/Arms

1. Circle the right shoulder. Moving forward and backward:

   a. Make small micro movements

   b. Make circle a little bigger

   c. Make large circles

   d. Circle whole arm

2. Repeat left shoulder

3. Clasp arms behind back, pull shoulders backwards.

   a. Pull shoulders backward and lift sternum upward in an arch.

   b. Repeat (a), and stretch arms behind you (two times). Hold the last one, and breathe in and out.

STRESSBUSTER:
TREATMENT FOR NECK AND SHOULDER PAIN

1. Heat or ice

2. Massage

3. Gentle stretching

RELIEVING PROBLEM HEADACHES

Everyone gets a headache now and then. For some women, however, headaches are an ongoing problem. In fact, tension headaches can painfully remind us we are pushing too hard or worrying too much.

There are many types of headaches. You may have one in reaction to a specific food, as part of flu or cold symptoms, or from a bump on the head. Osteoarthritis in the cervical spine can also cause headaches, as does a misalignment of your bite. The most common types of headache, though, are muscle tension and migraine. Women who suffer from these types find themselves unable to concentrate on the job and irritable and unable to function at home.

For those who suffer from chronic muscle tension headaches, relief is available. Studies have shown that even people who have suffered for years and taken a wide variety of medication can eradicate painful symptoms. This requires eliminating the body's response to stress, using relaxation techniques and coping strategies, and working directly on muscular tension in the neck and shoulders, by using movement exercises.

Women with migraines will also find these same techniques beneficial. Migraines are painful and debilitating. To date there is no agreement on their cause. What has been found, however, is that muscle tension is frequently present in migraine-type headaches. When you are in pain, you respond by tensing up. The frustration, annoyance, and anxiety you feel about getting another headache create even more pain, aggravation, and often perpetuate the symptoms. Migraine sufferers can therefore benefit from techniques that relieve tension.

Because migraines are considered vascular problems, countless experts have found that practicing hand-temperature control using autogenic training techniques can help migraine sufferers diminish their frequency. Autogenic training results in an increased blood flow to the extremities and decreases the flow to the head and scalp. Autogenics combined with visualization and breathing appear to have the best effect. However, practice must be regular rather than just during a headache attack.

In my work I have found that people need to use both relaxation techniques and work directly on the body part. Most of us have some tension in our neck and shoulders, but people suffering from tension headaches tend to have chronic unreleased or "frozen" tension that, when coupled with a stressor, triggers painful headaches.

To release held muscle tension, you must first learn to feel the tension you already have. Then you need to be aware of when and how you add more. You may be unaware of how much tension you put into your neck, but when you move your head very slowly, you can begin to feel just how much tightness is really there.

FOOD FOR THOUGHT

Headaches can be a symptom of food allergies. Pay attention to circumstances surrounding your headaches: Do they occur after you eat? You may not always be able to tell, however, because symptoms often take hours to show up. If you do suspect you have allergies, check with a specialist or try eliminating certain foods. Do not eat a food for a week, then eat it three meals in a row and watch your response.

Preventing Painful Headaches

1. Practice the exercises beginning on page 199 every day.

2. Practice regular relaxation techniques for ten to twenty minutes a day. Progressive relaxation helps you feel and release tension. Use passive relaxation once you have mastered the tensing. Use autogenics, especially the hand-warming exercises. Visualize yourself in a pleasant outdoor environment with the sun warming your arms and legs. Imagine a cool breeze on your forehead.

3. Watch the positions in which you sit; keep your neck lengthened and balanced on top of your shoulders.

4. Be aware of your tension level. Don't let your neck and shoulders get so tense that you can't avoid a headache.

5. Be aware of how you respond to stress.

6. Express your feelings appropriately. Don't hold things in and then explode with a headache.

7. If you are a migraine sufferer, it is important to avoid foods that trigger headaches, including alcohol (particularly red wine), cheese, chocolate, and citrus fruit.

STRESSBUSTER:
IMMEDIATE RELIEF FOR HEADACHE SUFFERERS

1. Use ice or a cool or warm cloth (whichever you prefer).

2. Massage your temples, forehead, jaw, and neck muscles.

3. Very slowly move your neck in all directions.

4. Do a relaxation exercise, particularly breathing exercises, visualizing yourself in a peaceful environment; use autogenic hand-warming phrases.

5. For migraine: lie down in a darkened room or wear dark glasses.

6. Avoid further tensing.

DE-TENSING YOUR JAW:
BRUXISM AND TMJ

Ever notice that your jaw tends to tire easily from chewing tough meat or gum? Do you hear clicking when you move your jaw or find a big yawn is uncomfortable? Has your husband or boyfriend told you that you make irritating noises with your teeth during the night? If so, you may be unconsciously grinding your teeth, which is called bruxism, or clenching your jaw, a common, though perhaps less noticeable, stress response.

Many women are unaware of the amount of tension they put into their jaw. Maggie, a client who had been seeing me for neck and shoulder discomfort, was surprised when her physician told her the constant ringing in her ears was from tension in her jaw. Although she was aware of tension in other parts of her body she hadn't noticed it in her jaw. This isn't uncommon.

Teeth grinding is frequently a response to stress among women, according to Harvey Perlow, DDS, a New York City dentist who treats many patients with bruxism. He says it's such a widespread problem (in New York City) that when a professional woman aged thirty or older makes an appointment, he usually finds her teeth worn down from grinding.

Bruxism And Its Negative Effects

By definition, bruxism is an involuntary excessive grinding, clenching, or rubbing of the teeth. Grinding wears off the enamel, leaving the teeth more sensitive, especially the lower front teeth, and affects the bite, causing muscle imbalance. Grinding and clenching result in jaw tension, which can lead to muscle spasm, pain, and headaches, and has been found to be a component in most cases of temporomandibular joint dysfunction, or TMJ. If your teeth are slightly loose, grinding will make them looser. Bruxism also can lead to inflammation and recession of the gums and an increased risk of periodontal disease (if you are predisposed to it).

Some dentists believe bruxism is the result of a physical problem within the mouth or jaw. The most predominant view, however, is that bruxism is related to stress or the perception of stress in one's life. When under stress, a person may unconsciously grind her teeth in her sleep and/or during the day, or clench her jaw. Individuals who are anxious, aggressive, or have a need for control tend to grind their teeth.

As I have stated before, stress is almost always a component in any physical problem. Therefore, you may have a genetic predisposition to teeth grinding, or a bite that is misaligned, and under stress this is where you will put your tension. Excessive caffeine and drugs such as cocaine and amphetamines, which trigger the stress response, have also been linked to bruxing.

Admittedly, grinding the teeth or clenching the jaw does seem to be a perfect place to hide your stress. After all, it's got to go somewhere. Some people shake or jiggle their legs or constantly fidget with their hands, but this is very noticeable and doesn't give the appearance of being in control or relaxed. Society gives women the message to hold back their anger, keep things to themselves, to be nice, and to look good. A woman can look very together and hold in all her feelings by clenching her jaw, yet at the same time have an outlet for the stress. Because the action feels as if it reduces tension, it's reinforced. Unfortunately there is a high price to pay for it.

The majority, if not all, of TMJ patients exhibit grinding or jaw clenching. Whether or not bruxism leads to TMJ or a similar syndrome known as myofascial pain dysfunction (MPD) is not adequately documented, but it is clearly a component, and certainly exacerbates the condition. Even if bruxism does not turn into the more painful condition TMJ, it has harmful effects in and of itself and

needs attention. If you think you may have jaw tension, doing the
exercises in this section will allow you to feel your muscles, and
assess your level of tension.

STRESSBUSTER: TMJ AND HEADACHES

Some experts have estimated that 10 percent of headaches
come from TMJ problems. If you have any limitations and
tension in your jaw, you may want to see a dentist who is
trained to diagnose bruxism and TMJ. A simple bite
adjustment may relieve your headaches.

TMJ Dysfunction And Disease

TMJ, or the temporomandibular joint, is a hinge joint formed by your
jaw, or mandible, and the temporal bone of the skull. The mandible
is attached on each side with ligaments. To feel this joint, put your
fingers directly under your earlobes and open your mouth, move
your jaw from side to side to feel the action of the joint. You may
feel tenderness in the muscles that open and close and inside as you
move around. The muscle above the jaw is also often involved and
contributes to headaches associated with TMJ.

The pain from TMJ can be debilitating, and eating and talking
become excruciating. TMJ sufferers often have difficulty concentrating, and their sleep is affected as well. In addition, TMJ usually causes the development of pain and tension in the neck and shoulders.

Currently dentists and doctors don't agree on the cause and
treatment of temporomandibular joint problems and pain. There are
three schools of thought: those who view emotional stress as a
cause; those who see TMJ as a condition related to irregular occlu-
sion (the relationship of the teeth when the jaw is closed) and/or
disc displacement; and practitioners who believe that stress exacerbates an already existing physiological problem, such as a misalignment of the bite, or temporomandibular joint. In the latter view,
stress is cumulative; the problem begins as a dysfunction, and when
stress is added, symptoms appear. For instance, you may start having difficulty chewing or have limited jaw movement; then when
under stress, TMJ pain occurs.

Because symptoms vary, a correct diagnosis is important. So if
you are experiencing jaw or facial pain, you need to find a compe-

tent practitioner; one who emphasizes prevention is a good bet. Though you may be experiencing pain, be sure to start with conservative measures. (Many patients undergo complex surgeries and procedures to raise the teeth, which may be more harmful than the symptoms themselves.) Although stress appears to be a component in many cases, other factors may be contributing to your pain and must be ruled out.

Whether or not stress is the cause or the trigger, it needs to be dealt with in treating the problem. Research has shown that practicing relaxation and doing simple movement exercises will reduce TMJ pain. Your practitioner may tell you that stress plays a role in your problem, but may not be trained to handle it. He or she may refer you to someone or have you learn techniques on your own. Identifying that stress is contributing to your problem and making a commitment to reduce or eliminate as many stressors as you can is the first step. Practicing relaxation is an important part of this. Avoid tranquilizers and muscle relaxers, which do not treat the cause and can cause problems of their own. Eventually you must learn not to put tension in that area.

Watch Muscle Tension In Your Neck And Shoulders

TMJ problems are also often related to head and neck posture. A habitual forward head posture, cervical deviations, and tension in the neck and shoulder muscles can cause imbalances and strain the muscles of the TMJ. Many practitioners, therefore, refer their patients to chiropractors for adjustments that will help balance the muscles and release the tension. TMJ dysfunction causes pain in other areas as well. Your headaches and neck and shoulder pain may be coming from the TMJ joint which needs to be checked. Learning to reduce tension in the entire area is important.

Treating Bruxism And TMJ Pain

1. SEE A DENTIST. Get a diagnosis to determine if you have bruxism or TMJ dysfunction. You may need a bite plate or bite adjustment. Look for a dentist who specializes in or is knowledgeable about TMJ and bruxism.

2. TAKE A STRESS INVENTORY. What are your current stressors? Determine what you can do to eliminate or cope with your stressors.

3. EXPRESS YOUR OPINIONS AND FEELINGS VERBALLY. Often women who clench their teeth are holding back saying what they want, think, and/or feel.

4. RESOLVE YOUR ANGER. Some experts feel women with jaw problems are holding in a lot of anger. Many women feel they shouldn't get angry or don't know how to express their anger. Find out why you are angry, and figure out what you can do about it. If you are angry at someone else, determine your role in it and how you can best handle it. Release pent-up anger by exercising; play racquetball or jog, beat a pillow. Vocalize, make sounds, yell (not at others, though).

5. PRACTICE REGULAR RELAXATION. Practice one or more of the relaxation techniques in this book to help lower your overall stress level.

6. PRACTICE THE RECOMMENDED JAW EXERCISES. These exercises will not only release the muscle tension in your jaw and face, they will help increase your awareness of your tensing or grinding your teeth.

7. PRACTICE THE RECOMMENDED NECK AND SHOULDER EXERCISES. If you have tension in your jaw, chances are you will also have neck tension as well and need to release it. Be sure to read the preceding section on neck and shoulder pain. Do the exercises beginning on page 199 daily. See a chiropractor if you have excess tension in this area.

8. MOVE YOUR JAW OFTEN. During the day move your jaw slowly in all directions. You may want to put a note above your desk or computer to remind you.

9. PRACTICE HEALTHY HABITS. Eat well, get plenty of rest, and exercise.

10. WATCH OPENING TOO WIDE. Watch yawning too wide, biting too hard, chewing gum or tough meat, grinding and clenching.

11. CHECK OUT BIOFEEDBACK. If you aren't able to release the tension in your jaw with relaxation and the exercises below, you may want to look into biofeedback training to help you learn to relax the muscles.

Jaw Exercises

All these exercises are to be done very slowly and gently. They are small movements. If you have a great deal of tension in your jaw, large or fast movement can aggravate the area; slow, small movements should feel good.

1. OPENING AND CLOSING

   ♦ Slowly open your jaw as far as it will go comfortably. Don't force. Slowly close.

   ♦ Open it to a relaxed position (slightly open, lips parted). Feel what this position is like. Close.

   ♦ Now move slowly between these three positions—all the way open, back to slightly open and closed. When you are in the relaxed position, hold it and notice how it feels.

   ♦ Do this four or five times.

   ♦ Rest your jaw.

2. MOVING SIDE TO SIDE

   ♦ Move into the relaxed position—lips slightly apart.

   ♦ Slowly and gently move your jaw right and left.

   ♦ Do this about 6 times or more (right and left equals one time).

3. MOVING IN ALL DIRECTIONS

   ♦ Explore all the movements your jaw can make, moving smoothly and gently. Take your time.

4. MOVING THE TONGUE

   ♦ Move the tongue all around your mouth; reach as far as you can go.

   ♦ Stretch your tongue out of your mouth and move it all around.

5. BREATHING

   ♦ Feel the breath in your mouth and throat. Keep your jaw relaxed.

6. SOUNDING

   ♦ Make sounds. Let the sound reverberate in your mouth.

7. MASSAGING THE JAW

   ♦ With your index and middle finger, massage all around the jawbone using circular motions. If you have a lot of stiffness or pain in this area, massage before and after doing these exercises.

8. USING HEAT OR ICE

   ♦ If you like the feel of heat, use a warm washcloth on the area to relax muscles before and/or after exercise, or use ice on the area.

While doing these exercises, remember to breathe and not to force, as it could further aggravate your discomfort. If you grind your teeth, be sure to do these exercises right before you go to sleep. It will relax your jaw and help inhibit the grinding. Suggest to yourself that you will keep your jaw relaxed throughout the night.

Being busy and concentrating at work may be the time that you're putting tension into the jaw area. During breaks, assess your tension levels, particularly on high-stress days, when meeting deadlines, and so on. These habits can be carried home with you— enabling you to prevent larger problems caused by TMJ or severe bruxism.

OVERCOMING INSOMNIA

Everyone has trouble falling asleep once in a while. As soon as your head hits the pillow and you are no longer physically active, your mind suddenly is, and all the day's events and worries come flooding in. You lie there unable to fall asleep, perhaps ruminating over the events of the day or worrying about the amount of work you have to do, taking an hour or more to fall asleep. Others find themselves waking up in the middle of the night unable to go back to sleep. Difficulty falling asleep, waking early, and sleeping poorly through the night are all forms of insomnia. People who have sleep difficulties are tired throughout the day and then find themselves wide awake at night. Although you can handle a night or two without sleep, chronic sleep disturbance leaves a person fatigued, depressed, and/or anxious. Lack of sleep decreases your ability to cope with daily stressors.

If you have difficulty sleeping, first check if what you are eating or drinking is keeping you awake. Caffeine stays in your system for many hours, so cut down on caffeinated beverages, with no intake after twelve noon. Although you limit your coffee drinking, for example, perhaps you've forgotten about the diet cokes you drink. Chocolate and sugar can keep you awake as well.

Don't make the mistake of trying to use alcohol to help you sleep. It will make you drowsy, but a few hours later it can wake you up and leave you feeling restless. Some experts recommend taking aspirin if you're worried you can't sleep. It is thought to enhance the passage of tryptophan, a chemical needed for sleep, to the brain.

Sleeping pills should be avoided except under extreme circumstances. Barbiturates are very addicting and potentially dangerous. You quickly build a tolerance to them and they become ineffective. They can actually aggravate the problem: they interfere with the body's ability to produce the chemicals necessary for you to fall asleep naturally, so they can prevent the body from falling asleep without them. Since depression can cause insomnia, using barbiturates (central nervous system depressants) makes the problem worse. Also, they leave you feeling hungover the next day and unable to concentrate.

If you're not falling asleep, chances are you're worrying about it; the anxiety you feel creates more tension, thereby preventing you from falling asleep and creating a vicious cycle. Anyone who has taken hours to fall asleep knows of the panic that sets in each evening, wondering if sleep will come. And the worry usually *guarantees* that it will not. Many people also overestimate the length of time it takes them to fall asleep. As they lie there awake, worrying about sleeplessness, it seems like hours, thereby increasing the anxiety.

There are several things you can do to break the insomnia cycle: changing your sleep habits, practicing regular relaxation, stopping your thoughts, and using visualization and affirmations.

We are all creatures of habit, but sleeping habits appear especially sensitive to conditioning. To improve your sleeping you will need to set up regular conditions for falling asleep. Develop a routine that encourages sleep. Take time to unwind from the day. Don't be working at your normal daily pace up until time to go to bed. Relax, do something you enjoy, keeping busy during the evening hours. If you have chores, slow down and do them at an easy pace. Then a half-hour or more before bedtime, start planning for sleep. Don't answer the phone, if possible, and don't start any projects. Make sure you've made a list of all the things you have to do the next day so you won't worry about them before you go to sleep. Take a hot bath. Brush your teeth, put on your sleeping apparel. Have some herbal tea. Read a good book if you enjoy reading. Try to do the same thing each night. When you are ready to fall asleep, get into bed and go through a relaxation sequence.

Relaxation And Visualization:
Setting The Conditions For Restful Sleep

One of the most effective methods of coping with insomnia is relaxation. Insomnia is most often caused by worry and not being able to turn off your thoughts, so any technique to reduce stress will prove beneficial. For best results, practice during the day, which lowers your general stress level and improves your ability to concentrate, blocking out distracting thoughts. Do this again at bedtime. In addition, twenty minutes of deep relaxation has been shown to be as restful as two hours of sleep. So practicing will help your fatigue when you are not getting enough rest.

Visualization is a powerful tool. With your imagination you can create a clear image of falling asleep effortlessly, and focusing on that picture will help give it reality. After you have achieved a relaxed state doing your regular relaxation method, see yourself going through your nightly routine, falling asleep easily, and sleeping through the night. Be sure to see yourself waking up the next morning feeling refreshed and feeling good about an effortless and successful night's sleep.

Use affirmations to support your visualization. Affirmations will "make firm" what you desire. If you are not sleeping well, you probably have many thoughts running through your head about not being able to sleep. Replace these negative ideas with positive ones. Re-read Chapter 4, and see sleep suggestions on page 215. When using visualization and affirmations, you may discover what is really bothering you and keeping you awake, if you don't already know. Be attuned to any problems you have in imagining yourself falling asleep. Write out your affirmations and notice what thoughts come up.

Doing a relaxation sequence before you go to bed will help you relax your muscles and remove your focus from distracting thoughts. You can do your relaxation exercise in your normal spot or in bed. I like to do relaxation in bed so I can just go on to sleep. When I have difficulty turning off my mind, I use a tape with a soothing voice; when I hear it I begin to drift off. When the tape is over I wake up just long enough to take off the headphones and go back to sleep. If you wake up during the night or in the early morning and can't go back to sleep, listen to a tape or do your own relax-

---

STRESSBUSTER: AFFIRMATIONS FOR BETTER SLEEP

◆ Visualize yourself falling asleep and sleeping through the night. See yourself awaken feeling rested in the morning.

◆ Put in the suggestion that you will fall asleep easily and sleep throughout the night. This will help counter negative thoughts about sleeping and set up the conditions for better sleep.

◆ Say to yourself during the day and with your relaxation: "I am setting the conditions for restful sleep," "I fall asleep easily and sleep soundly through the night," or "I am learning to fall asleep easily and sleep soundly through the night." If you wake early: "I sleep eight hours a night (or the amount you wish) and wake refreshed."

---

ation. You may want to put your relaxation on tape. Remember, even if you are still awake after doing a relaxation sequence, you are better off than staying awake worrying. Your body will be resting and you are practicing control and setting the conditions for sleep. Many sleep experts say if you can't fall asleep, get up and do something: read, watch TV. I recommend this only after you have practiced relaxation and are still feeling nervous about not sleeping.

If you find that, after reducing caffeine, changing your sleep habits, and practicing relaxation, you still can't get to sleep, you may want to try a brain-wave synchronizer, an instrument that can enhance your ability to induce sleep and return to sleep after waking during the night. (For information about how to order a brain-wave synchronizer, see "Resources" in the Appendix.)

How Much Is Enough?

Stress experts recommend seven to eight hours of sleep a night to allow your body to regenerate from daily stressors. Your sleep requirements do change with age. As a newborn baby, you slept about eighteen hours a day, but as an elderly woman you may need only six and a half hours or less each night. An adult woman needs at least seven hours to meet the many demands placed on her. Many women, in trying to balance multiple roles, stay up later or get up earlier or sometimes do both—often at their peril. If you are practicing relaxation regularly and exercising, you should be able to get by with seven hours of sleep. Everyone is different, though, and some people need a minimum of eight hours to feel refreshed and alert. Learn what your body needs and try to accommodate it.

Insomnia may be secondary to other conditions such as arthritis, migraines, chronic pain, ulcers, and asthma. If such conditions are affecting you, be sure to address each condition specifically. Some people have disturbances in their biological rhythm; they are awake at night and ready to sleep in the morning. They need to reprogram the body to a more normal rhythm.

If you're not sleeping, you certainly can't handle demands placed on you at work. Being tired magnifies small problems, needlessly adding to your stress level. Therefore, a stress-reducing plan should start with getting a good night's sleep.

COMBATING FATIGUE

"I'm so exhausted!" is an all-too-often complaint made by many women today. It may surprise you to know, however, that for the most part the fatigue we experience is not from being physically tired but from being over-worried and under-exercised. The stress of our daily lives, while often challenging, can also wear us out. We've all felt physical fatigue from tired muscles after a strenuous exercise class or game of tennis or from working all day in the yard. This is usually a pleasant tiredness that is accompanied by a sense of accomplishment. The fatigue that is most widespread today, however, comes from our emotions.

Frequently, it is anxiety and depression that cause fatigue. Feeling dissatisfied with or trapped within a job you hate or which is too taxing, or in a relationship you don't want to be in, can result in sensations of extreme fatigue. Emotions, when not expressed openly, become manifested through physical symptoms. Many women feel overwhelmed by having too many roles and from worrying about the future. They are tired from trying to be all things to

STRESSBUSTER:
FIFTEEN TIPS FOR BETTER SLEEP

1. Reduce caffeine.
2. Establish a sleep routine. Do the same thing every night.
3. Go to sleep and wake up at the same time every day.
4. Use earplugs to block out distractions and help you focus inward. Use them even if there is not a lot of loud distracting noise.
5. Don't take work to bed.
6. If possible, associate your bedroom with sleeping and sex only.
7. Regularly practice relaxation.
8. Practice visualization and positive sleep affirmations.
9. Get regular exercise. It will produce a healthy fatigue so you can fall asleep. Don't exercise before bedtime.
10. Use good time-management techniques. The better organized you are, the less stressed you will be about all you have to do. Use the strategies for time management in Chapter 8.
11. Make lists, so you don't have to worry about remembering what you need to do. Once you've made the list, forget about it, know that you are organized for the next day, and can handle what you have to do. Don't make your list immediately before you go to bed because it may trigger more worry.
12. Don't nap after work.
13. Don't eat a heavy meal before you go to sleep.
14. Drink a glass of milk; it contains tryptophan, which has sleep-inducing properties.
15. Use a brain-wave synchronizer if necessary to induce deep relaxation leading to sleep.

all people. That rundown feeling, then, is usually a sign that something is bothering you. Identifying the cause is the first step toward alleviating this condition.

Poor sleep habits contribute to fatigue. When you are worried, anxious, or depressed, your sleep is often disturbed and can leave you feeling chronically tired. You may have difficulty falling asleep or else sleep fitfully and wake up still feeling exhausted. Worry and sleeplessness can create a cycle of insomnia and fatigue.

Your diet also can contribute to fatigue. A diet high in sugar and fats can make you feel tired and rundown. Sugar gives you a quick energy boost and then a few hours later, when your blood sugar level drops below normal, you are left feeling drowsy, irritable, and nervous. You may be craving sweets because you are under stress, but eating sugar will make you feel even more stressed out. Starting your morning with coffee and a danish will set you up for a day of feeling sluggish and irritable and in need of more coffee and sugar to keep going.

Your diet, therefore, is the first place to start when dealing with fatigue. Each morning, be sure to eat a breakfast low in sugar and fat and high in protein. Studies have shown that eating protein prevents morning fatigue. For example, two eggs or one-half cup of cottage cheese or farmer's cheese, with whole-grain bread or rice cakes, or eight ounces of low-fat or soy milk with a bowl of whole-grain cereal (shredded wheat, grapenuts, oatmeal) will give you the boost you need. Have a piece of fruit at mid-morning, and continue eating healthfully throughout the day. One of the problems about being under stress and feeling fatigued is that you usually crave sweets and fats, which perpetuate the problem. Watch your snacks. See Chapter 6 on nutrition for more information.

You may think you're just too tired to exercise, but paradoxically exercise will give you more energy rather than tire you. Regular exercise helps fight the effects of the fight-or-flight response, and at night you will sleep sounder because you have released tension and worked your body in a healthful manner. Even when you're feeling tired, make time to exercise even if it is just some stretching or a short walk. Exercise also works as a tranquilizer and can increase your feeling of well-being. This is discussed further in Chapter 5.

If constant worry or negative thinking is fatiguing you, relaxation will help. Relaxation helps repair the effects of stress. Meditation can help you learn to clear your mind and feel calmer and peaceful. Breathing and progressive relaxation should prove beneficial in releasing muscle tension. Also, in a relaxed state with your conscious mind quieted, you may want to look within to determine what is troubling you.

Some women may just be tired from doing too many things and having too many roles. If this is the case in your life, you will benefit from good time-management skills, as well as some assertiveness skills. Many women feel they just can't say "no" and end up being overextended. Although you may get satisfaction from doing for others, it's a habit that may be draining, especially if you say "yes" when you want to say "no." Conversely, sometimes we become fatigued when there is nothing to look forward to, with no plans or goals to work toward. Having a clear sense of purpose is important for optimum health. Re-read Chapters 7 and 8 for better coping skills.

If your fatigue does not improve after addressing the underlying causes, using exercise, a nutritious diet, and stress-reduction methods, you may want to consider professional help, with a psychologist, clinical social worker, marriage counselor, or physician.

Eight Ways To Combat Fatigue

1. IMPROVE YOUR DIET. Eat a diet high in complex carbohydrates and low in sugar and caffeine. Every morning eat a breakfast that is low in sugar and high in protein. Watch your snacks; eat fresh fruit, raw vegetables, nuts, and seeds.

2. DO REGULAR AEROBIC EXERCISE. Exercise with your family, take a class, join a gym.

3. GET A GOOD NIGHT'S SLEEP.

4. PRACTICE RELAXATION TECHNIQUES. Use breathing exercises, progressive relaxation techniques, and meditation.

5. DETERMINE WHAT'S WORRYING YOU. In a meditative state, look inside yourself and find out what is troubling you and take steps to cope with it. Consult a professional, such as a therapist, if you're not sure how to handle it or are unable to figure out things on your own.

6. PRACTICE GOOD TIME MANAGEMENT. This will help you feel less overwhelmed and more in control. Be realistic about what you can handle. Make sure you schedule time for leisure activities.

7. LEARN TO SAY "No." Determine if you need help with assertiveness and learning to say "no."

8. SET GOALS. Have a purpose in life and goals toward which to work.

As you gradually incorporate the elements listed above into your lifestyle, you should experience more energy and enthusiasm—at least until the next uncontrollable stress-causing circumstance comes along. But when that happens, you'll be equipped to handle it—and subsequent fatigue will be a passing, short-lived side effect.

FOOD FOR THOUGHT

According to a 1986 study, people who exercise three or more days a week, drink little alcohol, and neither smoke nor watch television were the least likely to report headaches or back and muscle pain.

RELIEVING BACKACHES

Back pain is the stress disorder of our time. Daily, the back muscles tense against physical and emotional stressors. Unconsciously we brace ourselves against the world; by holding tight we feel in control. We contract our muscles to gear up, get moving, meet a deadline, or take action, all the while putting excess tension into the body and not releasing it. We drink coffee or soda to help this process along. If your back muscles are weak, overly tight, and inflexible, you won't be able to withstand these daily pressures.

Although women usually do less heavy lifting in their jobs, they are as susceptible to back problems as men. Women tend to sit for long periods of time in poor positions. Because of their hectic schedules they may not have time to exercise and keep their back and stomach muscles strong. Stress, poor posture, being overweight, constantly carrying heavy shoulderbags and briefcases, and wearing high heels all contribute to back strain and injury.

Chances are if you've ever suffered from back pain you know that sense of helplessness when suddenly you become confined to a bed or couch. For a while, every move is fraught with pain and agony. Normal daily routines of dressing, sitting in a chair, or washing dishes can be torture. Back pain often comes on "out of the blue," causes intense pain for a few days, and then goes away.

Unfortunately, after one attack, a person is often susceptible to future back strain or chronic backache. Therefore, ongoing attention and preventive measures are essential.

Learning Good Body Mechanics

Using your body correctly is the first step to preventing and eliminating back pain. Your spine is a uniquely designed structure that supports and transfers weight, protects your nerves, and provides shock absorption. When it meets no interference, this structure functions very efficiently. Unfortunately, all too often improper posture, poor body mechanics, overuse, positions held for too long—usually on the job—and/or sitting incorrectly cause awkward and inefficient movement, strain, and even injury.

When the spine conforms to unhealthy sitting and work habits, its function is compromised. Keeping the spine in unhealthy positions puts excess pressure on the discs, jams vertebrae together, and irritates nerves, causing aches and pains. Holding the spine out of balance places strain on the muscles, causing certain muscles to stay tense while others become underused and flabby, creating imbalances. The muscles are then unable to maintain proper alignment. For more information on body use and correct sitting habits, review Chapters 5 and 8.

Stress And Back Pain

In addition to such physical, or mechanical, stressors as improper posture, body mechanics, and sitting habits, emotional tension is a major contributor to back pain. Many experts believe the predominant cause of back pain is stress and worry. Canadian biofeedback expert Dr. John Basmajian has pointed out: "Back pain is just a tension headache that has slipped down in the back." Megan, who recently started her own business, suddenly found her back in painful spasms. Because of her previous body-awareness training, however, she knew that the pain in her back was a response to her taking on a great deal of financial responsibility. Since the business investment was a positive step for her, Megan was not overly concerned about her back, but made sure she paid extra attention to it, practicing relaxation, Kinetic Awareness, and back-care exercises.

Women who are unable to speak up for themselves and feel overburdened by work and home responsibilities often find themselves suffering from back pain. Some medical researchers have found that there are actually "backache personalities," people who are inclined to be hard-working but lacking in self-confidence. These individuals tend to repress anger and avoid conflicts, traits shared by many headache and ulcer sufferers.

Handling The Problem

The key to eliminating back pain is recognizing the role tension plays, initiating stress reduction methods, and keeping the back strong and flexible with regular exercise.

The traditional method of dealing with back pain has been to see the problem only in terms of muscular weakness. When back and stomach muscles are strong, they can support the back in daily activity; when the muscles are weak, they cannot give adequate support. Doctors and physical therapists, therefore, have sought to strengthen weak abdominal and back muscles with active exercise. Being out of shape contributes to back strain, and staying physically fit is a vital component of proper back care. To maintain a strong back, however, you must have flexible muscles, which are elastic and resilient, resist strain and injury, increase range of motion, improve comfort, and help guard against the effects of aging. The exercises in this section include those that aid strengthening and flexibility.

Try this:

1. Stand sideways in front of a mirror. Look at your posture, particularly the curve of your back. Now tighten your back muscles by shortening the muscles in the small of your back, bringing the buttocks closer to the upper back.

2. Notice what happens to your stomach muscles. If you have shortened your back muscles, your stomach will spill forward and the arch in your back will increase. It will look like you have a bigger stomach than you do and place strain on your lower back.

3. Now release, bend your knees slightly, let your pelvis relax.

If your back muscles are tight and you do stomach-strengthening sit-ups—which can sometimes aggravate an acute back problem—your abdomen will get firm, but if you do not release the muscles in your back as well, you will also increase the tightness and perpetuate the imbalance. When you have an exaggerated curve in your lower back, the transfer of weight to your lower body is compromised and all·the weight of your upper body presses on the small of the back, creating strain. If, conversely, there is no curve in the back, problems can result; gaining flexibility will keep the area mobile and better able to handle pressure.

The Pelvic Tilt

The mainstay of back care has been an exercise called the pelvic tilt. Anyone who has ever sought help for back pain has probably been taught this exercise. The tilt is designed to stretch out the curve in your back to reduce strain. Unfortunately, most people are taught to do this action by contracting all the muscles and holding the position.

Try this:

1. Curl your pelvis under, tightening the muscles in your stomach, buttocks, and back. Hold it.

2. Take a deep breath.

3. Notice how your body feels in this position. Can you breathe fully? Does this feel like a comfortable position? Do you feel your back would benefit from it?

Your answers to the above questions were probably "no." The tilt does reduce the curve and stretch out the back, but at a great price. I'll describe a similar but more beneficial action, the pelvic roll, which will be healthful for your back and will reduce back pain.

The goal of the pelvic roll is the same as that of the pelvic tilt, but you will do it very differently. You will be relaxing the buttocks and thighs and engaging the deep muscles of the abdomen that support the back. To do this, you imagine you are moving the sacrum (shield-shaped back bone we often refer to as the tailbone) and relaxing the superficial stomach muscles. Instead of tightening and holding a tense position, you will slowly roll into and out of the position. You can do this sitting, standing, or lying down.

Most people who experience back pain feel better when they lie down and bend their knees or bring the knees to the chest. Not all people feel better in this position, however. Some feel relief when lying on their stomach. The position you find comfortable is related to how you hurt your back. The position in which you hurt your back will not feel good, the opposite will. For example, if your back was in an arched position when you hurt it, rounding it will feel better.

Test which position is best for you. You want to put your back into positions that make it feel better. Lie on the floor and bend your knees. Does that feel better? Pull your knees to your chest; does it improve your condition? Lie on your stomach. How does that feel?

The pelvic tilt is designed to take the curve out of your back. Physical therapists sometimes tell people to hold the tilt in daily activities. However, this adds tension to your body and causes problems of its own. Some people's backs have little or no curve, or have just enough. They do not need to curl under more. Instead, they may need more arch. In fact, no position that is held is good for the back. You need to move the back in all directions, curling and arching. If you have pain in one direction, don't move in that way until you are ready.

Practicing The Pelvic Roll

To do a correct pelvic roll, you must engage the deep muscles of the abdomen. Keep your focus on your back, though, rather than stomach to do this. Most of us move the pelvis around with our thighs, or upper back. Learning to isolate and engage these deep muscles will take some practice and patience. You will be asked to do something you probably haven't done before. So stick with it.

EXPLORING THE MUSCLES THAT MOVE THE SACRUM.

1. Lie with your legs extended. Feel your sacrum (and coccyx— the tip of the tail bone). Get a sense of what it feels like. It is more mobile than you imagine.

2. Now try to move just the sacrum. Keep your thighs and upper back still. It will be very small movement. Go in any direction.

Notice which muscles want to get involved when you try to move. If you find you are unable to move separately, keep trying; your concentration on the area is beneficial. You may want to start by imagining the area moving. Visualize that part of your back slowly moving, seeing just the bones in the sacrum moving, one by one.

3. After attempting to move your sacrum while lying on your back, try it on your stomach, then on your side (knees slightly bent) and on your hands and knees.

THE CURL.

1. Bend your knees, which will enable you to move more easily.

2. Feeling the tip of your tailbone, begin to curl it upward very slowly, moving smoothly piece by piece, until the small of the back is on the floor. Don't force. Focus on using only the muscles around the bone.

3. Now release the curl slowly segment by segment. It helps to think about moving the bones rather than the muscles. Do not tighten the thighs. To find out if you are using your superficial stomach muscles, move your tailbone by pulling in your stomach.

4. If you have difficulty feeling the roll, slowly bring one knee to your chest and feel how the back rolls on the floor. This is the action, only you initiate it by using your deep muscles.

THE ARCH. This move is important because it is essential to always move in all directions, and the arch is the opposite of the curl.

1. Lying down with the knees bent, start at the tip of the tailbone (the coccyx), and move downward toward the floor. Move each section slowly. As you move downward the back will come off the floor and when you finish the small of the back will not be touching the floor. Release the position, starting again, at the tailbone, moving piece by piece, controlling the movement. Go back to "center" (the position your back is in when you stop moving).

2. Repeat the curling and arching.

Though it is important to move in both directions, some people need more curls than arches. If arching hurts, wait until your back is better before practicing.

Easy Back Care Exercises

These exercises are designed to help prevent back pain and relieve minor backache. When practiced regularly they will increase and maintain flexibility and help you to develop strength. They are to be done slowly and gently, paying attention to how your body feels. If you have pain from tension and stiffness, work through the exercises. If an exercise intensifies your pain do it smaller, slower, fewer times, or not at all. When you are in acute pain or have nerve pain, you may be better off not exercising or doing only a few exercises. Choose exercises that make you feel good. The pelvic roll should feel good when you are in pain, but twisting may aggravate your back, so stick to the pelvic rolls, knee folds, and exercises that relax the muscles in your back and neck. Be sure to practice relaxation techniques as your back heals.

There are no repetitions given for these exercises. You should work at your own pace, gradually increasing the number of times you do an exercise. The time you have to exercise will also be a factor. If you only have a short while in the morning, be sure to do each exercise at least once; if you have more time, increase repetitions. The exercises are sequenced to warm up and move through each part of your body and serve as an excellent warm-up to more vigorous exercise or aerobics. *Be sure to pay attention to your breathing during these exercises.*

BODY SCANNING.   Begin these exercises lying down, legs extended.

   ◆ Scan your body. Notice where you feel any tightness, if both sides feel the same, and how much curve is in the small of your back, what your breathing is like, and so on.

THE PELVIC ROLL.   This reduces tension, lengthens the back, and strengthens back muscles.

   ◆ Start with your knees bent, line your feet up with your hips. Relax the thighs.

♦ Do several curls.

♦ Do a few arches, followed by more curls.

KNEES TO CHEST. This exercise stretches out the lower back and increases hip flexibility. Do not use your hands to grab hold of your knee. Use your conscious awareness to focus on the release. It will be more lasting.

♦ Slowly bring one knee toward your chest. Feel your pelvis roll. Think of lengthening your spine. Release, or "soften" in the hip socket.

♦ Alternate knees.

HIP CIRCLES. This loosens up tight hip joints that hold the back rigid.

♦ Start with the knees bent. Take hold of your knees with each hand, right hand on right knee, left on left knee. Leave them there.

♦ Pull knees toward chest.

♦ Then gently open legs outward, away from each other, making a circle. Go in both directions.

    a. Leg extension: With knees at chest, extend one leg. Stretch flex foot, and let it release, gently bouncing. Alternate legs. This is a gentle stretch; do not force it.

THE BRIDGE. This exercise lengthens out and mobilizes the spine, strengthens your legs, buttocks, and abdomen, and stretches the front of the body and hips.

♦ Start with knees bent, feet pointed forward, at hip's width.

♦ Begin by doing a full pelvic curl. Instead of rolling down, lift hips off floor when the small of the back is on the floor. You will need to tighten the buttocks and thighs to do this action.

♦ Gently roll the vertebrae off the floor, keeping the pelvis moving upward. Don't let the back arch as you roll up. Keep the pelvis lifted.

♦ Go up into the lumbar (low back) vertebrae and then roll down, vertebra by vertebra.

♦ Now go further. "Peel" the vertebra off the floor like a chain. Go to the top of the spine if comfortable. Keep your hips lifted as you roll down, controlling the coming down.

KNEE DROP. This is an excellent overall stretch for the back and neck and shoulders.

♦ Start with knees bent and arms extended, shoulder height.

♦ Begin by rolling your head from side to side, moving slowly and gently. Repeat several times. Keep your head moving while doing the rest of the exercise.

♦ Extend your right arm, putting tension into your shoulder and extending it outward to your hand. Release the tension, starting at the hand, then moving up toward the shoulder. Repeat with left arm. Coordinate the rolling of your head and the reaching of your arm. Move head and arm several times right and left.

♦ Drop your knees together (in the same direction), moving them in the opposite direction of your head and arm.

♦ Twist from side to side gently, while slowly moving the head, arm, and knees.

HEAD CIRCLES. This is used to warm up the neck in preparation for the curl ups, which can place some strain on your neck.

♦ Gently circle your neck, keeping your head on the floor, moving head clockwise then counterclockwise.

♦ Curl head slightly forward and then stretch upward.

ABDOMINAL CURLS. Abdominal curls strengthen the muscles that support your back. There are many ways to do sit ups. Because most people who have chronic back pain also have neck and shoulder pain, I have presented a few variations. In doing any of these be aware of your neck and try not to tighten it when you move, tuck under too much, or lead with your chin. Choose a) or b) or c) or combine b) with c).

a. Knees bent, arms behind head (do not push head with hands; think of them as decoration). Lift upper back off floor slightly (shoulder blades should be off floor) and then release back down. The action should happen in the stomach muscles. Lengthen spine and relax throat and neck as much as possible.

◆ Move forward between knees.

◆ Twist and move toward knee; alternate sides.

◆ Extend legs in air, knees bent to 45 degrees; repeat action.

◆ Legs extended: This exercise can be done with legs extended in front of you if you have no back pain.

b. This variation is easier on the body for some and works the same.

◆ With knees bent, slightly lift head off floor and reach with your hands toward your knees, letting your arms pull you up. Reach both forward and toward each knee.

c. This exercise works the stomach muscles, lengthening them instead of bunching the muscles, but does not strain the neck as much.

◆ Using your arms and hands to help you, roll up to sitting. Push off with the elbows (arms at side), then your hands, as you come up to sitting. Come up evenly on both sides. Then slowly roll down, controlling the going down, feeling the stomach muscles working. It is in the rolling down that the strengthening happens. Halfway down, hold the position for an isometric contraction. You can also work your arms at the same time, crossing them in front of you as you count.

SITTING UP.

◆ Come up to sitting using the above exercise. Sit crosslegged.

◆ Circle the head in both directions.

◆ Use this time to work on releasing tension in the upper body.

◆ You may want to do the neck and shoulder sequence beginning on page 202 to increase mobility in your upper body.

FORWARD CURL. This is an important low back stretch and helps you gain control of your spine by moving each vertebra separately, greatly increasing flexibility and control.

◆ Start kneeling, sitting on your feet. If you have knee problems do this exercise from a crosslegged (sitting) position.

◆ Curl forward, starting with the top of the head, move forward vertebra by vertebra. Arms will go behind you. Move until you are folded over. Hold this position and breathe into your back, feeling the stretch. Soften in the hip sockets. Uncurl, beginning in the tailbone, and moving up the spine, vertebra by vertebra.

THE CAT. This is an excellent exercise for your back. It increases flexibility as well as control. Use your spine to move you. Think of moving the bones, not the muscles.

♦ Start on your hands and knees.

♦ Begin your movement in the tailbone at the very tip of your spine. Curl your pelvis under as you did with the pelvic roll. Continue curling into the lumbar spine.

♦ Next move into the thoracic vertebrae (upper body) and finally round your neck; your head is the last to move. You will be stretched in a complete curve, like a cat stretches.

♦ To reverse the position, begin again in the tailbone. Lift the tailbone upward, releasing into an arch. Slowly move into the lumbar spine creating a curve like a swayback horse. Move into the upper back and finally the neck which extends upward.

NOTE: Always start in the tailbone. The head is the last to move. Don't let your stomach muscles do all the movement; instead engage the back muscles. Keep the arms straight.

♦ Variation. Move side to side. Begin with back straight (on hands and knees). Move your head and hips in the same direction, shortening one side and lengthening the other, making a "C," moving side to side.

HIP FLEXOR STRETCH. This is a very important exercise for a healthy back.

♦ Kneel. Bring the right foot forward so the knee is bent in front of you, foot on floor. You will be kneeling on left leg with right leg bent in front.

♦ Put your hands on the floor in front of you.

♦ Extend the left leg back until you feel a stretch in the front of your hip and thigh.

♦ Change legs by bringing the right leg back to center and left leg forward.

THE ARCH. As I've said, it's important to move in all directions. This exercise increases flexibility and strength. It is especially important to move in this direction since so many of our daily movements are rounded over. If you are in acute pain you may not want to do this one until you are better, however.

◆ Start by lying on your stomach, arms bent, hands palm down and by your face.

◆ Start by pressing into your hands. As you begin to lift the arms slightly, lift the upper back in one piece, keeping the head in line with the back.

◆ Be sure not to overarch the low back.

◆ Keep the muscles in the lower back relaxed. Do not tense. Lower the spine. Repeat several times.

◆ As your back improves, increase the arch. Always make a lengthened movement rather than a shortened one.

HAMSTRING/LEG STRETCHES. Tight hamstrings pull the back out of alignment. Therefore, any back regimen must include some release exercises for this part of your body. Start with:

◆ Ankle Circles: Start with one knee bent, one leg in the air. Circle ankle clockwise and counterclockwise. Change legs or stay on same leg and continue on.

◆ Knee Release: Start with one leg in air, bend knee forward about two inches, without dropping the foot. Extend and stretch the hamstring, feeling the pull. Repeat several times (build up to as many as you can do). Hold the leg straight, flex the foot, then point it. Repeat several times. Lower the leg.

◆ Active Stretch: 1) bend knee in toward chest, 2) extend up in air, 3) flex foot, 4) extend leg out straight with foot flexed and lower to ground, keeping the back relaxed and close to the floor, 5) point toe and bend knee to chest. Repeat sequence. Change legs.

◆ Straight Leg Raises: Lift leg up and down. Keep other leg bent. Release from the back of the leg. Change legs.

◆ End with knees to chest.

NOTE: As your strength increases, to develop stamina, stay on one leg for more or all of the exercises. Then change.

HIP RELEASE. Tight hip muscles inhibit sitting and pull on the back. This exercise helps release them. Do as slowly as possible for maximum release.

+ Lie with knees bent. Slowly open the right knee outward to floor, then slowly return. Consciously release muscles in hip. This may feel jerky if you go slowly, but that is just tension and should improve the more you do this exercise.

+ Repeat several times and change legs.

FINAL TWIST.

+ Lie with legs extended, arms at side, shoulder height. Bring your right knee toward your chest, then twist it across your body, gently stretching your back. Keep your arms extended, shoulder on floor if possible.

+ Bring leg back by rolling the hip. Keeping the knee bent, open outward to the floor, making a triangle (with the other leg forming the base). Hold in that position. Extend your leg.

+ Repeat other side.

BODY SCAN.

+ With legs extended notice how your body feels. Take a few deep breaths.

Four Tips For Proper Back Care

1. SITTING. Sitting is perhaps the worst position for your back. (See Chapters 5 and 9 for proper sitting tips.)

2. DRIVING. Driving long distances can aggravate your back. Stop frequently and walk around. You may be in a rush to reach your destination, but you'll be better off—and enjoy yourself without a backache once you get there—if you take breaks. Use a pillow at the small of your back for support. Adjust the seats and keep your back as vertical as possible.

3. LIFTING. We all know we should lift objects properly and how to do it, but most people just lift something without thinking about it. When lifting, don't bend from the waist, bend the knees, keep the

STRESSBUSTER: ON THE JOB BACK CARE

The following variations of the exercises beginning on page 226 can be done on the job. Do them daily if you have had any type of back strain or discomfort. You can do them as a series on a break or periodically throughout the day.

1. The Pelvic Curl. While seated you can do this action to release tension and keep your back flexible. Move forward and backward (like you did lying down). Focus on moving from the back; don't collapse in the upper body.

2. Spine Roll. Sit forward in your chair. Starting with your head, curl forward vertebra by vertebra. Go as far as you can comfortably. Come up slowly. Repeat process arching backward as far as you can go, starting in the low back.

3. The Twist. Sitting forward, rotate your torso, leading with your ribs, then shoulders; let head follow. Hold twist, take a few deep breaths. Come back to center. Repeat other side.

4. Knee Lift. Standing feet apart hip width and holding on to your chair for support, slowly lift your right knee upward as far as it can go. Let the tailbone drop down, releasing and lengthening in the back. Keep weight as evenly on both legs as possible. Soften in the hip joints. Switch to the other knee.

5. The Cat. Stand with both hands on the back of your chair or on the desk. Curl your spine slowly and then release in an arch.

6. Hip Flexor Stretch. You want to stretch the front of your pelvis, one side at a time. To do this, pull out a bottom drawer of your desk just a little. Put your right foot on the front of the drawer. Lean forward pressing into your left hip. Feel the stretch. Change legs. You can also do the stretch by stepping forward with your right leg, bending it, and leaning into and stretching your left hip.

7. Neck and Shoulder Sequence. Do the exercises beginning on page 202. Keeping your neck and shoulders relaxed will take strain off your lower back.

8. Move Around Often. Staying in one position is hard on your back. Find excuses to move.

back straight. Be careful lifting items over your head; this places strain on the spine, even when you think it isn't a lot of weight. Don't reach for something away from your body. Keep it close.

4. SLEEPING. A good mattress is the key to a good night's sleep and to a healthy back. A firm but giving mattress that supports your body's curves is a must. Avoid sleeping on your stomach. Instead, lie on your side with your knees slightly bent. You need to move and stretch while you are sleeping. If you sleep with another person, consider a queen-size bed so you have plenty of room to turn.

Treatment For Back Pain

Often acute back pain goes away on its own after two weeks. For many people, however, backaches become an ongoing problem. The following are suggestions for preventing and treating back pain.

1. ICE (short-term treatment for acute pain). Ice is the preferred treatment for injuries these days. Heat causes swelling, and if pain is in the joint, it can aggravate the condition. Some people feel better using heat on an area, however, because it is soothing and helps muscles relax. If you prefer heat, use moist heat, either hot, wet towels or packs or a moist heating pad. Use no longer than twenty minutes. Some people like to take a hot bath and relax the muscles and then use an ice pack on the affected area. For general muscle stiffness, try a hot bath or shower.

2. GENTLE STRETCHING. Slow easy movements help lengthen a muscle, increase circulation, and increase your awareness of tension in the area.

3. RELAXATION TECHNIQUES. Practicing relaxation helps reduce the body's response to stress and breaks the stress cycle. Breathing, progressive relaxation, and visualization are especially beneficial for back pain.

4. MASSAGE. Deep tissue massage uses various strokes, rubbing, pulling, and kneading, to release tight, knotted muscles. The massage improves circulation and helps remove lactic acid in the muscles. It helps initiate overall relaxation. Although it is important to learn to release tension through relaxation techniques and therapeutic exercise, having a massage can be very beneficial in helping with this process. Many times a muscle or muscle groups are so tight and have been that way for so long that it requires a professional massage to help release the tension. It also feels great!

5. MANIPULATION. Back manipulation is the most popular treatment for backaches. Manipulation restores mobility to stiff vertebrae and improves function in the muscles and nerves. When the spine is out of balance, pain occurs. Tight muscles can pull bones out of place, and conversely bones out of place cause the muscles to spasm. A chiropractor or osteopath will adjust your spine, realigning the bones to relieve pressure on muscles and nerves. A chiropractor trained in applied kinesiology will balance bones, muscles, and tissues, using manipulation and deep release work. Chiropractic work should be combined with exercise to improve poor muscle patterns and maintain flexibility or your body may go back out of balance. Most pain clinics and back treatment centers use some type of manipulation for their patients.

6. ACUPUNCTURE. Acupuncture is a Chinese method of healing that involves inserting needles into meridians, specific points on the skin that are channels of magnetic energy. Inserting needles into these points has been shown to be helpful in treating specific disorders, including low back pain. Acupuncture works on balancing the energy flow. A Chinese dictum says, "There is no pain if there is free flow; if there is pain, there is no free flow." Recently the existence of meridians have been confirmed by electromagnetic research.

7. BODY AWARENESS TECHNIQUES. These techniques teach individuals to recognize and release poor muscular patterns and gain a better understanding of how to use their bodies. Techniques especially beneficial for back-pain sufferers are Alexander Technique and Kinetic Awareness.

FOOD FOR THOUGHT

Before you consider back surgery, check all your options. twenty to forty percent of back surgeries fail. Pain centers are full of individuals with histories of failed back operations. Surgery can make a condition worse. If you have ongoing chronic back pain, look into a comprehensive pain center. A comprehensive approach will include physical therapy, biofeedback, relaxation, manipulations, injections, body mechanics, and supportive psychotherapy.

There is probably no part of the body that can cause as much pain as the back. Its connection to stress makes it very vulnerable during difficult times. Doing these exercises can help strengthen the back, preventing it from falling victim to life's wear and tear.

As you now see, stress can make its presence known through all kinds of aches and pains. Chances are you're already experiencing some of the problems included in this chapter. These exercises can help relieve the pain. Practiced on a regular basis, and included in your overall stress-reduction plan, they can help decrease their reoccurrence.

Chapter Eleven

MASTERING THE WORK-HOME BALANCE

By now you may have read through most of this book and have, I hope, found the arguments for stress reduction very persuasive. You probably see that you need to do something to relieve your stress, but you may be wondering how you're supposed to fit even more activities into your already busy schedule. Isn't this why you're stressed—you have too much to do and too little time?

Now you'll find how the ideas in this book can work in your life. We'll look at many real-life examples of women who have discovered positive ways of coping with stress. Using these examples as guidelines, I have put together suggestions on how to make the techniques I've suggested work for you.

In this section, you'll find a discussion about each of the four major categories of working women: single, married, married mother, and single mother. What I talk about are specific problems and stressors frequently resulting from that particular lifestyle. To avoid repetition, however, each section provides specific information that is applicable to other situations as well. Therefore, if you are in an intimate relationship; single, or married with children, you will want to read about, "The Two-Career Household." Similarly, my discussion of married mothers addresses issues relevant to single mothers as well. Although there are differences, women do share many things in common. The same techniques, of course, can work in a variety of circumstances. The key lies in learning how to apply the solutions to your particular situation.

IF YOU'RE SINGLE...

Melanie, 43, an office manager for an interior design firm, is an attractive woman who looks much younger than her age. Embodying the true picture of health, she knows how to make her life work for her, using most of the stress-reduction techniques discussed in this book. Melanie was eating healthfully long before many of us jumped on the bandwagon. She manages her schedule efficiently and excels at setting priorities, recognizing that she needs a balance of work, social activities, exercise, and creative endeavors such as writing. Although Melanie supports herself as an office manager, she is a writer/performer and makes time to pursue this interest. Friendships have always been important to her, and she has an active social life, going to movies, meeting friends for dinner, attending art openings and performances, as well as visiting acquaintances in other parts of the country. Melanie never schedules appointments or dinner engagements, however, until after the end of her exercise class, which she takes twice a week. Acknowledging the importance of exercise, she rides her bicycle most places she goes. She also does stretching exercises to keep her back strong and flexible as she has had several injuries, and knows that stress can aggravate them. When Melanie finds herself having problems or encountering difficulties, she uses meditation to help her find the answers. When you meet Melanie, you see a vibrant woman, who exudes both physical and mental health.

Is Melanie too good to be true? No, like everyone else, she sometimes pushes too hard and gets overextended, but she knows when to pull back. She has the tools she needs to take care of herself, in addition to the good health to support her when she does too much. When her back starts aching, for example, she uses Kinetic Awareness techniques, such as ball work, and doubles up on her exercises. When she has scheduled too many activities, she feels comfortable (and guilt free) telling her friends "no."

Because Melanie is single, she has more control over her time and her responsibilities than, say, a married woman or working mother. With her 9-to-5 job, she can schedule time with friends or exercise classes. She doesn't have to plan around another person's schedule or be there for a child. While being single offers many opportunities to practice healthful habits, it brings with it its own problems and stressors, though. Remember Patricia and Linda from Chapter 9? Both were single working women suffering from unrelieved job stress; yet each had entirely different job stressors. Here, we will look at some of the scenarios single women face and solutions that can help.

How To Avoid Stress And Depression When A Job Is Only A Job

One of the stresses Melanie deals with is that her job is only that, a job, and not a career. She doesn't really enjoy being an office manager and often feels she's just babysitting the all-male staff. For the past two years, she has made her writing one of her priorities (cutting back some hours at work) and hopes someday to support herself writing and performing. Working on what she cares about keeps her from feeling trapped and angry, unlike Sally who hates her job and sees no way out.

Sally, 23, works as the receptionist at a magazine. She keeps hoping that she can move up into another position on the magazine staff, such as assistant to the fashion editor. After all, she took fashion and business courses at the community college she attended. Unfortunately, though, no one seems to think she is qualified for anything other than answering phones all day. This is her first job after finishing school, though, and with the economy in tatters she feels lucky to have a job. Her friends who work in offices remind her that their receptionists are being replaced by automated phone services. As much as she hates her job, she's terrified of losing it. And she feels guilty for disliking it and her boredom.

Fatigued from the monotony at work, Sally is restless sitting in one position all day in an uncomfortable chair. She feels unappreciated and is afraid that she's going nowhere. When she gets home in the evening, she's so drained that all she does is watch TV and eat potato chips, which has added to her weight problems. Her room-mate usually goes out with her boyfriend, or the two of them watch TV with Sally, drinking beer and smoking cigarettes. Sally never par-ticularly liked to drink, but finds herself joining in, and lately it's become a way to forget about how bad she's feeling. She looked into health clubs and gyms, but can't afford the steep membership fees. She feels stuck and can't see any way to get unstuck.

Sally may seem a lot like Patricia, from Chapter 9. Both are sin-gle women working in low-paying jobs for which they're overquali-fied and that offer few challenges and little advancement—like many jobs women hold. You may be able to identify with these women. Often single women struggle to cover rent, transportation, and cloth-ing costs with few dollars left over for vacations, entertainment, or improvements in their lifestyle. Feeling deprived, they often have lit-tle energy to motivate them to be creative with their time, resulting in ruts like the one Sally is in. Boredom destroys motivation, and unfortunately feelings of being trapped usually lead to sluggishness, inertia, and eventually depression.

After reading through this book, you may already have some ideas for Sally and, if you're like her in any way, for yourself. Sally's big concern is her job. She might volunteer to help out in the fash-ion department in some way or ask if she could take on additional duties. This will let the editors know her interest in moving up and give them a chance to see what she can contribute. To combat fatigue during the day, she needs to stand up and stretch when there are lulls. On her lunch hour she should spend some time outside get-ting fresh air and stretching. She also needs to lobby for a better chair!

Until her job situation improves, she should get involved in out-side activities that are intellectually stimulating. Most towns and cities have adult-education classes that are usually reasonably priced. She could get interested in an environmental or political group or vol-unteer her time. Many of us don't know where to begin when vol-unteering, but there are so many organizations that welcome volun-teers. For example, you could tutor people from other countries if you speak a foreign language, help with youth groups, devote time to an environmental group, or walk dogs at the animal shelter.

One of the best stress reducers is exercise, especially if you're fatigued from boredom. If you, like Sally, can't afford a gym, you might do as Abby did. After two years of working and going to graduate school full time, Abby, 35, found herself more than twenty pounds overweight, her cholesterol level rising, and her doctor concerned about her heart and cardiovascular fitness. Since her funds were depleted from school, she decided to begin exercising on her own until she could afford to join a health club. Instead of taking the bus, she walks to and from work, about two-and-a-half miles a day. Sally could, in addition, get together with several friends for an exercise group, take a stroll after work, or rent or purchase a work-out video instead of watching a constant stream of TV shows every night.

In the area of nutrition, Sally would do better to restrain herself from purchasing junk food and sweets, and instead have plenty of carrot and celery sticks and raw sunflower seeds around to munch on. Sparkling juices would be a healthy alternative to beer and soda. Being depressed can create a craving for sweets, a difficult habit to break. That's why exercise is so important; it helps alleviate depression, and working out makes you feel better about yourself, and less likely to crave junk. In addition, Sally might be happier if she makes plans with friends for those nights when her roommate's boyfriend comes over to watch TV. At home alone would be the ideal time to practice relaxation exercises.

Will it be easy for Sally, or anyone else, to implement these suggestions? No. If you've gone beyond being down occasionally to having pervasive feelings of helplessness and lack of control, it is very difficult to motivate yourself. Being fatigued from work, you don't feel like going out, so you stay home and eat junk food—which leaves you feeling sluggish the next day so after work you stay in and watch TV and eat more junk food. Soon you're depressed, not only from the food and lack of activity but because you never do anything and don't have the energy to change. I'm not condoning the behavior, but I am saying that it is a vicious cycle, which takes a strong effort to break. You will need to be motivated to change and, hopefully, if you are in this situation, reading this book will help you find the incentive.

How To Combat Stress When Work Is All There Is

Some of you may be thinking, Right now I'd give anything to be bored with my job and go home at 5:00 with nothing to worry about! You represent the other side of the coin. Like Cindy, the TV production assistant (from Chapter 9), you put in long hours working your way up the professional ladder. Such is the case for Debbie, an ad salesperson for a trade magazine. She works in a large company, and as the only woman on the sales staff, she toils long hours, often during lunch, feeling extra pressure to land as many ad sales as the men on the staff do. She often works into the evening on special projects, struggling to come up with new ways of making sales. The other part of her job consists of meeting advertisers, wining and dining them, in an effort to convince them to buy ad space during difficult economic times. She often lunches with clients or meets them for drinks or dinner after work, if they're from out of town. Sometimes these dinners last well into the evening, so Debbie gets home just in time for bed—and with no time for herself. Debbie is young, 28, but wonders how long she can keep up the pace. She doesn't exercise regularly and realizes her diet, which lately includes a lot of alcohol, could be better. She also knows that the cigarettes she's been smoking do more harm than just leaving her out of breath. But Debbie likes her work, enjoying the competition and continually meeting new people, plus she feels the need to get ahead.

Career women like Debbie often find themselves not only having to compete with men, but to be more competent than their male counterparts. At the same time, they're expected to look good and have a sunny disposition. Like Debbie, your day may start at 8:30 and not end until 7:00 or later, and then you still take work home. You only have time for a quick dinner and a little television or reading before you fall into bed exhausted. Under these conditions, it seems difficult to make plans for socializing with friends or exercise after work. But it is important to make time for yourself as well as for work.

Most career women find their jobs stimulating and challenging. But your job can take its toll physically and mentally. To continue enjoying a productive and satisfying professional life, you need to counteract the effects of long hours and demanding work with stress-reducing techniques. No one ever said you couldn't work hard and excel in your career, but make sure you spend some time exercising, relaxing, having hobbies, and going out with friends.

Start with finding an exercise class that is late enough in the evening to accommodate your work schedule. This may be harder if you live in a small town. If that is the case, try to get together with other working women and see about adding a later class. Having a regular class, especially one you paid for, will help motivate you. Go with a friend; it's a way of socializing and you can support one another's efforts. It's also a way to meet people. Wendy, a lawyer from New England, met her husband in a dance class. You need to learn to make your health habits, as well as the demands of work, a priority. Wendy, for example, realizing the benefits of daily exercise, runs or takes ballet classes daily. You may not be able to leave at a reasonable hour every evening, but at least once or twice a week make sure you get to your exercise class or meditation group.

Joining a gym may fit into your schedule better than an exercise class. At a gym you will have access to stationary bicycles and treadmills for aerobic exercise, machines for strength training, and usually classes. Be sure, though, to plan on going at a regular time and stick to it. It's easier to put off visiting the gym than a scheduled, already paid-for class. Again, going with a friend, male or female, will help motivate you.

You may find you want to exercise before or during your work day. Lena, a designer for a top clothing manufacturer, has found a 7:30 A.M. yoga class she can take before she starts her work day. Sara, a magazine editor, has arranged her hours so she can run during the day. She takes a shower (there is one at work) and returns to her desk refreshed. And, of course, you can get up and do your stretching exercises every day before work.

Because of the high stress of maintaining long hours and demanding work, it is especially helpful to practice relaxation techniques regularly. Meditate or do relaxation for ten to fifteen minutes in the morning before work. It's often harder to fit relaxation into your schedule after work because there are always numerous distractions and things to do. You can, however, come home and immediately do relaxation exercises—before reading mail, eating, making phone calls, and so on. It may help to change into something comfortable right after you get home. You can combine relaxation with a hot bath (see page 74, which discusses bathtub relaxation). Join a meditation group or start a relaxation group with friends. Rotate houses, and use taped exercises or have one person lead the group.

If you're working late and eating a lot of take-out food, pay attention to what you order. Choose Chinese food without MSG, selecting from items such as vegetables and chicken that are not fried, or vegetables with bean curd or black beans. More and more

Chinese restaurants serve brown rice. In some areas you can get Middle Eastern food, which is inexpensive and a healthful choice. A platter of babaghanouj (made from eggplant, spices and tahini sauce) and hummous (ground chickpeas) with tabouli salad (made from parsley, onion, tomatoes, and grain) is a good choice. Avoid the gyro sandwich (roasted meat) and shish kebab; falafel is a better choice, although it is fried. Refer to the recipes and food ideas in Chapter 6 to add to your repertoire of easy things to make. Drink lots of water, and try to avoid overdoing it on soda and/or alcohol when socializing.

Your Social Life—An Essential Stressbuster

Social supports are important whether you're like Sally or more like Debbie. We all need friends we can depend on—to laugh and be silly with, tell our troubles to, commiserate with. Although it's important to have buddies who will listen to your problems, watch that you strike a balance. Don't always complain about your relationship or lack of one, your job, or mother, just because they will listen. Sometimes you will need to escape and not think about anything but having fun, laughing over dinner or seeing a movie; other times you will want more serious conversations and pursuits.

When your job is unrewarding, your activities outside of work become even more important. Find recreation that is fun as well as affordable. Boredom and feelings of loss of control may come into play in your job. So outside activities should be challenging, but also things that you enjoy and at which you can succeed. If you're feeling particularly bored at work, visualize yourself after work engaged in an activity you enjoy. Find hobbies and activities that include others. Adult-education centers and Y's offer a wide array of everything from cooking, to learning massage, to astrology, to ballroom dancing. Try something that interests you, and where you can make friends. You can also get together with a buddy to pursue an interest or exercise.

If your job is demanding, you need friends and leisure activities to create a balance in your life. When your work is greatly challenging, you may want to pick activities that help you relax. A meditation group or yoga class is a good way of winding down; you have quiet time with yourself while engaging in a group activity.

Swimming is a physical activity that will relax and revitalize you. Taking a walk or run in the park with a friend will let you exercise, socialize, and feel more relaxed.

Being single, of course, doesn't necessarily mean you live alone. Many women choose to have roommates for company or from financial necessity. If your work requires that you deal with people all day, going home to a roommate may not be the best way to relax or it may be the only way you relax—by chatting over a glass of wine. Often your roommate may distract you from taking time to do relaxation or getting the solitude you need. Therefore, you will need to find a way to practice relaxation that is best for you. If it is after work, explain that although you enjoy your roommate's company, your relaxation is extremely important, and ask for her help in giving you the time and space you need. Or, see if you can interest your roommate in doing a relaxation tape with you. But do take time alone for yourself. If you lack privacy, you will not have enough time to get in touch with how you feel.

Everyone needs privacy, and everyone needs a social life; the key is finding a balance. It's important to keep this in mind when it comes to your living situation, because it will affect how you will cope with stress. If you lack privacy, work out with your roommate when you can each have the place to yourself. If you live alone, on the other hand, you may have so much time to yourself that you are not disciplined and are not exercising and practicing relaxation. You will need to create a structure and perhaps take classes with friends. The point is to identify if your living conditions are affecting you, and then find a solution for what you might do about it.

Your Love Life And Stress

Perhaps the outstanding characteristic of being single is going it alone. Ultimately, you have only yourself to depend upon; we all do, but when you are single you are clearly responsible for yourself. Sometimes, this responsibility gives a feeling of independence and freedom. Other times, it adds pressures and makes one feel alone and overwhelmed—even when life seems fulfilling in many ways. Many single women feel uncomfortable when they are not in a relationship and they worry about the future.

Thirty-four-year-old Linda, for example, sometimes feels she has no one to turn to. A freelance artist and photographer, she struggled through a long period without much work. Having plenty of time on her hands, she worried constantly, feeling lonely and wondering if she'd ever get married. Her four-year relationship with another photographer who had been adamantly noncommittal had ended badly; he'd left her for a young college student. Linda slept constantly but always felt tired anyway. Listless, she couldn't get motivated to develop new ideas for paintings. Instead of using this time to garner assignments or gallery shows, she could barely get out of bed. She felt achy and even got tested for Lyme disease, thinking she must be ill. When the results came back negative, her doctor told her she was suffering from depression.

Occasionally, Linda would meet a guy who interested her, but she was uncertain as to how to become better acquainted. Indeed, protocol for dating is not as clear as it once was. In the past, the man asked a woman out and paid for the evening. Now more women feel comfortable asking a man out, although this brings with it the stress of possible rejection as well as the anxiety of an often unfamiliar action, as in Linda's case. And of course, the AIDS epidemic, another of Linda's concerns, has added yet another dimension to the already emotionally charged dating scene. Single women, therefore, are having to find their way without clear guidelines. In addition, the question of "who pays" has become hazy. Expenses are often split, no matter who asks whom out. This may be based upon how much each person makes, the type of date, and your comfort level and his about expense sharing. Often women have been, wrongly, made to feel they owed the man something if he paid. Sharing expenses takes away that pressure.

Could Linda learn anything from Melanie, the writer/performer who works as an office manager? Probably. Melanie had a series of unfulfilling relationships. Three years ago, she decided to concentrate on her career rather than putting her energy into dead-end relationships. She had found that unavailable men drained her emotionally. Not only did she do all the work in the relationships, but she spent much time and energy wondering why they weren't giving her what she wanted, continually trying to figure out how to get it. She, therefore, decided to invest her energy in herself instead.

Melanie knew that she would have a relationship someday and that there was someone for her, but she made a decision not to date until she found someone with whom she really wanted to become involved. Her priority became her writing and performing. Because Melanie had never cut off her friendships when she was in a relationship, she had numerous friends and social supports that sustained her. Although it would have been nice to have a man around, she was satisfied with herself and her friends and knew that her time would come. It did; two years later she met the man to whom she is now engaged. She had become very clear on the type of guy she wanted and what kind of relationship she expected. Now that she has that, she is enjoying the growing relationship.

Learning to be comfortable with independent living will give you strength and enhance any relationship you will undertake. The stronger and more self-motivating you are, the more you can bring to a relationship. Prioritizing yourself and your interests only makes you more attractive and interesting. Use meditation and visualization to become clear on how you want your life to look and the qualities you seek in a relationship. Then pursue yourself! Remember, being in a relationship won't guarantee that you will no longer feel lonely, depressed, or isolated. Although having a satisfying relationship is a good buffer against stress in the workplace, it brings with it its own set of stressors. In the next section, I discuss qualities of a healthy relationship and your role in maintaining them.

Being a single working woman is a challenge. You want to be accepted in the work place; at the same time you want to be attractive to men and establish and maintain a relationship. For women there often appears to be different rules and behaviors for each. In addition, many women feel pressure because time needed for connectedness conflicts with the amount of hours required for a successful career. Feeling good about yourself and having a clear sense of purpose will help guide you in finding a balance. Being single is an opportunity to focus on the most important aspect of your life: You. Use the time you have to improve the quality of your life; exercise, set and visualize goals, make lasting friendships and develop hobbies. Learning to live a satisfying, productive life will set up the conditions to continue to have a fulfilling life whether you remain single or enter into a relationship.

THE TWO-CAREER HOUSEHOLD

When you are married or living with a "significant other," you no longer have to worry about having a date on Saturday night or finding the person with whom you want to spend your life. New concerns arise, however. Balancing work, quality time with your spouse, seeing friends, and having time for yourself are all primary concerns. Living with another person creates time and space demands that are often not an issue when you are single. For example, the time you spend with the other person may take away from what you spend on yourself, or you may be distracted from practicing relaxation with another person around. You may find that between work and your relationship, you no longer see your friends and have cut out recreation that you enjoyed. Many times being in a relationship can cause stress itself. Therefore, to implement a stress-reduction program, you will need to evaluate your situation and prioritize activities, people, and responsibilities.

Is Your Relationship Causing You Stress?

Involvement in a relationship is a great source of strength and support and contributes to your well-being. In addition, being in a happy, satisfied relationship is an excellent stress reliever. Conversely, however, a relationship in which your needs are not getting met, where you constantly feel angry, or where you feel emotionally distant can create stress in your life. Being in a satisfying relationship takes work. It demands attention, good listening skills, staying in touch with your emotions and being able to express them, asking for what you want (as well as knowing what you want), and respecting the needs of the other person. It also involves having a good sense of yourself as a separate individual as well as a part of a couple.

Finding the balance between separateness and togetherness is one of the major challenges facing couples. It's natural when a couple first meets that they want to spend all their time together. Problems arise, however, if you continue that level of togetherness. Conversely, there are some couples who from the beginning are very independent and stay that way. Their task, then, is to learn to develop closeness. It takes a great deal of learning and practice to balance the two.

We often tend to think relationships will take care of themselves and simply loving each other is what's important (and it is, but not exclusively). Relationships, like anything else, demand work and commitment to be satisfying and productive. This seems foreign to many women like myself who grew up in the Fifties, and had our ideas about relationships shaped by the media. I watched film after film where the woman schemed and connived to "catch" her man, and then as the bride and groom kissed, "The End" came onto the screen. Marriage seemed to signify a time where you would now live happily ever after. Even today, young people seem to have an idealistic view of what it takes to maintain an intimate relationship. This, I believe, is because we have had little preparation for what is necessary to make a relationship work, except the example of our parents who struggled through with no preparation either, or viewing TV and films (certainly not a reliable source).

Much of our behavior in relationships has been defined by societal roles. Women have traditionally been given the message that they should be nurturing and, if necessary, self-sacrificing, no matter what. We have been taught to be nice and keep the peace. This has left many women with a lot of anger. Harriet Lerner, Ph.D. in her book, *The Dance of Anger*, notes that in this traditional view, women have two choices: they fall into the "Nice Lady" syndrome, remaining silent or becoming tearful and hurt, while accumulating a "storehouse of unconscious anger," or they become the "Bitchy Woman," nagging and complaining and stuck in patterns of ineffective fighting. Neither accomplishes its purpose and both keep women in old patterns of communicating and responding. Couples become caught in a "dance," where each person's behavior, not just the man's, maintains the status quo. Observing patterns of communication, taking responsibility, and changing old responses to familiar situations will help break old patterns.

When you begin to work toward positive changes, the other person will often attempt to transform you back. You change because your old patterns were stressful, but in doing so it's important to be aware that changing will also cause stress. Understanding this will help you get through the transition. Pam, for example, was always there for other people, but didn't get her needs met most of the time. After a particularly exhausting day working at the hospital, she visited a friend before going home. The friend spent the whole time talking about her problems. When Pam finally got home, she had to fix dinner and do household chores. Right then, she decided that instead of tending to everyone else's needs, she was going to take care of her own, beginning with an exercise class after work and enlisting her husband's help more around the house. Sounds like a good plan, but Pam wasn't prepared for her feelings of guilt when her friend called to meet for a drink or her mother needed something for the third time that week. Her husband had always agreed to help with housework, but when it came down to brass tacks, he put up a fuss. Pam spent a while saying "no," then feeling guilty, or over-functioning in another caretaking role to compensate, but eventually friends and family came to accept the change. Pam is happier and healthier for it, has made some new friends at the gym, and still has time to get together with her old ones.

Many women find that when they start focusing on themselves rather than on changing their partner, the relationship improves. When you start making plans with friends, taking classes, and exercising, you will find your partner will respond. Once the pressure is off him, he will feel more comfortable and it may be easier for him to take more responsibility around the house, come home when he says he will, make plans to spend some quality time with you, find a job he is happier with, and so on.

Not only do we learn our patterns of responding from our family, we learn roles and rules that we carry into our present relationships; we may frequently reenact our early ones. In certain situations, old wounds and feelings get triggered. Your partner's working late generates a violent reaction because you unconsciously respond as you did as a child when your father was never home. Perhaps the lateness of your mate brings up the feelings of abandonment you felt when your father said he'd be home on Saturdays but didn't show up until dinner. Or, like Pam, you are reenacting your mother's role of caretaker. Complicating matters is the fact that people tend to marry a person who has qualities their father and mother had. We gravitate to what is familiar, even if it is unhealthy.

How To Reduce Relationship Stress

The first step to reducing stress is to evaluate your relationship. Look at the roles each of you takes. Are you nagging your partner all the time (or keeping quiet when things bother you)? Does he become distant when you seek contact (or vice versa)? Are you overfunctioning in the relationship? What is your role in your fights? If you never argue, ask yourself why. Reflect on your family's "scripts," or belief systems. Choose books from the "Reading List" Appendix to help you in these areas. Individual or group psychotherapy can help you sort through issues of dependency and individualization and help you discover if old patterns are being played out in your current relationship while giving you the support to function both as an individual and a partner. Perhaps you feel trapped in old family roles and patterns; if you can't seem to break the cycle yourself, using some of the techniques listed below, couples therapy can help. Sometimes in just a few sessions, problems can be worked out. A family-centered therapist will view the relationship as a system with roles, rules, and boundaries that become problematic when they remain fixed. Therapy can help you get unstuck. Some couples find that when a third party is present they can communicate with each other better, expressing their concerns and needs rather than simply blaming and yelling. I've found that often a person hears her spouse in a different way in this setting. Things they may have said to each other might not have been taken seriously, or they were unable to share good feelings because of other problems. I've seen women cry when their husbands expressed tenderness in a session because it was the first time in ages that they had heard it; indeed they had been questioning whether the partner still cared.

The time you spend with your partner isn't always quality time. Most couples get so caught up in work and responsibility that they have few moments to spend together when they are not exhausted. By bedtime, neither usually wants to talk about feelings or sharing ideas, let alone have sex. It's important to be together when you feel good and have energy. If you're tired at night try to find another time to be together. Meet for lunch. Make a date to do something fun and keep it. You may do errands or chores in unison, but this doesn't count for quality, relaxing time. If you're working overtime during the week, save Saturday or Sunday for the two of you to spend together in a leisure activity. Reward yourselves with a romantic weekend away from home. You deserve it!

The same goes for seeing friends. Often when women become part of a couple, they rarely see their old friends. Obviously, relationships change; you may not be able to see a friend as frequently as when you were both single, but that doesn't mean you can't maintain an active friendship. Your mate cannot and should not provide all your social and emotional support. Make regular plans to go to dinner, see a movie, go to a museum, or take an exercise class. Use a friend to help motivate you in your stress reduction by joining a fitness program together or attending a meditation group.

It's important that each of you have personal goals and goals as a couple—and that they are in sync with one another. Suppose you choose to work on weekends to earn extra money to buy a new car, but your partner prefers that you relax together on days off and buy a used one instead. What do you do? Talk it out. Articulating your goals and working toward them gives you a common purpose and direction. Use the techniques in Chapter 8 on goal planning and time management to help you.

Evaluate your responsibilities. Look at those you both have. Make a list, then categorize the items into the order of their importance. Share your list with your mate. Be sure to pay attention to those things on the list that are priorities for each of you.

Exercise is a sure way to help with stress, and being a couple offers opportunities for exercising together. Janet and Bill, for example, go horseback riding every weekend. On a polocross team, they get a good workout. Most importantly, it's something they enjoy doing together. With their busy work schedules, they see little of each other during the week. Riding allows them to leave the city, be together, and get exercise. Your activity obviously doesn't have to be as exotic as polocross. You may want to bike ride or hike, play tennis or racquetball, join a gym or study martial arts.

Remember, too, that relaxation training is an essential component of stress reduction. Achieving a relaxation response not only helps fight stress, it improves concentration, and gives you a sense of control as well as calm. In addition, by calming your mind and going inward, you may become more in touch with anything that is bothering you.

Finding time to exercise and practice relaxation takes scheduling for sure, but both are vital for good health. It is, of course, more difficult to meditate and exercise in the morning when both you and your spouse are getting ready for work. I lived alone for a long time and could meditate or practice relaxation whenever I desired and wasn't disturbed except by the phone. When I started living with my fiancé, I found I had to be more disciplined since we share a small New York City apartment. Since he went to work later than I did, I got up earlier and was able to do my relaxation in the morning while he was still asleep. When we got on the same schedule, though, it became harder. Now I have to wake up very early or find time after work, which isn't as easy for me. One solution I have found for relaxing when another person is around is "bathtub meditation" (see page 74). I can go in, close the door, and be undisturbed (when it doesn't conflict with our morning routine), giving me time not only to soak my muscles but to relax my mind and body as well.

As you can see, it is very important to work on your relationship; a healthy relationship with the man you love can strengthen your ability to cope effectively with the many stressors in life. And vice versa, striving to deal effectively with stress accrued at work can enable you to be in a good place when facing the inevitable disagreements and problems that arise in any relationship. Just as you should not put off your relaxation exercises, don't delay in working on improving your relationship.

IF YOU'RE MARRIED WITH CHILDREN...

As a working woman with a child or children, you've certainly experienced the challenges and strains of trying to function effectively in both the workplace and within the family. Freud said that a person should love and work. Yet, love and work for a woman requires many responsibilities and obligations: to children, spouse, home, extended family and friendships, to work and co-workers. While combining both work and family can be very fulfilling, it also can be quite stressful as you attempt to succeed on all fronts.

The goal is balance. If you have the support and comfort gained through loving relationships, you are free to achieve the mastery you seek in the workplace and vice versa. Feeling good about yourself on the job allows you to feel self-confident and better able to attend to your family.

Most working mothers are responsible for the children and household. In the majority of two-career families it is the woman who keeps everything running smoothly. Women are the ones who most often adjust their work schedules to be home for the kids and to fix dinner. This is often because husbands' jobs tend to be high-er-paying positions and therefore take priority. Even in families where chores are shared, the woman usually takes the main respon-sibility for the children. This is, of course, changing, and more and more fathers are doing laundry, shopping, and picking up the kids.

For some women the most stressful part of the day is coming home to household responsibilities and keeping the peace. Yes, you've made the choice to do this, but how can you do it without feeling overwhelmed by the pressure? First you may need to look at your attitudes. Ask yourself if you feel you are the only one who can do it (get the kids to school, do the washing, go to that meeting, fix a healthy dinner). Do you feel your self-esteem will be affected if you don't attend to something personally? Do you have difficulty saying "no"? Do you need to be perfect? Your perceptions of moth-erhood and what you should accomplish could be causing extra pressures.

List all your responsibilities at home and work, then have your husband list his. Are you sharing household and family chores? Determine where you need assistance and what you can eliminate. Learn to delegate and share tasks. What can your children do to help? Can you afford to hire someone to come in and help with some of the household chores? Look into a drop-off laundry service. We tend to forget that running a household with children used to be a full-time job. Now you're trying to do two jobs!

Norma, an office manager in a mental health clinic, found her-self worn out working all day and caring for the house and her three children. She liked her job, finding it challenging, but doing house-hold chores left her irritable, with no time leftover for her kids. She had no help from her husband, who came from a country that cul-turally did not encourage men to do housework. Her solution: They hired a housekeeper/nanny, leaving Norma free to make extra money occasionally working overtime.

Don't try to be supermom. (Later I'll describe a single working mother who attempted to be the perfect supermom and the price she had to pay.) You can't be perfect in all areas. Prioritize responsibili-ties and eliminate those nonessential ones, especially those you don't like, which will leave you with more time for your kids. Pool resources with other mothers. Do you have to go to that birthday party with your children or can they go with another child and mother? Then next time, you take the kids. Make play dates for your kids. See page 259 for suggestions on managing your responsibilities and determining which you most enjoy.

Perhaps one of the hardest things a working mother has to deal with is guilt. Working takes time away from being with your children, or spending time together in the evening because you must do household chores. But research studies tell us that what is important is the quality of your time together. A mother may stay home with her kids all day, but be disinterested, distracted, and irritable. Are the children better off with this mother or in a day care situation where they are being responded to and interact with other children, returning home to a mother who is happy to see them?

Obviously not all time you will spend with your kids will be quality time, nor will you be able to listen to each and every word they utter. But do plan to spend some time each day when you sit down and really listen to their concerns. Schedule time if necessary. Too often you are busy and tired and only half listen as you go about your chores. Children know when you are paying attention and when you are not. I am constantly impressed by one mother I know who lovingly and patiently addresses her children's concerns. She is really there for them emotionally, and they know it. She works full-time and has live-in help, so she isn't with them constantly, but when she is, she's attuned to their needs.

Be sure to do fun things together. I always admired Jody, a dental assistant who worked about thirty hours a week and was the mother of two young boys. She scheduled time every week to spend alone with each of her boys, doing something they wanted to do. It was their special time and made them feel important and cared about.

As a married working mother, not only are you the main emotional support for your children; you must also seek to maintain a satisfying relationship with your mate. Therefore, the information I have shared and will share with you should help in your attempts to balance family and work. The section on "Two-Career Families" deals with relationship issues, the importance of communicating your needs, and tips for implementing stress reduction if you are part of a couple.

With all your responsibilities, you will need some form of stress release. Exercise is one of the best, and it will increase your stamina and give you the extra energy you need to meet your obligations. Here's what one mom I know has to say about exercise. Anne, the mother of two daughters, declares that exercise will save your relationship—with your husband, kids, and yourself! She advises: "If you are a working mother, you need to have a way of releasing (stress) before you interact with your kids." Otherwise, you end up arguing. Her solution is to jog to and from work each day (a total of about seven miles). She says "you sleep better, have more energy, and can tackle more problems." In fact, her husband can usually tell if she hasn't had her run and always offers to take care of the kids so she can catch up!

If it's not practical for you to jog or walk to or from work, try to walk after work. If you drive to work, walk before you leave for home, if possible. All you need are walking or running shoes. If the area isn't suitable, drive to a park or school track before going home. Or pick up your kids and take them too. Anne learned to jog with her father, and it's a tradition they are both committed to. Exercising together is a healthy way to spend time with your kids and helps them develop good habits. If your children are young, you may want the company of another adult and exercise with another mother while the kids play.

Obviously, finding time to practice relaxation is difficult when balancing a career and family, but all the more necessary. You may want to try a meditation group that takes you out of the house and gives you quiet time. After the kids go to bed, meditate once or twice a week in a quiet place you have set aside.

Too many working mothers resort to fast food for their families. One night it's Taco Bell, the other Wendy's, then Captain Bill's fried fish. One woman told me that when she was in graduate school, her family lived on McDonald's. If you're doing this, not only are you depriving yourself (and your family) of the nutrition you need to meet your demands (plus contributing to future health problems), but you are instilling poor lifetime habits in your kids. Enlist your family's aid in preparing healthful meals. I loved to cook as a child and was happy to help in the kitchen. Mom enjoyed it and made it fun, not a chore. For starters use the recipes in Chapter 6, then buy some cookbooks and experiment. There are some books with recipes especially appropriate for kids.

Goal planning, time management, and setting priorities are most important when managing a career and family. Using those skills plus the steps described here should start you on the path to reduced stress. And, remember, the lessons you are learning can be taught by example to your children—preparing them for their own adult lives.

IF YOU'RE A SINGLE MOTHER...

As a single mother, you are doing it all—supporting and parenting a family—and you certainly don't need to be told you have a great deal of stress. That's obvious. What you probably wonder is how in the world you're supposed to find time to do anything about it. Here are some suggestions that I hope make reducing stress a little easier.

Being a single mother offers the most challenges for practicing stress reduction since your time and energy go into working and parenting. If you don't have help from your children's father or other family members, the problem intensifies. And even if your children's father may be cooperative, you are predominantly responsible for the real day-to-day parenting responsibilities. If you have a young child or children, you may find that you aren't able to practice all the methods in this book, but you should be able to use some of them.

The demands of work and family responsibilities require strength, stamina, emotional commitment, time, organization, perseverance, and an ability to deal with your conflicting demands. Start by putting into practice time management and assertiveness techniques. Although I realize there are only so many hours in a day, time management can help. The assertiveness chapter should assist you in standing up for your rights, asking for what you need, or saying "no," even to well-meaning but intruding relatives who think they have the answers for you. For the sake of both you and your children, the better your diet, the better able you'll be to withstand the effects of stress. Enlist your child or children in preparing healthful meals. Look for recipes that are both tasty and healthy. See Chapter 6 for some suggestions.

Don't think you have to do it all yourself. Relatives—sisters, aunts, in-laws—may want to help out and are just waiting to be asked. You may even have a single friend who would love to be a parent for an afternoon or evening. I know one young woman who spends every Tuesday with her nephew. They usually go to the movies, which he loves, as well as occasional camping trips. Make use of other mothers in a similar situation. Find a few with children the same age as yours, and trade off taking care of the kids. This will free some of your time and save on having to pay a babysitter. Alternate who drives to parties and activities. Of course, it may not give you enough time to take an exercise class, but getting the shopping or laundry done might make you feel less behind.

Exercise will increase your strength and stamina and improve how you feel about yourself. Here's how one mother, Alex, with a teenage daughter manages to incorporate exercising into her hectic schedule: She combines exercise and solitude in an early morning routine. Rising early, she walks briskly for forty-five minutes before breakfast. Listening with headphones to relaxing music, she goes into a somewhat "meditative" state. Since she lives by the beach, she can simply watch the scenery or take a more inward focus. Alex uses this time to reflect on work, family, how she's feeling, or sometimes she will just "zone" out. When she finishes, she showers and has breakfast with her daughter before they both leave the house. Alex is an early riser and likes to have time alone for herself, so it's not difficult for her. If you awaken early and don't have a long commute, you may want to exercise in the morning before work. You might alternate relaxation and exercise each day. If getting you and your child out of the house in the morning, however, is all you can manage (and that's enough), you'll need to figure out other ways of getting exercise. Sherry, for example, doesn't have time to exercise during the week, but makes sure she does so on the weekend with her son. She also tries to walk any chance she gets, but she admits that walking doesn't meet her exercise needs. If you have kids that can play together without constant supervision, ask another mother over for a work-out, while the kids play. Realize that exercise will make you feel better in the long run (and you'll just have to experience this to know it's true), and then make a commitment to fit it in. Even then, it's not always easy. See page 256 to learn how one mother feels about exercise and good parenting.

Another problem for working mothers is the struggle to find time for themselves to socialize. Often boyfriends and others compete for your attention, and this is hard on all concerned. The children often feel they are being slighted, as do friends, leaving you feeling torn and guilty. Children need to know you love them, will listen to them, and that they can count on you. You don't have to spend all your time with your kids to achieve this, but when you do, be sure to be there in mind, body, and spirit. M. Scott Peck, MD, in *The Road Less Traveled,* discusses the appropriate ways to listen and respond to your children according to their age. Communicating well with your children and loved ones is also important. You must be able to discuss with all those around you your feelings, needs, and expectations.

When you're a mother, especially a single one, your needs often come last. Combining multiple roles and being everything to everyone is a clumsy juggling act that can take a physical and mental toll.

Take Julie, for instance. A single mother with two young boys, Julie, 39, found herself in a chronic-pain clinic dealing with physical problems that were directly related to the stress of trying to do it all. Her injuries from a car accident had not healed, and she had developed some serious psychosomatic symptoms as well. Julie felt she had to be the perfect mother, teacher, daughter, and lover, a task few can accomplish, let alone a single mother struggling to support her family with no help (only hassles) from her husband and no relatives in the area. Julie took her kids to Little League and after-school activities. She made sure they had the right clothes, lived in a perfectly ordered household, had help with their homework, ate nutritious meals, and spent quality time with her. In addition, she tried to spend time with her boyfriend who also wanted to see her more. Trying to fit everything in was more than she could cope with, and her body let her know it.

To deal with her stress-related physical symptoms, heal from her accident, and continue to perform her many roles, Julie had to learn to set priorities, schedule, and pace herself—skills she learned at the clinic. She was also given assertiveness training, which helped her in dealing with her ex-husband and in situations where she had difficulty saying "no." An important lesson for her was not to judge herself as a mother by her kids' clothes or her home's condition, or her ability to drive her kids to all their activities.

When you feel overloaded, not enjoying what you are doing, and having no time for fun or for yourself, some things have to go. If you have volunteered to be the scout leader and really get pleasure out of it, do it and enjoy. If you find it is too much work and not rewarding or it's not your thing, give it up without guilt. It is not a reflection of your devotion or capability as a mother. Analyze your mothering responsibilities. Look at the ones that are important to you and the ones that aren't. Is there anything that you can cut out? You may want to discuss your thoughts with your kids. They might not think PTA is important, but that your coming to Parents' Night is. But ultimately you need to make the decision for yourself. If you continually drive your kids to their activities, as Julie does, find other mothers with whom to take turns.

Use less energy trying to make your kids perfect. They will like it better too. Rather than constantly nagging your children, use criticism constructively. At least one week night when the kids are in bed, do something that you enjoy or find relaxing, rather than trying to catch up on chores. Read a novel, paint your nails, talk on the phone (for fun—not to return a call). Feel indulged.

It's important to really understand yourself and your situation to put into place a successful stress-reducing plan. By looking carefully at the structure of your life, you can start making beneficial changes. And not only will you find your own stress reduced, you should also discover a most positive effect on your children's lives as well.

YOUR JOURNEY BEGINS

I hope I've offered some clear methods and approaches to stress reduction that you can implement immediately, and that I've motivated you to do so. Keep in mind a piece of wisdom from the Congo, called "the three T's"—Things Take Time. Don't expect overnight miracles. You've probably been experiencing stress for a while, and/or old habits are contributing to your stress level. Or you may be responding to a new stressful situation. As I have said throughout, anytime you make changes, even changes for the better, you put new demands on your system—and this will require an adjustment. The time you spend cutting up raw vegetables, going to your exercise class, or waking a little earlier to practice relaxation, will place new demands on you. I'm not saying "don't change," but only that you should be aware that though you will be benefiting, you will also have to accommodate the change in lifestyle.

Another thing we all tend to do is to judge ourselves. We can improve no matter where we are in our health habits, but healthful living is a way of life. It evolves over time. Accept yourself, and don't focus on, say, the peanut butter you eat in the middle of the night. You are a healthy person who happens to need a snack (certainly better than ice cream or candy). Get a clear picture of where you want to be, then move toward it without struggle, seeing yourself as healthy.

This book is to be used as a guide. In the Appendix, I have included a list of recommended readings for subjects covered throughout the book, so you can pursue in depth areas of interest. The more you learn, the more you will be reminded to take time to practice the skills and attitudes presented here.

Of all the skills in this book, learning to relax will be the most valuable. It takes only fifteen minutes a day to reverse the effects of the stress response. If you don't have ten or fifteen minutes, take five. Once relaxation is familiar to you, you can indulge in mini-relaxation breaks during the day to revive you and keep your stress level from rising.

You may find it difficult to take time out to practice relaxation, or to concentrate when you do. There are many reasons for this, which vary from simple to complex, but the end result is that this may be the hardest part of relaxation training to implement. We are accustomed to being active and accomplishing things. When you practice relaxation, you stop your momentum and focus inward, something at which few of us are any good. We perhaps feel that if we relax we'll have difficulty getting going again. Also some people are not comfortable with the feeling of relaxation because it is so foreign to them.

If you are experiencing physical symptoms you think are related to stress, it is important to see a doctor for a check-up before beginning to practice these techniques. Should depression, anxiety, or addictive behaviors be a problem, seek help from a trained therapist. Periods of major life change, such as divorce, the birth of a child, or the death of a loved one, also can warrant consultation with professional help to support and guide you through the changes. If you find that you are practicing the exercises in the book and not seeing any difference in your stress level, consider finding a relaxation class or group, or consult a professional trained in stress management and biofeedback.

Sometimes when you practice relaxation regularly and continue to have symptoms, they may represent more than just a stress response. You may have "secondary gains," that is, you benefit from the symptom in some way, even though you consciously don't wish to have it. Backaches and headaches, for example, may exonerate you from going to your relatives or doing the housework. Often our symptoms are a way that our body lets us know we are not dealing with some issue in our life that needs to be addressed. Because we learn from our parents to cope with stress, we sometimes adopt their physical ailments as we identify with them. Again, the more inward you go through practicing awareness techniques, the more answers you will gain, but don't feel badly if you can't work it out on your own. My journey to better physical, emotional, and spiritual health has been paved with supportive and knowledgeable professionals who have all contributed in some way.

It's clear that it's not easy being a working woman today. You do have the ability to deal with a multitude of stressors, though, by following the suggestions in this book. Incorporating effective job-stress management skills into your life may take from a few months to a year. The important thing is to start now.

In your journey, believe you can change your habits, have the desire, and enjoy the experience.

APPENDIX

READING LIST

I recommend all the books on this list and within these pages have referred to many. The ones that are starred especially support or extend the information in this book.

About Stress

Pelletier, Kenneth. (1977). *Mind as Healer, Mind as Slayer.* NY: Delacorte Press.

Selye, Hans. (1974). *Stress Without Distress.* Philadelphia, PA: Lippincott.

Stress and Meditation

Benson, Herbert. (1975). *The Relaxation Response.* NY: Avon Books. (Stress and Meditation.)

Benson, Herbert and William Proctor. (1985). *Beyond the Relaxation Response*. NY: Berkley Press.

*Borysenko, Joan. (1987). *Minding the Body, Mending the Mind*. Reading, MA: Addison-Wesley Publishing. (Stress, emotions, and meditation.)

*Kabat-Zinn, Jon. (1990). *Full Catastrophe Living*. NY: Delacorte Press. (Mindfulness and healing.)

Nuernberger, Phil. (1985). *Freedom From Stress*. Honesdale, PA: The Himalayan International Institute of Yoga Science and Philosophy. (Excellent information on breathing.)

Managing Your Stress

*Davis, Martha, Elizabeth Robbins Eshelman & Matthew McKay. (1988). *The Relaxation and Stress Workbook*. Oakland, CA: New Harbinger Publications.

Mason, John L. (1980). *Guide to Stress Reduction*. Culver City, CA: Peace Press.

Roggenbuck Gillespie, Peggy. (1986). *Less Stress in 30 Days*. NY: A Signet Book.

Shealy, C. Norman. (1977). *90 Days to Self-Health*. NY: Bantam Books.

*Tauraso, Nicola M. (1979). *How to Benefit from Stress*. Frederick, MD: Hidden Valley Press.

Positive Attitudes/Creative Visualization

Burns, David. (1992). *Feeling Good: The New Mood Therapy*. NY: Avon Books.

Epstein, Gerald. (1989). *Healing Visualizations, Creating Healing Through Imagery*. NY: Bantam Books.

*Gawain, Shakti. (1978). *Creative Visualization*. NY: Bantam Books.

Jampolsky, Gerald. (1983). *Teach Only Love*. NY: Bantam Books.

*Siegal, Bernie. (1986). *Love, Medicine and Miracles*. NY: Harper & Row.

————— (1986). *Peace, Love and Healing*. NY: Harper & Row.

Psychology/Improved Well-Being

*Borysenko, Joan. (1990). *Guilt Is The Teacher, Love Is The Lesson*. NY: Warner Books. (Women and perfectionism explored.)

*Bradshaw, John. (1988). *Bradshaw On: The Family*. Deerfield Beach, FL: Health Communications, Inc. (Helpful in understanding our behavior in relation to our origins.)

*Bradshaw, John. (1988). *Healing the Shame That Binds You*. Deerfield Beach, FL: Health Communications, Inc.

Cousins, Norman. (1984). *The Healing Heart*. NY: Avon Books.

Friz, Robert. (1984). *The Path of Least Resistance, Learning to Become the Creative Force in Your Own Life*. NY: Fawcett Columbine.

Kaplan-Williams, Strephon. (1988). *Transforming Childhood, A Process Book For Personal Growth*. Berkeley, CA: Journey Press.

*Lerner, Harriet Goldhor. (1985). *The Dance of Anger*. NY: Harper & Row. (Helps identify behavior, yours and others, in important relationships.)

* Miller, Alice. (1981). *The Drama of the Gifted Child: The Search for the True Self*. NY: Basic Books.

*Peck, M. Scott. (1978). *The Road Less Traveled*. NY: Simon and Schuster. (Highly recommended for anyone in an intimate relationship. He devotes an entire section to love—what it is and how to maintain it.)

Women/Coping Skills

Berg, Barbara J. (1986). *The Crisis of the Working Mother*. NY: Summit Books.

*Davis, Martha, et al. (1988). *The Relaxation and Stress Reduction Workbook*. Oakland, CA: New Harbinger Publications. (Especially good for assertiveness, time management and work stress.)

*Lerner, Harriet Goldhor. (1985). *The Dance of Anger*. NY: Harper & Row. (A must for every woman, looks at all types of relationships.)

————. (1989). *The Dance of Intimacy*. NY: Harper & Row.

Phelps, Stanlee and Nancy Austin. (1987). *The Assertive Woman: A New Look*. San Luis Obispo, CA: Impact Publishers.

Nutrition

Brody, Jane. (1981). *Jane Brody's Nutrition Book*. NY: W.W. Norton.

Tessler, Gordon S. (1984). *Lazy Person's Guide to Better Nutrition*. La Jolla, CA: Better Health Publishers.

The Physical Body

Anderson, Bob. (1980). *Stretching*. Bolinas, CA: Shelter Publications.

Baker, Sarah. (1978). *The Alexander Technique: The Revolutionary Way to Use Your Body For Total Energy*. NY: Bantam Books.

Bertherat, Therese and Carol Bernstein. (1979). *The Body Has Its Reasons*. NY: Avon Books.

*Brown, Stephanie. (1993). *The Hand Book: Preventing Computer Injury*. NY: Ergonome. (May be ordered directly by calling 1-800-222-6996.)

Caplan, Deborah. (1987). *Back Trouble: A New Approach to Prevention and Recovery*. NY: Triad. (The Alexander Technique.)

*Donkin, Scott. W. (1986). *Sitting on the Job: How to Survive the Stresses of Sitting Down to Work—A Practical Handbook*. Boston, MA: Houghton Mifflin Company.

Feldenkrais, Moshe. (1977). *Awareness Through Movement*. NY: Harper & Row.

Katz, Jane, Ed.D. (1985) *Fitness Works!* A Blueprint for Lifelong Fitness. Champaign, Illinois, Leisure Press.

Lynch, Jerry. (1987). *The Total Runner: A Complete Mind-Body Guide to Optimal Performance*. Englewood Cliffs, NJ: Prentice Hall.

Masters, Robert and Jean Houston. (1978). *Listening to the Body*. NY: Delacorte Press.

Millman, Dan. *The Warrior Athlete, Body, Mind & Spirit*. (1979). Walpole, NH: Stillpoint Publishing.

Saltonstall, Ellen. (1988). *Kinetic Awareness, Discovering Your Bodymind*. NY: Kinetic Awareness Center. (Order directly, 17 E. 16th Street, New York, NY, 10003.)

Tobias, Maxine and John Stewart. (1992). *Complete Stretching: A New Exercise Program for Health and Vitality*. NY: Knopf. (Yoga.)

Stress and Work

Veninga, Robert L. and James P. Spradley. (1981). *The Work Stress Connection*. NY: Ballantine Books.

Breathing

Speads, Carola. (1978). *Breathing: The ABC's*. NY: Harper & Row.

Nuernberger, Phil. (1985). *Freedom From Stress*. Honesdale, PA: The Himalayan International Institute of Yoga Science and Philosophy.

Biofeedback

Brown, Barbara. (1977). *Stress and the Art of Biofeedback*. NY: Harper & Row.

Karlins, Marvin and Lewis M. Andrews. (1972). *Biofeedback: Turning on the Powers of Your Mind*. NY: J. B. Lippincott.

Magazine

Natural Health Magazine
P.O. Box 57320
Boulder, Co 80322-7320
(303) 447-9330

Mail Order Catalog

Many of the above books are listed in this catalog.

East West Books
78 Fifth Avenue
New York, NY 10011
(212) 243-5995

AUDIOCASSETTES

Music

Steven Halpern
Dawn
Eastern Peace
Comfort Zone

Golden Voyage Series, Vols 1, 2 & 3

For these music selections and many of the audiocassettes write or call:

Music Design
4650 N. Port Washington Rd.
Milwaukee, WI 53212
1-800-862-7232

or

Self-Health Systems (write or call for catalog)
Route 1, Box 216
Fair Grove, MO 65648
(417) 267-2900
FAX 417-267-3102

Spoken Word

Attitudes for Attunement
  Freedom From Fear
  Love (self-love)
  Stress-Conversion
    Dr. Henry Rucker
    P.O. Box 10551
    Chicago, IL 60610
    (312) 374-0087
Psychology of Success Series
  Brian Tracy
  Nightingale-Conant Corp.
  1-800-323-5552

Creative Visualization

> Shakti Gawain
> Whatever Publishing Inc.
> P.O. Box 13257
> Northgate Station
> San Rafael, CA 94913

Letting Go of Stress

> Emmett Miller
> Music Design
> 4650 N. Port Washington Rd.
> Milwaukee, WI 53212
> 1-800-862-7232

Guided Meditations: Love Is the Lesson Series

> Mind/Body Health Sciences
> Joan Borysenko
> 393 Dixon Road
> Boulder, CO 80302
> (303) 440-8460

Balancing Body Feelings

> Basic Schultz (Autogenic Training)
> Self-Health Systems (write or call for catalog)
> Route 1, Box 216
> Fair Grove MO 65648
> (417) 267-2900

RESOURCES

Aerobic Exercise

> Step Aerobic and Abdominal Workout
> (Video)
> Jane Fonda Workout
> 1-800-824-7148

Back and Neck Pillows

Inflatable, self adjusting back support pillow

Medic-Air Corp of America
16 North Chatsworth Avenue
Larchmont, NY 10538
1-800-247-7455

Self Care
5850 Shellmound Street
Emeryville, CA 94662
1-800-345-3371
Offers a variety of pillows for low back and neck

Biofeedback

For practitioners in your area call or write

The Biofeedback Society of America
10200 W. 44th Avenue, Suite 304,
Wheat Ridge, CO 80033
(303) 422-8436

Hand Temperature Devices

Thought Technology Ltd.
7 Hundred Oaks Lane
Ashland, MA 01721
1-800-361-3651

J&J Enterprises
22797 Holgar Court, N.E.
Poulsbo, WA 98370
(206) 779-3853

Body Therapies

For practitioners in your area call or write

The Alexander Technique
The North American Society of Teachers
    of The Alexander Technique
P.O. Box 5536
Playa deRey, CA 90296
1-800-473-0620

Feldenkrais Technique
The Feldenkrais Guild, Inc.
706 Ellsworth Street
P.O. Box 489
Albany, OR 97321-0143
1-800-775-2118

Kinetic Awareness
The Kinetic Awareness Center
P.O. Box 1050, Cooper Station
New York, NY 10276

Body-Mind Centering Association, Inc.
16 Center Street, Suite 530
Northampton, MA 01060
(413) 582-3617

Brain Synchronizers

Shealy RelaxMate
Self-Health Systems
Rt.1, Box 216
Fair Grove, MO 65648
(417) 267-2900

Other models may be ordered through:

Tool for Exploration
1-800-456-9887

Tai Chi Videocassette Tapes

Tai Chi For Health with Terry Dunn
Yang Long Form
Healing Arts
321 Hampton Drive
Venice, CA 90291

Five Elements with Al Huang (short form)
Living Tao Foundation
P.O. Box 846
Urbana, IL 61801
(217) 337-6113

Yoga Videocassette Tapes

Yoga Journal Practice Series (Video)
   Yoga Practice for Beginners
   Yoga Practice for Flexibility
   Yoga Practice for Strength
   Yoga Practice for Relaxation

For books, tapes and video catalog, write or call

Yoga Journal
Book and Tape Source
2054 University Avenue #600
Berkeley, CA 94704-1082
1-800-359-YOGA

The W.E.T. (Wader Exercise Techniques) *Workout*®
Video by Dr. Jane Katz
1-800-967-5469

INDEX